THE H(

A TREATISE ON THE

BREEDS, MANAGEMENT, FEEDING, AND MEDICAL TREATMENT OF SWINE;

WITH DIRECTIONS FOR

SALTING PORK AND CURING BACON AND HAMS,

BY WILLIAM YOUATT, V. S.,

Author of "The Horse," "Cattle," "Sheep," "The Dog," &c.,

AND

W. C. L. MARTIN,

Member of the Royal Zoological Society.

ILLUSTRATED WITH ENGRAVINGS, DRAWN FROM LIFE BY WILLIAM HARVEY, ESQ.

EDITED BY A. STEVENS.

NEW-YORK:

ORANGE JUDD & COMPANY,

No. 245 BROADWAY.

Printing Statement:

Due to the very old age and scarcity of this book, many of the pages may be hard to read due to the blurring of the original text, possible missing pages, missing text, dark backgrounds and other issues beyond our control.

Because this is such an important and rare work, we believe it is best to reproduce this book regardless of its original condition.

Thank you for your understanding.

SF576
G7Y6
1855

PREFACE.

In undertaking this work, the author was influenced by an anxious desire to extend the views of medical science generally, and of his own profession in particular, and a wish to draw the attention of agriculturists and veterinary surgeons to a too much neglected and undervalued class of animals, and by the hope of materially increasing the amount of knowledge already possessed.

It has been his task to collect all the various brief and cursory notices which have been accorded to swine by ancient as well as modern agricultural and medical writers; to select those which were valuable and worthy of record; and then, by weaving them into the groundwork of his own ideas and experience, to bring the before scattered rays into one focus, so that the eye of science may be attracted towards this hitherto neglected branch, and, from contemplating, may be led to study it; and practical men may be induced to aid, by their experience, in elucidating a subject which is as yet so little understood.

In short, he has endeavored to act as a pioneer, to lead the way to, and break up, a new and fertile spot; one that will amply reward the labors of those whom he hopes to induce by his example to bestow some little of their care upon it.

Many talented and valued friends have kindly assisted him by hints and information; to them he tenders his sincere thanks. Should it be deemed that he has succeeded in throwing some portion of light, faint though it may be, on the management and diseases of animals whose value is becoming more and more acknowledged every year, he will consider his labors amply rewarded.

WILLIAM YOUATT.

EDITOR'S PREFACE

THE Publisher having committed to the editor the task of combin-
ing in one, the two volumes of "Youatt on the Hog," and "Martin
on the Hog," he has endeavored to so unite them, as to offer in one
the full substance of both. These two works are the best in our, or
any language, on the subject of the Hog. Youatt is eminent and
superior in his historical, descriptive, and veterinary portions,
and Martin in his Natural History of Swine. The Editor has taken
Youatt's work as the basis, which he has preserved entire, and has
incorporated therewith such portions of Martin as are not in Youatt,
and are not repetitions.

The volume now presented is superior in its material to any other
on the subject of the Hog now extant, in all its departments of
natural history, in the history of the relations of the animal to man,
in its veterinary, or surgical and medical treatment, and in the
breeding, feeding, fattening, and general economy of the Hog.

A. STEVENS.

CONTENTS.

THE HOG.

CHAPTER I.

THE HOG, (*Suidae Sus* of the ancients and Linnæus,) according to Cuvier, belongs to "the class MAMMALIA, order PACHYDERMATA, genus SUIDAE or SUS, having on each foot two large principal toes shod with stout hoofs, and two lateral toes much shorter and scarcely touching the earth; the incisors variable in number, the lower incisors all levelled forwards; the canines projected from the mouth and recurved upwards; the muzzle terminated by a truncated snout fitted for turning up the ground; the stomach but little divided; the body square and thick, and more or less covered with bristles and hairs; the neck strong and muscular; the legs short and stout." (Cuvier's Animal Kingdom, vol. iii.)

The *suidæ* are robust and massive in their form, low in the limbs, flat-sided, with immense muscular development in the neck and fore-quarters. The head is wedge-shaped, with an elongated snout, terminating in a round or oval disc of cartilage, called in common language the button; this disc is pierced by the nostrils, and possesses great power of mobility, being supplied by several strong muscles; it is, moreover, strengthened and supported by a small extra bone, as in the instance of the mole also, and is used with great facility as an instrument for ploughing up the ground in quest of roots for food. The lower jaw is deep and strong, and the symphysis of the chin is completely ossified, and not, as in ruminants, united by suture. The mouth is wide, opening to a degree almost unparallelled among terrestrial mammalia. The jaws are armed with tusks, which grow to a large size, pass from between the lips, and are weapons of tremendous effect; the tusks of the lower jaw advance before those of the upper, which turn obliquely upwards and outwards. In the peccaries, the tusks are but little developed;

in the male babiroussa those of the upper jaw pierce through the skin of the snout, and are greatly elongated. The eyes are small, but quick and shrewd in expression ; the ears are moderate, erect, and pointed. The tongue is elongated and smooth. The tail is short, slender, and apparently of little utility. The senses of smell, sight, and taste are in high perfection, more especially that of smell, and the olfactory nerves are large. The sense of hearing is acute. In their diet the *suidæ* are omnivorous, vegetable and animal substances being equally acceptable ; still it is on vegetable aliment that they chiefly feed. The skin is coarse, covered with bristles, and destitute, or nearly so, of the subcutaneous muscular expansion common to most other animals, termed the *panniculus carnosus*, and so highly developed in the hedge-hog. On looking at the skull we find its base or occipital portion forming a right angle with the obliquely rising upper surface, and a bold transverse ridge is formed by the union of the occipital to the parietal bones, which latter advance above the frontal bones, and form the most elevated portion of the skull. The nasal bones are prolonged to the end of the snout, and the symphysis of the lower jaw is consolidated. In proportion to the elevation of the occipital bone are the length and strength of the spinous processes of the dorsal vetebræ. Those of the anterior dorsal vertebræ in particular are remarkable for their development, and indicate the volume of the muscles for supporting and moving the head. These are the agents by which the dreadful tusks are brought into play. Rushing on his antagonist, the boar strikes obliquely upwards, right and left, with irresistible violence, in a direction harmonizing with that of the tusks, and in the mode best suited for the exertion of the animal's strength. The neck is short, and with this shortness is necessarily connected that of the limbs, and especially of the interior pair, otherwise the animal would not without difficulty reach the ground with its snout. Their strength must be in proportion to the weight to be sustained, and the weight depends upon the size of the head and the muscular development of the neck and shoulders.

All this species feed on plants, and especially on roots, which their snout or trunk enables them to grub out of the earth; they will devour animal substances, but rarely hunt or destroy animals for the purpose of devouring them. They are thick skinned ; said to be obtuse in most of their faculties, excepting in the olfactory and oral senses; voracious, bold in defending themselves ; and delight in humid and shady places.

To this order belong the elephant, the rhinoceros, the hippopotamus, &c., the general characteristics of all of which are very similar.

From among the cloven-footed or many-toed animals of the pachydermatous order of mammalia, man has subjugated and reclaimed only two—viz., the hog and the elephant.

The domestic hog .s the descendant of a race long since subjugated; yet while a race of domesticated swine has been and is kept under surveillance, the wild type whence this race sprung has maintained itself in its native freedom, the fierce denizen of the forest, and one of the renowned beasts of "venerie." Its wild source still exists, and is universally recognized; it roams through the vast wooded tracts of Europe and Asia. The wild stock of the hog is most extensively spread throughout Europe and Asia, and has been known, described, and celebrated from the earliest ages, alike by sacred and classical writers; it is the *sus scrofa* of Linnæus, the *sus aper* of Brisson.

Under the generic term SUIDAE or SUS many zoologists have included, besides the true hog as it exists in a wild or tame state in Europe, Asia, and Africa, the peccary, the babiroussa, the phaco choere, and the capibara; we will, therefore, slightly glance at each of these varieties before proceeding to the actual subject of the present work.

THE PECCARY.—This appears to be the nearest approach to swine among the animals indigenous to the New World; and the Collared Peccary (*Dicotyles torquatus*) and the White-lipped Peccary (*Dicotyles labiatus*) actually do at first sight appear to bear a very close resemblance to the common hog, but a more careful examination soon enables us to detect material differences. The head is thicker and shorter, the body not so bulky, the legs shorter, the hoofs longer, the ears shorter, and the tail is supplied by a slight, and, at a cursory glance, almost imperceptible protuberance. But the great difference arises from a small gland on the back, which, although partially concealed by the hair, is nevertheless evident, and hence it is that the term *Dicotyles*, which signifies a double navel, has been given to this species. This gland secretes a fluid which is emitted in great abundance whenever the animal is irritated, and gives out a very strong odor, pronounced as fetid and disagreeable by some authors, and by others compared with musk.

Cuvier remarks that the external toe on the hind feet is wanting in the peccary. The body is of a grayish hue, and thickly covered with strong coarse bristles, stiff enough to penetrate a tolerably firm substance, and shaded black and white. These are longest on the back, where some will be found measuring four or five inches; they become gradually shorter and shorter on the sides, and disappear altogether on the belly, which is nearly bare. On the head is a large tuft of black bristles. The eyes and snout are small, the ears erect.

This animal is found in vast numbers in Paraguay and Guiana, and has been termed by some writers the Mexican hog. It has nearly the same habits and tastes as the common hog; feeds on seeds and roots; digs with its snout; expresses its emotions by grunts; is fierce in defence of its young; very prolific; and the flesh is similar to ordinary pork, but harder, less sweet and juicy and not so fat.

The peccary may be tamed if taken when young, and will attach itself to those who are kind to it, and to dogs and other animals; is fond of being caressed and scratched, and will answer to its keeper's voice.

The European hog, when transplanted to the wilds of America, will herd with the peccaries, but is never known to breed with them; the two races, although resembling each other in certain points, are, and remain distinct. The hog is the larger, stronger, and more useful animal, and will thrive in almost any part of the world: the peccary is smaller, weaker, and cannot be made to live in a foreign climate without very great care and attention.

The BABIROUSSA, (*sus baby-roussa,*) or Hog-deer, or, as it has been termed by some foreign authors, the Indian hog, is chiefly found in the Moluccas, Sumatra, Java, and other islands of the Indian Archipelago.

This animal stands higher than the common hog; its legs are long and slender; its skin thin and scantily furnished with short woolly hair of a reddish brown on the back, and lighter and more inclined to fawn-color on the belly. It is chiefly remarkable for the strange position of its upper tusks, which come through the skin of the muzzle and curve backwards almost like horns, until they nearly or quite touch the skin again; they are sometimes as much as nine inches in length and five in circumference. Pliny (b. 8, chap. lii.) evidently alludes to this animal when he says that wild boars are found in India which have two horns on the face, similar to those of a heifer, and tusks like the common wild boars.

There are all the family characteristics of the hog in this animal; the heavy awkward gait, thick neck, small eyes, head terminated by a snout, and grunting voice; it feeds, too, on roots, plants, and leaves, and some say shell-fish; but some authors assert that it does not grub roots out of the ground like most of the swinish varieties. Sparrman informs us that the natives would rather attack a lion than this animal, for it comes rushing on a man swift as an arrow, and, throwing him down, snaps his legs in two and rips his belly up in a moment. (Voyage, vol ii.)

The flesh of the babiroussa is very fine eating, and the Malays melt down the fat to use instead of butter and oil.

Cuvier has given an account of a pair that were at the Menagerie at Paris, the female of which was much younger and more active than the male; he was old and fat, and only ate, drank, and slept. When the male retired to rest, the female would cover him completely over with straw or litter, and creep in after him, so that both were concealed from sight. The specimen at the Zoological Gardens in the Regent's Park used to cover himself up with straw in the same way.

THE PHACO-CHOERES.—There are two recognized species of this variety of the hog family, the one found in Guinea and the interior of the Cape, and spoken of by various writers as the Wark-hog, and the other first seen in Kordofan and afterwards in several parts of Abyssinia, and referred to by Ælian as the hog with four horns. Of the habits of these creatures little is known, save that they are inhabitants of forests, and their food is vegetable.

They are remarkable for the two warts or fleshy excrescences which disfigure the face on either side; the eyes are small; a bristly mane of a pale brown color rises between the ears and extends itself along the back, many of the hairs of which are from eight to ten inches in length; the body is bare; the tail thin and terminated by a tuft of hair; and the tusks very large and powerful.

THE CAPIBARA—is an animal which is often classed by modern zoologists among the Cavies; it also resembles a two-year old hog in shape and color, but its head is longer, its eyes larger, and its nose cleft like the lip of a rabbit, instead of being round. It has thick, coarse whiskers, a narrow mouth, and no tusks. The front hoofs are divided into four parts, and the back ones into three, and these divisions or toes are connected together by skin, and thus in a manner webbed, and adapted for swimming; indeed so much does it delight in the water that by some it has been called the water-hog. It lives upon fruit, corn, and sugar-canes, and eats all the fish it can catch. These animals associate in herds and seldom go out of their lair excepting in the night time, or quit the borders of some lake or river, for their short legs and strangely-formed feet prevent them from running with any degree of speed, so their only safety is in the water, wherein they plunge on the least alarm.

If taken young this animal may easily be tamed, and is capable of great attachment. We are informed that its flesh is tender, juicy, and fat, but has a fishy flavor; the head is, however, said to be excellent.

Cuvier refuses to admit this last-mentioned animal among the PACHYDERMATA, but places it in the order RODENTIA, genus *Cavia*.

The animal, too, so well known to us by the name of Guinea-pig, or among the French as the *Cochon d'Inde*, he also classes among the Rodentia. (Cuvier's Animal Kingdom.)

The name Hog has been given by different nations to various animals which have no affinity whatever with the actual family *Sus*: thus the Spaniards call the *tatous*, hogs in armor; the Hollanders term the *porcupine*, the iron-hog; the *porpoise* has frequently been designated the sea-hog; and Aristotle speaks of a hog-ape, which has been since supposed to refer to one of the baboon tribe; while among our common animals we have the hedge-hog. This has led to much confusion and misapprehension; but the genus *Suidae* or *Sus* is now very generally allowed to apply only to the actual swine as they exist in a wild or domesticated state throughout the greater part of the known world.

Martin says :—That the wild hog is the source of our ordinary domestic race cannot be disputed; and as little can we doubt its extreme antiquity. The hog has survived changes which have swept multitudes of pachydermatous animals from the surface of our earth. It still maintains an independent existence in Europe, and presents the same characters, both physical and moral, which the earliest writers, whether sacred or profane, have faithfully delineated. The domestic stock has indeed been more or less modified by long culture, but the wild species remains unaltered, insomuch that the fossil relics of its primitive ancestors may be identified by comparison with the bones of their descendants.

The fossil relics of the genus *sus* have been found in the miocene and also in the pliocene deposits of the tertiary system of Lyell. Kaup, for example, has described fossil bones of the genus *sus* from the miocene Eppelsheim sand, in which they were associated with those of the mastodon and dinotherium ; and MM. Croizet and Jobert, in their account of the fossils of Auvergne, describe ano figure the fossil bones of a species of hog, which, as was satisfactorily proved, must have lived coëxistent with and on the same locality as extinct elephants and mastodons. According to these geologists, the facial part of the fossil hog discovered by them is relatively shorter than in the existing species; hence, under the supposition that their fossil animal might have been distinct, they conferred upon it the title of *aper* (*sus*) *Avernensis.* How far this distinctiveness is real, yet remains to be seen ; at all events, Professor Owen, in his valuable work on British fossil mammalia, places the *sus Avernensis*, with a query, as one of the synonyms of the *cochon fossile* of Cuvier, *sus scrofa fossilis* of Von Meyer (*Palæologica,* p. 80,) *sus priscus* of Goldfuss (*Nova Acta Acad. Nat. Car.,* t. xi., pt. 2, p. 482,) the *fossil hog* of Dr. Buckland, and the *sus scrofa,* Owen, in *Report of British Association,* 1843, p. 228.

With reference to the fossil remains of the hog, Professor Owen thus writes :—" When Cuvier communicated his memoir on the fossil bones of the hog to the French Academy, in 1809, he had met with no specimens from formations less recent than the mosses, or turbaries and peat-bogs, and knew not that they had been found in the drift associated with the bones of elephants. He repeats this observation in the edition of the *Ossemens Fossiles,* in 1822; but in the additions to the last volume, published in 1825, Cuvier cites the discovery by M. Bourdet de la Nièvre of a fossil jaw of a *sus,* on the east bank of the lake of Neufchatel, and a fragment of the upper jaw from the cavern at Sundwick, in Westphalia, described by Professor Goldfuss.

" Dr. Buckland includes the molar teeth and a large tusk of a boar found in the cave of Hutton, in the Mendip hills, with the true fossils of that receptacle, such as the remains of the mammoth, Spelæan bear, &c. With respect to cave-bones, however, it is sometimes difficult to produce conviction as to the contemporaneity of extinct and recent species."

This observation applies merely to cave-bones, and not to such as are imbedded in deposits with other remains.

The oldest fossil remains of the hog, from British strata, which Professor Owen has examined, were from fissures in the red crag (probably miocene) of Newbourne, near Woodbridge, Suffolk :— "They were associated with teeth of an extinct *felis*, about the size of a leopard, with those of a bear, and with remains of a large *cervus*. These mammalian remains were found with the ordinary fossils of the red crag ; they had undergone the same process of trituration, and were impregnated with the same coloring matter, as the associated bones and teeth of fishes, acknowledged to be derived from the regular strata of the red crag. These mammaliferous beds have been proved by Mr. Lyell to be older than the fluvio-marine, or Norwich crag, in which remains of the mastodon, rhinoceros, and horse have been discovered ; and still older than the fresh-water pleistocene deposits, from which the remains of the mammoth, rhinoceros, &c., are obtained in such abundance." To this the Professor adds :—" I have met with some satisfactory instances of the association of fossil remains of a species of hog with those of the mammoth, in the newer pliocene fresh-water formations of England."

The most usual situations however, in which the fossilized bones of the hog are met with, are in peat-bogs, often at the depth of many feet, and in association with the remains of the wolf, the beaver, the roebuck, and a gigantic red-deer ; generally they underline the bed of peat, and rest on shell-marl or alluvium. Of the identity of these bones with those of the ordinary wild hog, all doubt has been removed by the most rigorous comparisons ; nevertheless, we do not assert that no other species of *sus* may not have anciently existed, which, like the mammoth and the mastodon, has become extinct ; we mean only to say that the bones of the *sus scrofa* are among the fossil remains of our island and the continent of Europe. Professor Owen gives an excellent figure of the fossil skull of a wild boar, from drift in a fissue of the free-stone quarries in the Isle of Portland.

Leaving the wild hog, let us direct our attention more immediately to that breed which, time immemorial, has been reared in captivity, and valued for the sake of its flesh, prepared in different ways as food for man.

"One of the most singular circumstances," says Mr. Wilson (*Quarterly Journal of Agriculture*,) "in the domestic history of this animal is the immense extent of its distribution, more especially in far removed and insulated spots inhabited by semibarbarians, where

the wild species is entirely unknown. For example, the South Sea
Islands, on their discovery by Europeans, were found to be well
stocked with a small black-legged hog ; and the traditionary belief
of the people, in regard to the original introduction of these animals,
showed that they were supposed to be as anciently descended as the
people themselves. Yet the latter had no knowledge of the wild
boar or any other animal of the hog kind, from which the domestic
breed might have been supposed to be derived. The hog is in these
islands the principal quadruped, and is more carefully cultivated
than any other. The bread-fruit tree, either in the natural state or
formed into sour paste, is its favorite food, and it is also abundantly
supplied with yams, eddoes, and other vegetables. This choice of a
nutritive and abundant diet, according to Foster, renders the flesh
juicy and delicious; and the fat, though rich, is not less delicate to
the taste than the finest butter. The Otaheitans and other South Sea
Islanders were in the habit of presenting pigs at the *morais*, as the
most savory and acceptable offering to their deities which they had i:
in their power to bestow. They covered the sacred pig with a piece
of fine cloth, and left it to decay near the hallowed spot."

The pigs of these islands are evidently of the Cochin-Chinese or
Siamese variety, or at least are closely allied to it, and were no
doubt introduced at some remote period by the colonists of Malay-
an origin. Cook found the fowl, as well as the hog, at Ulietea and
others of the Society Islands.

It has been doubted, and not without some reason, whether the
domestic breed, so widely spread, is in every country attributable
to the same specific origin. Certain it is that the various domestic
races offer marked distinctive peculiarities, and if Mr. Eyton be
correct, differences not only in the length of the snout, size of the
ears, and symmetry of the body, but also in the number of the vertebræ of the spinal column. In the *Proceedings of the Zoological
Society* for February 28th, 1837, p. 23, will be found the following
observations by T. C. Eyton, Esq., on the osteological peculiarities
to which we have alluded :—" Having during the last year prepared
the skeleton of a male pig of the pure Chinese breed, brought over
by Lord Northampton, I was surprised to find that a very great
difference existed in the number of the vertebræ from that given in
the *Leçons d'Anatomie Comparee*, vol. i., ed. 1835, p. 182, under the
head either of *Sanglier*, or *Cochon Domestique*. A short time
afterwards, through the kindness of Sir Rowland Hill, Bart., M. P.,
I prepared the skeleton of a female pig from Africa; this also differ-
ed, as also does the English long-legged sort, as it is commonly
called.

"The following table will show the differences in the number of
the vertebræ in each skeleton with those given in the work above
quoted :—

Vertebræ.	English Male	African Female.	Chinese Male.	Legons d'Anat. Comp. Sanglier.	Coch.Dom.
Cervical,	7	7	7	7	7
Dorsal,	15	13	15	14	14
Lumbar,	6	6	4	5	5
Sacral,	5	5	4	4	4
Caudal,	21	13	19	20	23
Total,	55	44	49	50	53

"It is possible that some of the caudal vertebræ may be missing.

"The Chinese was imported into this country for the purpose of improving our native sorts, with which it breeds freely, and the off-spring are again fruitful. I, this winter, saw a fine litter of pigs by Sir Rowland Hill's African *boar*, imported with the female I describ-ed, the mother of which was a *common pig*; time will show whether they will be again fruitful.

"From what has been stated, the result appears to me to be, that either of the above three pigs must be considered as distinct species, (and which, should the offspring of the two latter again produce young, would do away with the theory of Hunter, that the young of two distinct species are not fruitful,) or we cannot consider osteo-logical character a criterion of species.

"I have been induced to offer the above, not with any desire of species-making, but of adding something towards the number of recorded facts, by which the question what is a species, must be answered."

Closely-allied species *may* produce offspring fertile *inter se*, although we have no proof positive of the fact in the case in question; for when domestication produces decided differences of external form, why should it be difficult to admit of the extension of the differ-ences to internal parts also, and especially to the osseous frame-work, on which the form and symmetry of the body so greatly depend, or why the law of variation should be confined in its influence to one part, and restricted from another. If it be admitted that the bones may be somewhat modified in length or stoutness, we see not why it is that a numerical variation in the bones of the vertebral column should be so great a stumbling-block, especially seeing that accidental (and perhaps hereditary) variations are far from being uncommon, both in men and others of the mammalia. We can easily conceive that a portion of the osseous system, offering in al-most every species of quadruped some variation in the number of its constituent parts, should be also the most likely to exhibit such variation, where a species long subjected to the modifying influence of human control, has branched out into various breeds or races, distinguished by decided external characteristics. It would be interesting and important to know, whether the numerical ratio of the vertebræ, as given in the foregoing table, is constant in each race; and also whether the same variation does not obtain among others of our domestic animals, divided into numerous breeds or races, as the dog, the sheep, and the goat. The subject has not been treated so fully and extensively as it deserves. With respect to the caudal vertebræ, indeed, we know that they are subject to great numerical variation in most of our domestic animals; witness the dog and even the common fowl, of which latter, a tailless breed, perpetuated from generation to generation, is far from being uncommon. What takes place in one part of the spinal column may, we conceive, occur also in another and more important portion, to some, if not to so great an extent; and the modification may moreover be transmitted from one generation to another.

Examples of extraordinary modification in other parts of the skeleton, transmissible from generation to generation, may be here adduced in confirmation of our views. Aristotle notices a race of hogs with undivided toes, or rather with hoofs consolidated together; and Linnæus informs us that a similar variety of the hog is not unfrequent in the neighborhood of Upsal, in Sweden. A still more extraordinary case of modification of the osseous framework, is recorded in the *Proceedings of the Zoological Society for* 1833, p. 16, where will be found the notice of a race of pigs with only two legs, the hinder extremities being entirely wanting. The communication, with drawings of two individuals, was made by Colonel Hallam, who states that these animals were observed " at a town on the coast in the Tanjore country, in the year 1795; they were from a father and mother of a similar make, and the pigs bred from them were the same." Thus, then, accidental malformations, either by excess or deficiency, may become transmissible, and so perpetuate themselves.

The views of a writer in the *Penny Cyclopædia*, on the subject of the osteological differences observable in domestic swine, are much in accordance with our own. Undoubtedly, he remarks, such records as those given by Mr. Eyton are valuable, but he thinks that the inference is precipitate; adding, that John Hunter's theories are not so easily done away with, and that osteological character will continue to be a criterion of species, notwithstanding the differences set forth. He says, " By the term *pig*, we understand the African and Chinese varieties of the hog. *Phacochœrus* cannot be meant, or it would be stated. The pure Chinese breed was imported long ago; and for years its stock, bred from its union with our English varieties, has been known in our farm-yards. The varieties bred by man from the wild hog, are spread all over the world in a domesticated state; and there is no more reason to doubt that the result, a union of an African pig with a Hampshire hog, would be fruitful, than that a breed composed of the Berkshire, Chinese, and Neapolitan, would produce a good litter. Now, if we take little or no note of the differences in the caudal vertebræ, for the reason assigned by Mr. Eyton among others, what remain? Differences not exceeding two in the dorsal vertebræ, two in the lumbar verte-tebræ, and one in the sacral vertebræ, after a course of domestication no one knows how long. We know what breeding will do with dogs. Take a greyhound and a true shepherd's dog, for example, to say nothing of tailless cats. We know what it will do among poultry : it will take away the drooping feathers of the cock's tail in those bantams known to fanciers as hen-cocks, (Sir J. Sebright's breed,) and remove the tail-feathers altogether (rumpless fowls); whilst in the top-knotted varieties an osteological difference is produced in the cranium. Man has occasionally an additional lumbar vertebræ. This accidental excess was first detected in the negro, and was laid hold of by those who would have made him a different species; but by-and-by they found a white man with one more vertebra than he ought to have had, and wisely said no more about it.

We have, then, no solid or sufficient grounds for believing that, widely as the domestic hog is spread, and remote and insulated as are some of the localities in which it has been discovered by voyagers, it is derived from different sources; although, as we have shown, there are more wild species of the restricted genus *sus* than zoologists formerly suspected. In making these remarks, we may add, that as to every general rule there are exceptions, so some are to be found here. The Papuan hog, caught and reared in captivity, is distinct, and it is probable that the domestic hogs of Borneo, and of some of the islands adjacent, are derived from the wild races there indigenous. Be this as it may, we do not mean to insist upon the fact; our subject is the ordinary hog, as we see it in its state of contented domestication in Europe, and especially our own country.

CHAPTER II.

Derivation of the term Hog—The Hog was greatly esteemed by the Romans—Worshipped by some of the ancients—Swine's flesh prohibited by the law of Moses—By that of Mohammed —Despised by the Egyptians.

THE term Hog is stated by Carpenter, to be derived from the Hebrew word חֲזִיר, by which this animal was designated among the Hebrews, a word derived from חָזַר, to *encompass* or *surround*, suggested by the round figure, in his fat and most natural state. Bochart and Schultens, however are more inclined to refer the Hebrew noun to the Arabic sense of the verb, *viz.*, *to have narrow eyes*, and there is much of the probability in their supposition. In some respects swine seem to form an intermediate link between the whole-footed and cloven-footed animals, and the others to occupy the same ground between the cloven-footed and the digitative; but look at them in what point of view we may, these animals present various peculiar characteristics, and are of vast importance as affording the means of sustenance to millions of human beings in all parts of the world. The hog is a perfect cosmopolite, adapting itself to almost every climate; increasing rapidly, being more prolific than any other domestic animal, with the exception of the rabbit; easily susceptible of improvement, and quickly attaining to maturity.

As far back as the records of history enable us to go, the hog appears to have been known, and his flesh made use of as food. 1491 years before Christ, Moses gave those laws to the Israelites which have occasioned so much discussion, and given rise to the many opinions which we shall presently have to speak of; and it is quite evident that had not pork then been the prevailing food of that nation, such stringent commandments and prohibitions would not have been necessary. The various allusions to this kind of meat, which occur again and again, in the writings of the old Greek authors, plainly testify the esteem in which it was held among this nation, and it appears that the Romans actually made the art of breeding, rearing, and fattening pigs a study, which they designated *Proculatio.* Every art was put in practice to impart a finer and more delicate flavor to the flesh; the poor animals were fed, and crammed, and tortured to death in various ways, many of them too horrible to be described, in order to gratify the epicurism and gluttony of this people. Pliny informs us that they fed swine on dried figs, and drenched them to repletion with honeyed wine, in order to produce a diseased and monstrous-sized liver. The *Porcus Trojanus*, so called in allusion to the Trojan horse, was a very celebrated dish, and one that eventually became so extravagantly expensive that a sumptuary law was passed respecting it. This dish consisted in a whole hog, with the entrails drawn out, and the inside stuffed with thrushes, larks, beccaficoes, oysters, nightingales, and delicacies of every kind, and the whole bathed in wine and rich gravies. Another great dish was a hog served whole, the one side roasted and the other boiled.

Varro states that the Gauls produced the largest and finest swine's flesh that was brought into Italy; and, according to Strabo, in the reign of Augustus, they supplied Rome and nearly all Italy with gammons, hog-puddings, hams, and sausages. This nation and the Spaniards appear to have kept immense droves of swine, but scarcely any other kind of live stock; and various authors mention swine as forming a part of the live stock of most Roman farms.

In fact the hog was held in very high esteem among the early nations of Europe, and some of the ancients have even paid it divine honors.   In the island of Crete it was regarded as sacred. This animal was always sacrificed to Ceres at the beginning of harvest, and to Bacchus at the commencement of the vintage, by the Greeks; probably, it has been suggested, "because this animal is equally hostile to the growing corn and the ripening grape."

The Jews, the Egyptians, and the followers of Mohammed, alone appear to have abstained from it.   To the former nation it is expressly forbidden by the laws of Moses.   Leviticus xi. 7, says: "And the swine, though he divide the hoof, and be cloven-footed, yet he cheweth not the cud; he is unclean unto you."   Mohammed probably founded his prohibition on this one, or was induced, by the prejudices of his followers, to make it.   Numerous theories have been advanced by different authors to account for this remark-able prohibition uttered by Moses against a species of food generally so wholesome and nutritious as the flesh of the hog.   Maimonides says: "The principal reason why the law prohibited the swine was, because of their extreme filthiness, and their eating so many impu rities; for it is well known with what care and precision the law forbids all filthiness and dirt, even in the fields and in the camp, not to mention in the cities.   Now, had swine been permitted, the public places, and streets, and houses, would have been made nuisances."

Tacitus states that the Jews abstained from it in consequence of a leprosy by which they had formerly severely suffered, and to which the hog is very subject.   And several other writers concur in this view, stating that it was on account of the flesh being strong, olea-ginous, difficult of digestion, and liable to produce cutaneous diseases, that it was forbidden.   Michaelis observes, that throughout the whole climate under which Palestine is situated, leprosy is an endemic disease; and the Israelites being overrun with it at the period of their quitting Egypt, Moses found it necessary to enact a variety of laws respecting it, and the prohibiting the use of swine was one of these.   Plutarch (de Iside) affirms that those who drank the milk of swine became blotchy and leprous.

M. Sonnini states that in Egypt, Syria, and even the southern parts of Greece, swine's flesh, although white and delicate, is so flabby and surcharged with fat, as to disagree with the strongest stomachs, and this will account for its prohibition by the priests and legislators of hot climates, such an abstinence being absolutely necessary to health beneath the burning suns of Egypt and Arabia. "The Egyptians," he says, "were only allowed to eat pork once a year, on the feast-day of the moon, and then they sacrificed a num ber of these animals to that planet.   If at any other time an Egyp-tian even touched a hog, he was obliged to plunge into the Nile.

clothes and all, to purify himself. The swineherds formed an isolated race, outcasts from society, forbidden to enter a temple, or
intermarry with other families." Hence it probably is, that, in the
beautiful parable of the Prodigal Son, this unhappy young man is
represented as being reduced to the office of a swineherd, that being
considered as the lowest possible degradation.

Others are of opinion that this and many other of the prohibitions
and ordinances established by Moses were solely for the purpose of
distinguishing the Jews from other nations, and making them what
they are to this day in all countries and under all climates, "a peculiar people." Others, again, assert that it was with a view to
correct their gross and gluttonous habits that none but the simplest
and mildest kinds of animal food were permitted to the Jews. And,
lastly, another maintains that the swine was thus declared an abomination in the sight of God, as a lesson to the Jews to abstain from
the sensual and disgusting habits to which this animal is given.

The aversion to swine has descended to the Jews, Egyptians, and
followers of Mohammed of modern times. The Copts rear no
pigs, indeed this animal is scarcely known in most of the cities of
Lower Egypt; and the poorest Jew would sooner starve than touch
a morsel of this forbidden food, even though the presumed cause of
prohibition has long ceased to exist, and he is removed to colder
climes, where pork is both wholesome and nutritious.

By the precepts, warnings, and threatenings of the prophets, we
read that, so great was the detestation excited in the minds of the
Jewish nation against this animal, that they would not even pollute
their lips by pronouncing its name, but always alluded to it as "that
beast," "that thing;" and we read in the history of the Maccabees,
that Eleazer, a principal scribe, being compelled by Antiochus Epi-
phanes to open his mouth and receive swine's flesh, spit it forth, and
went of his accord to the torment, choosing rather to suffer death
than break the divine law and offend his nation,

And yet it is well known that immense numbers of swine were
reared in the country of the Jews, probably for the purpose of gain,
and in order to supply strangers and the neighboring idolaters; and
it has been supposed, that it was in order to punish this violation of
the Divine commandments that our Saviour permitted the herd of
swine to be affected with that sudden disorder which caused them to
rush headlong into the lake of Genesareth.

Martin says—at what period the hog was reclaimed, and by what
nation, we cannot tell. As far back as the records of history go, we
find notices of this animal, and of the use of its flesh as food. By
some nations it was held in abhorrence, and prohibited as food;
while among others its flesh was accounted a great delicacy. By
the Mosaic law, the Jews were forbidden to use the flesh of the swine
as food—it was unclean; and the followers of Mohammed, borrow-

ing their ritual from the institutions of Moses, hold the flesh of the hog in utter abhorrence. Paxton, in his *Illustrations of Scripture*, vol. i., says, " The hog was justly classed by the Jews among the vilest animals in the scale of animated nature ; and it cannot be doubted that his keeper generally shared in the contempt and abhorrence which he had excited. The prodigal son in the parable had spent his all in riotous living, and was ready to perish through want, before he submitted to the humiliating employment of feeding swine."

We pass over Paxton's description of the hog as the "vilest of animals," because there is no sense in the expression, and its presumed meaning is unworthy notice. It cannot, however, be doubted, from the passage in Luke, (xv. 15,) and from others well known, that herds of swine were kept by the Jews, perhaps for sale and profit. Dr. J. Kitto says, "There does not appear to be any reason in the law of Moses why the hog should be held in such peculiar abomination. There seems nothing to have prevented the Jews, if they had been so inclined, to rear pigs for sale, or for the use of the *lard*. In the Talmud there are some indications that this was actually done ; and it was probably for such purpose that the herds of swine, mentioned in the New Testament, were kept, although it is usual to consider that they were kept by the foreign settlers in the land. Indeed the story which accounts for the peculiar aversion of the Hebrews to the hog, assumes that it did not originate until about one hundred and thirty years before Christ, and that previously some Jews were in the habit of rearing hogs for the purposes indicated.

The same writer, in a note upon Luke viii. 32, enters at greater length into this subject. "We have already," he says, "intimated our belief that there was much error in supposing that the law which declared that certain kinds of animals were not to be used for food, should be understood as prohibiting them from rearing, for any other purpose, the animals interdicted as food. There was certainly nothing in the law to prevent them from rearing hogs, more than from rearing asses, if they saw fit to do so. It appears, in fact, that the Jews did rear pigs for sale to their heathen neighbors, till this was forbidden after the principle of refining upon the law had been introduced. This prohibition demonstrates the previous existence of the practice ; and it did not take effect till about seventy years B.C., when it is alleged to have originated in a circumstance which occurred between Hyrcanus and Aristobulus, the sons of King Alexander Janneus. Aristobulus was besieging Hyrcanus in Jerusalem ; but not wishing to interrupt the services of the temple, he permitted an arrangement under which money was let down from the temple in a box, in return for which the lambs required for the daily sacrifices were sent up. It at last occurred to a mischievous

old man, 'who understood the wisdom of the Greeks,' that there
would be no overcoming the adverse party while they employed
themselves in the service of God; and therefore one morning he
put a hog in the box, instead of a lamb. When half way up, the
pig reared himself up, and happened to rest his fore feet upon the
temple wall, whereupon continues the story, Jerusalem and the land
of Israel quaked. In consequence of this, two orders were issued
by the Council: 'Cursed be he that breedeth hogs;' and 'Cursed
be he who teacheth his son the learning of the Greeks.' Such is
the origin of the order against rearing hogs, as related in the Baby-
lonian Talmud. One of the enforcements of this prohibition is
curious, as showing for what purposes besides sale, hogs had been
reared by the Jews. 'It is forbidden to rear any hog, even though
hogs should come to a man by inheritance, in order to obtain profit
from its skin or from its fat, for anointing or for light.' From this
it would seem that the Jews had been wont to make ointments with
hog's lard, and that they did not exclusively use oil for lights, but
fat also, which was probably done according to a method we have
often seen in the East, by introducing a wick into a lump of grease,
which is set in a lamp, or in a round hollow vessel, made for the
purpose; the heat of the kindled wick, as in a candle, gradually
melts as much of the fat as is required to feed the flame. The inconvenience of the deprivation of the useful lard of hogs for this
and other purposes, seems to have given occasion to an explanation,
that the prohibition was not to be understood to imply that the fat
of hogs might not be obtained by purchase from the Gentiles. The
prohibition of keeping hogs does not appear to have had complete
effect, as regulations are made concerning towns in which hogs were
kept; and the keepers of swine are mentioned as contemptible and
infamous wretches, so that it was a favorite term of abuse to call
a person a hog-breeder or a swineherd. Although, therefore,
it may be likely that the herds of swine here mentioned were the
property of the heathen, who certainly did live with the Jews in
the towns of this neighborhood, (the country of the Gadarenes,) it is
not impossible that they belonged to the Jews, who kept them in
despite of the prohibitions we have mentioned."

Among the ancient Egyptians, although the figure of the hog
occurs several times well drawn at Edfou, this animal was held in
detestation. "Swine," says Herodotus, "are accounted such impure
beasts by the Egyptians, that if a man touches one even by accident, he presently hastens to the river, and in all his clothes plunges
himself into the water. For this reason, swineherds alone of the
Egyptians are not suffered to enter any of their temples; neither
will any man give his daughter in marriage to one of that profession,
nor take a wife born of such parents, so that they are necessitated
to intermarry among themselves. The Egyptians are forbidden to

sacrifice swine to any other deities than to Bacchus and to the moon, when completely at full, at which time they may eat of the flesh. When they offer this sacrifice to the moon, and have killed the victim, they put the end of the tail, with the spleen and fat, into a caul found in the belly of the animal, all which they burn on the sacred fire, and eat the rest of the flesh on the day of the full moon, though at any other time they would not taste it. Those who, on account of their poverty, cannot bear the expense of this sacrifice, mould a paste into the form of a hog, and make their offering. In the evening of the festival of Bacchus, though every one be obliged to kill a swine before the door of his house, yet he immediately restores the carcass to the swineherd who sold it."

This aversion towards the hog, among the ancient Egyptians and the Jews, (we need not here notice the Mohammedans or the Brahminical tribes of India,) is very remarkable. Among the Greeks and Romans the flesh of the swine was held in estimation, although the swineherd attracted little notice from the poet. Why, then, in Western Asia and Egypt should it have been forbidden? We attribute it entirely to mystical or religious motives, which we are not quite able to appreciate.

The following passage from Griffith's Cuvier is worthy our consideration, although it does not bring conviction to our mind; it is rather plausible than demonstrative:—" In hot climates the flesh of swine is not good. M. Sonnini remarks, that in Egypt, Syria, and even the southern parts of Greece, this meat, though very white and delicate, is so far from being firm, and is so overcharged with fat, that it disagrees with the strongest stomachs. It is therefore considered unwholesome, and this will account for its proscription by the legislators and priests of the East. Such an abstinence was doubtless indispensable to health, under the burning suns of Egypt and Arabia. The Egyptians were permitted to eat pork only once a year—on the feast day of the moon—and then they sacrificed a number of these animals to that planet. At other times, if any one even touched a hog, he was obliged immediately to plunge into the river Nile, with his clothes on, by way of purification. The swineherds formed an isolated class, the outcasts of society. They were interdicted from entering the temples, or intermarrying with any other families. This aversion for swine has been transmitted to the modern Egyptians. The Copts rear no pigs, any more than do the followers of Mohammed. The Jews, who borrowed from the Egyptians their horror of pigs, as well as many other peculiarities, continue their abstinence from them in colder climates, where they form one of the most useful articles of subsistence."

If the hog in warm climates is so unwholesome as food, how happens it that the Chinese rear this animal in such numbers for the table? and how happens it that the hare (if indeed this animal be intended) was forbidden by the Mosaic laws as food? Surely the same objection could not apply to this latter animal as to the hog. Whatever the motive might have been, both among the Egyptians and the Jews, which led them to forbid the use of swine's flesh on the table, a regard to the health of the people was not one. Locusts were permitted by the latter, but creeping things in general denied, as were also fishes destitute of apparent scales. Among the ancient Greeks and Romans, the flesh of the pig was held in great estimation. The art of rearing, breeding, or fattening these animals, was made a complete study; and the dishes prepared from the meat were dressed with epicurean refinement, and in many modes. One dish consisted of a young pig whole, stuffed with beccaficoes and other small birds, together with oysters, and served in wine and rich gravy. This dish was termed *Porcus Trojanus*, in allusion to the wooden horse, filled with men, which the Trojans introduced into their city—an unpleasant allusion, one would think, seeng that the Romans boasted their Trojan descent. However, such was the name of this celebrated and most expensive dish, so costly, indeed, that sumptuary regulations were passed respecting it.

Esteemed, however, as the flesh of the hog was by the Greeks and Romans, commonly as the animal was kept, and carefully and even curiously as it was fed, in order to gratify the appetites of the wealthy and luxurious, yet the swineherd, as may be inferred from the silence of the classic writers, and especially of the poets who painted rural life, was not held in much estimation. No gods or heroes are described as keeping swine. Theocritus never introduces the swineherd into his idyls, nor does Virgil admit him into his eclogues, among his tuneful shepherds. Homer indeed honors Eumæus, the swineherd of Ulysses, with many commendations; but he is a remarkable exception. Perhaps a general feeling prevailed, and still in some measure prevails, that the feeders of the gluttonous and wallowing swine became assimilated in habits and manners to the animals under their charge; or, it may be, that the prejudices of the Egyptians relative to this useful class of men, extended to Greece or Italy, giving a bias to popular opinion.

From the earliest times in our own island, the hog has been regarded as a very important animal, and vast herds were tended by swineherds, who watched over their safety in the woods, and collected them under shelter at night. Its flesh was the staple article of consumption in every household, and much of the wealth of the rich and free portion of the community consisted in these animals. Hence bequests of swine, with land for their support, were often made; rights and privileges connected with their feeding, and the extent of woodland to be occupied by a given number, were granted according to established rules. In an ancient Saxon grant, quoted by Sharon Turner in his *History of the Anglo-Saxons*, we find the right of pasturage for swine conveyed by deed :—" I give food for seventy swine in that woody allotment which the countrymen call Wolferdinlegh." The locality of the swine's pasturage, as here described, has a somewhat ominous title, referring as it does to the haunt of an animal, from incursions of which, on flocks of sheep and herds of swine, during the Saxon period of our history, both the shepherd and the swineherd had to preserve their respective charges. The men employed in the duties—generally thralls, or borne slaves of the soil—were assisted by powerful dogs, capable of contending with a wolf, at least until the swineherd came with his heavy quarter-staff or spear to the rescue. In Sir Walter Scott's novel of *Ivanhoe*, the character of Gurth is a true, but of course somewhat overcolored picture of an Anglo-Saxon swineherd, as is that of his master of a large landed proprietor, a great proportion of whose property consisted in swine, and whose rude but hospitable board, was liberally supplied with the flesh.

Long after the close of the Saxon dynasty, the practice of feeding swine upon the mast and acorns of the forest was continued, till our forests were cut down and the land laid open for the plough; even yet, in some districts, as the New Forest of Hampshire, the custom is not discontinued, and in various parts of the country, where branching oaks in the hedgerow overshadow the rural and secluded lanes, the cottagers turn out their pig or pigs, under the care of some boy, to pick up the fallen acorns in autumn. Pigs turned out upon stubble fields after harvest, often find in oak copses, in October and November, a welcome addition to their fare.

The large forests of England were formerly royal property; nevertheless the inhabitants of the adjacent towns, villages, and farms enjoyed both before and long after the Conquest, under certain conditions of a feudal nature, and probably varying according to circumstances, and the tenures by which lands were held, the right of fattening their swine in these woodlands. The lawful period for depasturing swine in the royal forests extended from fifteen days before Michaelmas, to forty days afterwards, and this was termed the pawnage month. This term was not, however, very strictly adhered to; many herds were suffered to remain in the forest during the whole year, the consequence of which was that numbers became feral, and were not collected by their owners without difficulty. Little damage would be done in the woods by these swine, but, no doubt, like their wild progenitors, they would take every opportunity of invading the cultivated grounds, and of rioting in the fields of green or ripening corn.

3*

CHAPTER III.

The early history of Swine—Legendary and authentic records respecting the keeping of them in England—Ancient Welsh laws relative to Swine—The forests of England—Swineherds—Their mode of managing their herds—Calabrian Swineherds—Horn used to assemble the grunting troop—The Schwein-General—Herds of Swine kept in France—Value of Pigs—Some vindication of them—Anecdote proving their teachability—Sagacity of a Pig—Some demonstration of Memory in one—Attachment to individuals—Swine not innately filthy animals—They are possessed of more docility than they usually have credit for—Their exquisite sense of smell—Pigs said to foretell rain and wind.

In Greece and the neighboring islands, swine were common at an early period, and were kept in large droves by swineherds; for we read in Homer's Odyssey, which is supposed to have been written upwards of 900 years B. C., that Ulysses, on his return from the Trojan war, first sought the dwelling of Eumæus, his faithful servant, and the keeper of his swine: and that office must then have been held in high esteem, or it would not have been performed by that wise and good old man.

The rude tables of the ancient Britons were chiefly supplied from their herds of swine, and the flesh of these animals furnished them with a great variety of dishes. (Cæsar, book i. chap 1.)

Sharon Turner, in his History of the Anglo-Saxons, while enumerating their live stock, states they had "great abundance of swine;" and adds, that although horned cattle are occasionally mentioned in grants, wills, and exchange of property, swine are most frequently spoken of. The country then abounded with woods and forests, and these are seldom particularized without some mention being made of the swine fed in them. These animals appear in fact to have constituted a considerable item in the wealth of an individual, for legacies of them often occur in wills. Thus Alfred, a nobleman, bequeathed to his relatives a hide of land with one hundred swine, and directs that another hundred shall be given for masses for the benefit of his soul; and to his daughters he leaves two thousand. So Elfhelm left land to St. Peter's at Westminster, on the express condition that they should feed a herd of two hundred swine for the use of his wife.

In the original Doomsday-Book for Hampshire, where an estimate of the value of the lands and forests belonging to the king, the monasteries, the hundreds, and other divisions is given, the number of hogs which can be fed on each separate portion is invariably specified.

In the oldest of the Welsh Triads, (which treat of the events of Britain in general,) we find evidence of the early domestication of swine, for one of these contains a recital of the actions of three powerful swineherds in the Isle of Britain, "over whom it was not possible to prevail or gain," and who restored the swine to their owners with increase. Some of the fabulous narrations blended with the history of these swineherds have been attributed by antiquarians to a period antecedent to Christianity.

In the laws of Howel Dha, there is a chapter on the value of animals, in which it is stated "that the price of a little pig from the time it is born until it grows to burrow, is one penny; when it ceases sucking, which is at the end of three months, it is worth twopence; from that time it goes to the wood with the swine, and it is considered as a swine, and its value is fourpence; from the Feast of St. John unto the 1st day of January, its value is fifteenpence; from the 1st of January unto the Feast of St. John, its value is twenty-four pence; and from that time forward its value shall be thirty pence, the same as its mother."

"The qualities of a sow are, that she breeds pigs and do not devour her young ones. The seller must also warrant her sound against the quinsy for three days and nights after she is sold. If she should not possess these qualities, one third of her price must be returned. The value of a boar is equal to the value of three sows."

The British forests, which formerly occupied the greater part of England, were peopled by the swinish multitude. Hertfordshire was nearly covered with wood and forest land; Buckinghamshire boasted its magnificent Bern Wood; Hampshire, its extensive New Forest; nor were the other counties destitute of these sylvan retreats, which have latterly vanished before the axe of the woodman and the industry of the husbandman.

In 1646 Norwood in Surrey is described as containing 830 acres from which the inhabitants of Croydon "have herbage for all kinds of cattle, and mastage for swine without stint."

The right of the forest borderers to fatten their swine in the various forests, formerly royal property, is very ancient, being evidently anterior to the Conquest. At first a small tax or fee was paid by those holding this right; but whether this went to the crown, or consisted in a certain gratuity to the forest ranger or the swineherd, is nowhere specified in the records. This privilege, like all others, was greatly abused; for many of the keepers availed themselves of it, and kept large herds of swine which they suffered to run the forests during the whole of the year, doing exceeding damage to the timber as well as to the land.

The actual period for which it was lawful to turn swine into the royal woods and forests for *masting*, was from fifteen days before Michaelmas to forty days afterwards, and this was termed the pawnage month.

Nor was the practice of feeding swine in herds, peculiar to this country. In Calabria they are grazed in herds, and the keeper uses a kind of bagpipe, the tones of which, when the period arrives for their being driven home, quickly collects the scattered groups from every part. In Tuscany it is the same.

In Germany almost every village has its swineherd, who at break
of day goes from house to house collecting his noisy troop, blowing
his still more noisy cow-horn, and cracking his clumsy whip, until
the place echoes with the din. The following very amusing account
of that important personage, the *Schwein-General*, has lately been
given in a popular work :—

"Every morning I hear the blast of a horn, when, proceeding
from almost every door in the street, behold a pig! The pigs generally proceed of their own accord; but shortly after they have
passed, there comes a little bare-headed, bare-footed, stunted child
about eleven years old. This little attendant of the old pig-driver
facetiously called at Langen-Schwalbach the 'Schwein-General,
knows every house from which a pig ought to have proceeded: she
can tell by the door being open or shut, or even by footmarks,
whether the creature has joined the herd, or is still snoring in its sty
A single glance determines whether she shall pass a yard, or enter
it; and if a pig, from indolence or greediness, be loitering on the
road, the sting of the wasp cannot be sharper or more spiteful than
the cut she gives it.

"Besides the little girl who brought up the rear, the herd was
preceded by a boy of about fourteen, whose duty it was not to let
the foremost advance too fast. In the middle of the drove, surrounded like a shepherd by his flock, slowly stalked the 'Schwein-
General.' In his left hand he held a staff, while round his right
shoulder hung a terrific whip. At the end of a short handle, turning upon a swivel, there was a lash about nine feet long, each joint
being an iron ring, which, decreasing in size, was closely connected
with its neighbor by a band of hard greasy leather. The pliability,
the weight, and the force of this iron whip, rendered it an argument
which the obstinacy even of the pig was unable to resist; yet, as
the old man proceeded down the town, he endeavored to speak
kindly to the herd.

"As soon as the herd had got out of the town, they began gradually to ascend the rocky, barren mountain which appeared towering
above them, and then the labors of the *Schwein-General* and his
staff became greater than ever; in due time the drove reached the
ground which was devoted for that day's exercise, the whole mountain being thus taken in regular succession.

"In this situation do the pigs remain every morning for four hours,
enjoying little else but air and exercise. At about nine or ten
o'clock they begin their march homeward, and nothing can form a
greater contrast than their entry does to their exit from their native
town.

"Their eager anxiety to get to the dinner trough that awaits them
is almost ungovernable, and they no sooner reach the first houses of
the town than away each of them starts towards his home.

"At half-past four the same horn is heard again; the pigs once more assemble, ascend the mountains, remain there for four hours, and in the evening return to their styes.

"Such is the life of the pigs, not only of Langen-Schwalbach, but those of every village throughout a great part of Germany : every day of their existence, summer and winter, is spent in the way described."

In France, swine are kept in herds, and in many districts the feeding of them in the woods and forests, (*le glandage*,) under certain conditions and restrictions, has been a source of no inconsiderable emolument to the forester. Indeed, to such an extent was it carried in certain localities, that it became an object of political economy. But of late years it has much diminished; the progress of agriculture is fast sweeping away those immense tracts of woodland country which formerly existed in England and France, and with them depart the denizens of the forest, wild or tame.

Nature designed the hog to fulfil many important functions in a forest country. By his burrowing after roots and such like, he turns up and destroys the larvæ of innumerable insects that would otherwise injure the trees as well as their fruit. He destroys the slug, snail, snake, and adder, and thus not only rids the forest of these injurious and unpleasant inhabitants, but also makes them subservient to his own nourishment, and thus to the benefit of mankind. The fruits which he eats, are such as would otherwise rot on the ground and be wasted, or yield nutriment to vermin; and his digging for earth-nuts, &c., loosens the soil and benefits the roots of the trees. Hence, hogs in forest-land may be regarded as eminently beneficial, and it is only the abuse of it which is to be feared. The German agriculturist, Thaër, does not, however, advocate the forest feeding of swine unless they are kept in the woods day and night and carefully sheltered; as he conceives that the bringing them home at night heats their blood, and nullifies the good effects of the day's feeding. He likewise considers that, although acorns produce good firm flesh, beechmast makes unsound oily fat.

But if he is a useful animal in this public point of view, how much more so is he to individuals? Among the poorer classes ot society how often is the pig their chief source of profit. In Ireland is this especially the case; there he is emphatically "*the gintleman what pays the rint*," better treated often than the peasant's own children. The small cost at which these animals can be reared and fattened, and their fecundity and wonderful powers of thriving under disadvantages, render them an actual blessing to many a poor cotter, who, with his little savings, buys a young and ill-conditioned pig, fattens it on all the refuse he can beg or spare, or collect, and sells it at a good profit, or occasionally, perhaps, kills it for the use of his family, who thus obtain an ample supply of cheap, nutritious diet.

Were it not for this animal, many of the laboring poor would

2*

scarcely be able to keep a roof over their heads, therefore, we may with justice designate the hog "the poor man's friend."

With the exception of the rabbit, swine are the most prolific of all domesticated animals, and this is another argument in their favor Nor does its value cease with its life; there is scarcely a portion of the pig that is not available for some useful purpose. The flesh takes the salt more kindly than that of any other animal, and, whether dried as bacon, or salted down as pickled pork, forms an excellent and nutritious food, exceedingly valuable for all kinds of stores. The fat, or lard is useful for numerous purposes—the housewife, the apothecary, and the perfumer in particular, know how to value it; the head, the feet, and great part of the intestines, all are esteemed as delicacies. Brawn, that far-famed domestic preparation—which is evidently no recently invented dish, for at the marriage of Henry IV., in 1403, and of Henry V. in 1419, we find, among other records quoted by Strutt, that brawn and a kind of hashed pork formed the staple dishes—is made from the hog. The bristles, too, are another important item in the matters furnished by swine; they are used by brushmakers, and are necessary to the shoemaker, and some idea may be formed of the extent to which they form an article of use and of commerce, when we state that in the year 1828 alone, 1,748,921 lbs. of hog's bristles were imported into England, from Russia and Prussia. As these are only taken from the top of the hog's back, each hog cannot be supposed to have supplied more than 7680, which, reckoning each bristle to weigh two grains, will be one pound. Thus, in Russia and Prussia in 1728, 1,748,921 hogs were killed to supply the consumption of bristles in England. The skin is formed into pocket-books, employed in the manufacture of saddles, and of various other things, and even the ears are eaten in pies.

It has been too much the custom to regard the hog as a stupid, brutal, rapacious, and filthy animal, grovelling and disgusting in all his habits; intractable and obstinate in temper. But may not much of these evil qualities be attributable to the life he leads? In a native state swine seem by no means destitute of natural affections; they are gregarious, assemble together in defence of each other, herd together for warmth, and appear to have feelings in common; no mother is more tender of her young than the sow, or more resolute in their defence. Besides, neglected as this animal has ever been by authors, there are not wanting records of many anecdotes illustrative of their sagacity, tractability, and susceptibility of affection. How often among the peasantry, where the hog is, in a manner of speaking, one of the family, may this animal be seen following his master from place to place, and grunting his recognition of his protectors.

The well-authenticated account of the sow trained by Toomer, a gamekeeper to Sir Henry Mildmay, testifies to the teachability of these animals; and therefore, as it is our intention to defend them from many of the aspersions cast upon them, we will quote it.

"Toomer actually broke a *black sow* to find game, and to back and stand. Slut was bred in, and was of that sort which maintain themselves in the New Forest without regular feeding, except when they have young, and then but for a few weeks, and was given, when about three months old, to be a breeding sow, by Mr. Thomas to Mr. Richard Toomer, both at that time keepers of the forest. From having no young she was not fed or taken much notice of, and, until about eighteen months old, was seldom observed near the lodge, but chanced to be seen one day when Mr. Edward Toomer was there. The brothers were concerned together in breaking pointers and setters, some of their own breeding, and others sent to be broke by different gentlemen; of the latter, although they would stand and back, many were so indifferent that they would neither hunt, nor express any satisfaction when birds were killed and put before them. The slackness of these dogs first suggested the idea that, by the same method, any other animal might be made to stand, and do as well as any of those huntless and inactive pointers. At this instant the sow passed by, and was remarked as being very handsome. R. Toomer threw her a piece or two of oatmeal roll, for which she appeared grateful, and approached very near; from that time they were determined to make a *sporting pig* of her. The first step was to give her a name, and that of Slut (given in consequence of soiling herself in a bog) she acknowledged in the course of the day, and never afterwards forgot. Within a fortnight she would find and point partridges or rabbits, and her training was much forwarded by the abundance of both which were near the lodge; she daily improved, and in a few weeks would retrieve birds that had run as well as the best pointer, nay, her nose was superior to the best pointer they ever possessed, and no two men in England had better. She hunted principally on the moors and heaths. Slut has stood partridges, black-game, pheasants, snipes, and rabbits, in the same day, but was never known to point a hare. She was seldom taken by choice more than a mile or two from the lodge, but has frequently joined them when out with their pointers, and continued with them several hours. She has sometimes stood a jacksnipe when all the pointers had passed by it: she would back the dogs when they pointed, but the dogs refused to back her until spoke to, their dogs being all trained to make a general halt when the word was given, whether any dog pointed or not, so that she has been frequently standing in the midst of a field of pointers. In consequence of the dogs not liking to hunt when she was with them, (for they dropped their sterns and showed symptoms of jealousy,) she did not very often accompany them, except for the novelty, or

when she accidentally joined them in the forest. Her pace wa:
mostly a trot, was seldom known to gallop, except when called to
go out shooting; she would then come home off the forest at full
stretch, for she was never shut up but to prevent her being out of
the sound of the call or whistle when a party of gentlemen had appointed to see her out the next day, and which call she obeyed as
regularly as a dog, and was as much elevated as a dog upon being
shown the gun. She always expressed great pleasure when game,
either dead or alive, was placed before her. She has frequently stood
a single partridge at forty yards' distance, her nose in an exact line,
and would continue in that position until the game moved : if it took
wing, she would come up to the place, and put her nose down two
or three times; but if a bird ran off, she would get up and go to
the place, and draw slowly after it, and when the bird stopped she
would stand it as before. The two Mr. Toomers lived about
seven miles apart, at Rhinefield and Broomey lodges; Slut has
many times gone by herself from one lodge to the other, as if to
court the being taken out shooting. She was about five years old
when her master died, and, at the auction of his pointers, &c., was
bought in at ten guineas. Sir Henry Mildmay having expressed a
wish to have her, she was sent to Dogmersfield Park, where she
remained some years. She was last in the possession of Colonel
Sykes, and was then ten years old, and had become fat and slothful,
but could point game as well as ever. She was not often used, excepting to show her to strangers, as the pointers refused to act when
out with her. When killed she weighed 700 lbs. Her death-war-
rant was signed in consequence of her having been accused of being
instrumental to the disappearance of sundry missing lambs.
(Daniel's *Rural Sports.*)

Colonel Thornton also had a sow which was regularly taught to
hunt, quarter the ground, and back the other pointers.

Some thirty years since, it was mentioned in the public papers,
that a gentleman had trained swine to run in his carriage, and drove
four-in-hand through London with these curious steeds. And not
long since the market-place of St. Albans was completely crowded,
in consequence of an eccentric old farmer, who resided a few miles
off, having entered it in a small chaise-cart drawn by four hogs at a
brisk trot, which pace they kept up a few times round the area of
the market-place. They were then driven to the wool-pack yard,
and after being unharnessed were regaled with a trough of beans
and wash.

A gentleman present offered 50*l.* for the whole concern as it stood,
but his offer was indignantly declined. In about two hours the ani
mals were reharnessed, and the old farmer drove off with his ex
traordinary team He stated that he had been six months in train
ing them.

Nor are these cases without parallel, for Montfaucon informs us that Heliogabalus, the Roman emperor, trained boars, stags, and asses to run in his chariot; and Pennant states that in Minorca, and that part of Murray which lies between the Spey and Elgin, swine have been converted into beasts of draught, and that it is by no means unusual to see a cow, a sow, and two young horses yoked together in a plough, and that the sow is the best drawer of the four In Minorca, the ass and hog may be regularly seen working together in turning up land.

Henderson gives another, and a very simple account, illustrative of the tractability of swine :—

" About twenty-five years ago my father farmed very extensively in various parts of the kingdom, and upon one of his farms in Redkirk, in the parish of Gretna Green, Dumfriesshire, kept at times upward of one hundred swine. It so happened that the keeper of that flock was either taken unwell or abruptly left his service one harvest, when every creature able to work was employed in reaping. A brother and I, being the only idlers about the premises, the above flock was given in charge to us for a few days, until the proper keeper was found; we were then reluctantly obliged to march off with our 'hirsel' early every morning to a clover-field about a mile distant, with our dinners, books, and great-coats, &c., packed upon our backs: we, however, soon began to think it was a great hardship for us to be groaning under our loads while so many stout, able ponies were trotting along before us at their ease, and immediately set about training one of them to relieve us of our burdens, which we accomplished in a few days by occasionally scratching the animal and feeding it with bread, &c., out of our hands. It became at last so docile as to stand every morning until it received the burden girted upon it, and then marched on in the rear, which place it was trained to keep, as we had more than once lost our dinners when it was allowed to join the herd; and in the same manner we soon trained two or three more into carrying the baggage in turns. Having been so successful in this training exploit, we then thought it would be turning our punishment into pleasure if we could train each of us one to ride: this was no sooner thought of than commenced, and although we received many a tumble, yet we soon accomplished our design, and succeeded in breaking in each two or three chargers. At length our system became so complete, that we not only rode to and from the field, but whenever any of the herd were likely to stray, or go into some adjoining field of corn, &c., each alternately mounted his charger, and went off at full gallop to turn back and punish the transgressors.

" Such as were trained, seldom or never went astray, being always about hand, and in readiness to be mounted; in short, such days as my father was from home, it was not unusual for a group of servants to receive amusement from my brother and I running set matches with our steeds, which were determined in the usual manner, with whip and spur; and in this latter management there was no such thing as bolting or tumbling going on, which occurred frequently during the training season. This system however, came at length to my father's ears, for one or two of the racers happening to die in consequence of too severe heats, or too much weight: when we were immediately disbanded from our office, and (our holidays being expired) ordered off to school again, which we set about with as much reluctance as we did the first morning in driving the hundred swine to the clover-field." (Henderson's *Practical Grazier*.)

The learned pig is another illustration of this same quality. This creature had been taught to pick up letters, written upon pieces of card, at command, and arrange them into words. It was first exhibited in the vicinity of Pall-Mall, in 1789, at 5s. each person. The price of admission was afterwards reduced to 2s. 6d., and finally to 1s.

The showman stated that he had lost three hogs in the course of training. Since then there have been many successors of the "learned pig" exhibited at different places, but none equal in talent to the original.

The next thing which we shall claim for our porcine clients is sagacity; nor are we here in want of illustrative evidences of their possession of it. But in general there is nothing in the life of a hog, in his domesticated state at least, which calls for any exercise of reasoning powers. His sole business is to eat, drink, sleep, and get fat; all his wants are anticipated, and his world is limited to the precincts of his sty or of the farm-yard. Yet even in this state of luxurious ease, individuals have shown extraordinary intelligence.

Mr. Craven, relates the following anecdote of an American sow: "This animal passed her days in the woods, with a numerous litter of pigs, but returning regularly to the house in the evening, to share with her family a substantial supper. One of her pigs was, however, quietly slipt away to be roasted; in a day or two afterwards another; and then a third. It would appear that this careful mother knew the number of her offspring, and missed those that were taken from her, for after this she came alone to her evening meal. This occurring repeatedly, she was watched out of the wood, and observed to drive back her pigs from its extremity, grunting, with much earnestness, in a manner so intelligible, that they retired at her command, and waited patiently for her return.

Surely this must be the result of something very like reasoning powers? "A gentleman residing at Caversham bought two pigs at Reading market, which were conveyed to his house in a sack, and turned into his yard, which lies on the banks of the river Thames.

"The next morning the pigs were missing. A hue and cry was

immediately raised, and towards the afternoon a person gave information that two pigs had been seen swimming across the river at
nearly its broadest part.

"They were afterwards observed trotting along the Pangbourn
road, and in one place where the road branches off, putting their
noses together as if in deep consultation. The result was their safe
return to the place from which they had originally been conveyed
to Reading, a distance of nine miles, and by cross roads.

"The farmer from whom they had been purchased, brought them
back to their owner, but they took the very first opportunity again
to escape, recrossing the water like two dogs, thus removing the
stigma on their race, which proverbially disqualifies them for 'swimming without cutting their own throats,' and never stopped until
they found themselves at their first home."

Here we see difficulties overcome, and a strange element encoun-
tered, in order to arrive at a far distant spot—the home to which
the animals were attached. Some recollection of that place or some
association of ideas must have influenced the proceedings of these
animals; but to what faculty shall we attribute their swimming the
river in a direct line with their old master's house, and then finding
their way so immediately thither? And how shall we account for
their thus acting in concert, if pigs are to be considered as the stupid
obtuse brutes most persons are in the habit of designating them?
Such instances of sagacity in the dog and the horse scarcely astonish
us, because we allow to them a certain degree of reasoning power.
But is not the great development of it in them as much arising from
their intercourse, if such we may term it, with man?—from their
being his companions, educated and ordered by him? "I have observed great sagacity in swine," observes Darwin, in his "Zoonomia,"
"but the short lives we allow them, and their general confinement,
prevent their improvement, which would otherwise probably equal
that of the dog."

"The Naturalist's Library" gives another anecdote of a hog
which is indicative of no small degree of instinct or intelligence :—

"Early in the month, a pig that had been kept several days a
close prisoner to his sty, was let out for the purpose of its being
cleaned and his bed replenished. On opening the sty-door, he anticipated the purpose of his liberation by running to the stable, from
which he carried several sheaves of straw to his sty, holding them
in his mouth by the band. The straw being intended for another
purpose, it was carried back to the stable ; but the pig, seizing a
more favorable opportunity, regained it, to the amazement of several
persons, who were pleased to observe the extraordinary instinct of
this wonderful pig.

Swine have also been repeatedly known to attach themselves to
individuals, and to other animals, and   of great docility
gentleness, and affection.

Mr. Henderson says, "I have a young sow of a good breed, so docile that she will suffer my youngest son, three years of age, to climb upon her back and ride her about for half an hour at a time, and more; when she is tired of the fun, she lays herself down, carefully avoiding hurting her young jockey. He often shares his bread and meat with her."

A pig belonging to a baker in Kinghorn, county Fife, became so attached to a bull-dog that it would follow and sport with him, and follow her master, when he was accompanied by this dog, for five or six miles. The dog was fond of swimming, and the pig imitated this propensity; and if any thing was thrown into the water for the dog to fetch out, the pig would follow and dispute the prize with him very cleverly and energetically. These two animals invariably slept together.

M. de Dieskau tells us that "he made a wild boar so tame that the animal, although nearly three years old, would go up stairs to his apartment, fawn upon him like a dog, and eat from his hand. He also endeavored to bring up one which he caught very young, and which formed such an attachment to a young lady in the house that he accompanied her wherever she went, and slept upon her bed. Once he attacked her maid as she was undressing her mistress, and, had he been strong enough, would have done her some mortal injury. This lady was the only person in the house for whom the creature showed any affection, and yet he was not fed by her. At last he fretted himself to death on account of a fox which had been taken into the house to be tamed."

A very amusing account of a "pet pig" is given by a lady, in "*Chambers' Edinburgh Journal :*"—

"Being at a loss to know what to do with the refuse of our garden, Aunt Mary suggested that a pig should be purchased. Accordingly our little damsel Annette was despatched to a neighboring farmer, and, in exchange for a few shillings, she brought home a fat, fair, round pig, just six weeks old; and in her haste to display her bargain she tumbled it out in the sitting-room. Nothing daunted by the splendor of its new abode, the pig ran up and down, snorting and snuffing at every chair and table in the room, overturning with his snout my aunt's footstool, and trying his teeth on her new straw work-basket. After the pig had been duly admired and commented on, Annette was desired to install it in its own domicile; but this was more easily said than done; for being, I suppose, pleased with his new quarters, Toby—for so we named him—ran hither and thither, now scudding behind a chair or table, now whisking under the sofa; at length Annette succeeded in dragging him from his hiding-place while he roared out 'Murder!' as plain as a pig could speak. Annette was very fond of dumb creatures, as she called them; the pig [darling, and for want of a companion of

her own species, Toby became her constant associate; and finding
his visits to the kitchen were winked at, he made use of the privilege, and would bask himself at full length before the fire. He
even ventured occasionally to follow her into the front lobby; and
if, as sometimes was the case, she put him into the yard, he would
kick up such a row at the kitchen door to be let in, thumping on it
with his snout, that she was fain to admit him to his old quarters.
Toby was of a very social disposition, and so fond of Annette, and so
grateful for her kindness, that he would follow her about everywhere;
indeed to my great surprise, one day I found him standing sentry over
her while she was putting down the stair carpet, and he seemed to be
watching her proceedings with a very sagacious air. In process of time
there came another proof that the course of true love never did run
smooth. Annette fell into bad health, and returned to her home;
the damsel who replaced her, had no taste for the society of pigs;
so she thumped Toby away from the kitchen door, and many were
the blows he got from her broom, or whatever missile first came to
hand. Toby was soon exiled to his sty, much against his inclina
tion, for he evidently would have preferred bivouacking in the back
premises. We seldom passed to the garden without throwing him
some comfort in the shape of a few cabbage-leaves, a handful of
acorns, or a bunch of turnip-tops. It was truly amusing to see
Toby make his bed. As the straw which was furnished for it was
rather long and coarse, Toby used to take it bunch by bunch in his
teeth, and run into a corner, breaking it into small pieces; and
having accomplished this feat, he proceeded to arrange his couch in
the most methodical manner. One day, Betty having omitted to
give him his dinner, Toby in a great passion, jumped out of his sty,
and came running to the kitchen door to see what was the reason
of his being so shamefully neglected, and loud and long were his
remonstrances on the subject. Finding it difficult to get the poor
animal properly attended to, he was transferred to a neighbor; and
we never gave him a successor, as we scarcely expected to find in
another of his species that gratitude for kindness and affection for
his friends, which shone so conspicuous in the character of poor
Toby."

It may appear absurd to claim cleanliness as a swinish virtue; but
in point of actual fact the pig is a much more cleanly animal than
most of his calumniators give him credit for being. He is fond of
a good cleanly bed; and often, when this is not provided for him, it
is curious to see the degree of sagacity with which he will forage for
himself. "A hog is the cleanliest of all creatures, and will never
dung or stale in his sty if he can get forth," says a quaint old writer
of the sixteenth century, and we are very much of his opinion. But
it is so much the habit to believe that this animal may be kept in
any state of filth and neglect, that "pig" and "pig-sty" are terms

usually regarded as synonymous with all that is dirty and disgusting.

His rolling in the mud is alleged against him as a proof of his
filthy habits; if so, the same accusation applies to the elephant, the
rhinoceros, and other of the Pachydermata.   May this not rather be
for the purpose of cooling themselves and keeping off flies, as we
admit it to be in the case of the animals above mentioned ? Savages
cover themselves with grease in hot climates in order to protect their
skins; may not instinct teach animals to roll themselves in mud for
a similar purpose ?

Pigs are exceedingly fond of comfort and warmth, and will nestle
together in order to obtain the latter, and often struggle vehemently
to secure the warmest berth.

They are eminently sensitive of approaching changes in the
weather, and may often be observed suddenly to leave the places in
which they had been quietly feeding, and run off to their styes at
full speed, making loud outcries.   When storms are overhanging,
they collect straw in their mouths, and run about as if inviting their
companions to do the same; and if there is a shed or shelter near
at hand, may be seen to carry and deposit it there, as if for the purpose of preparing a bed.   Hence has arisen the common Wiltshire
saying, " Pigs see the wind."   Virgil, in enumerating the signs of
settled fine weather, notices this peculiarity in swine :—

> " Nor sows unclean are mindful to provide
> Their nestling beds of *mouth-collected* straw !"

Foster says—" When hogs shake the stalks of corn, and thereby
spoil them, it indicates rain ; and when they run squeaking about
and throw up their heads with a peculiar jerk, windy weather is about
to commence."

Darwin observes—" It is a sure sign of a cold wind when pigs
collect straw in their mouths, and run about crying loudly.   They
would carry it to their beds for warmth, and by their calls invite
their companions to do the same, and add to the warmth by nume
rous bedfellows."

In their domesticated state, swine certainly are very greedy
animals; eating is the business of their lives; nor do they appear
so very delicate as to the kind or quality of the food which is set
before them.   Although naturally herbiverous animals, they have
been known to devour carrion with all the voracity of beasts of
prey, to eat and mangle infants, and even gorge their appetites with
their own young.

Low, however, says—" Instances have occurred in which a sow
has been known to devour her young ; but rarely, if ever, does this
happen in a state of nature.   It is not unreasonable to believe that
when an act so revolting does occur, it arises more from the pain

and irritation produced by the state of confinement, and often filth, in which she is kept, and the disturbances to which she is subjected, than from any actual ferocity: for it is well known that a sow is always unusually irritable at this period, snapping at all animals that approach her. If she is gently treated, properly supplied with sustenance, and sequestered from all annoyance, there is little danger of this ever happening."

Roots and fruits are the natural food of the hog, in a wild as well as in a domesticated state; and it is evident that, however omnivorous this animal may occasionally appear, its palate is by no means insensible to the difference of eatables, for whenever it finds variety it will be found to select the best with as much cleverness as other quadrupeds. "In the peach-tree orchards of North America," says Pennant, "where hogs have plenty of delicious food, they have been observed to neglect the fruit that has lain a few hours upon the ground, and patiently wait for a considerable time for a fresh windfall."

According to Linnæus, the hog is more nice in the selection of his vegetable diet than any of our other domesticated herbivorous animals. This great naturalist states that—

		eats	plants	and rejects	
The Cow	eats	276	plants and rejects	218
" Goat	"	449	"	126
" Sheep	"	387	"	141
" Horse	"	262	"	212
but that the Hog only	"	72	"	171

They are gifted with an exquisite sense of smell as well as touch, residing in the snout, and this enables them to discover roots, acorns, earth-nuts, or other delicacies suitable to their palates, which may be buried in the ground.

In some parts of Italy swine are employed in hunting for truffles, that grow some inches below the surface of the soil, and form those pickles and sauces so highly esteemed by epicures. A pig is driven into a field, and there suffered to pursue his own course. Wherever he stops and begins to root with his nose, truffles will invariably be found.

The last charge which we shall endeavor to refute is that of intractability. All the offences which swine commit are attributed to an innately bad disposition; whereas they too often arise solely from bad management or total neglect. Would horses or cattle behave one iota better, were they treated as pigs too often are? They are legitimate objects for the sport of idle boys, hunted with dogs, pelted with stones, often neglected and obliged to find a meal for themselves, or wander about half-starved. Can we wonder that, under such circumstances, they should be wild, unmanageable brutes? Look at the swine in a well-regulated farm-yard—they are as peaceable, and as little disposed to wander or trespass, as any of the other animals that it contains. Here, as in many other things, man is but too willing to attribute the faults, which are essentially of his own causing, to any other than their true source.

Martin says :—It has been usual to condemn the domestic hog, in no very measured terms, as a filthy, stupid brute, at once gluttonous, obstinate, and destitute of intelligence. Against this sweeping censure we beg to enter our protest. With regard to the filthiness of the hog in a state of confinement, every thing will depend on the trouble taken by its keeper. He may allow the sty or the yard to be covered with filth of every description, as disgraceful to himself as it is injurious to the animals. In this case the hog is the sufferer, for naturally it delights in clean straw, luxuriating in it with evident pleasure, its twinkling little eyes and low grunt expressing its feelings of contentment. In fact, the hog, so far from being the filthiest, is one of the cleanliest of our domestic quadrupeds, and is unwilling to soil the straw bed of his domicile if any thing like liberty be allowed him. It may be here said, is not the hog fond of wallowing in the mire ? Undoubtedly it is; and so are all the genuine *pachydermata*, as the elephant, the rhinoceros, and the tapir. The skin of these animals, thick as it may be, is nevertheless sensitive, and a covering of mud is doubtless intended as a protection to the skin in the heat of summer, (the time in which the hog chiefly delights to wallow,) both against the scorching rays of the sun and the attacks of myriads of puny but intolerable winged persecutors. No animal delights more to have its hide rubbed and scratched than the hog—a circumstance which every one practically conversant with pigs must have very frequently noticed.

With respect to the gluttony of the pig, we acknowledge him to be " a huge feeder ;" but so is the horse or the ox, and indeed every animal that has to support a bulky carcass ; and not only so, but become fat upon vegetable aliment. To a certain extent, indeed, the hog is omnivorous, and may be reared on the refuse of the butchers' slaughter-houses ; but such food is not wholesome, nor is it natural; for though this animal be omnivorous, it is not essentially carnivorous. Vegetable productions, as roots and grain, beech-mast, and acorns, constitute the staple of its natural diet; hence, the refuse of the dairy farm is more congenial to the health of the animal, to say nothing of the quality of its flesh. All animals eat with a keen relish—the hog amongst the rest ; besides, his appetite is pampered, the object being to make him fat: and certainly a well-fed, plump hog is a more comely-looking beast than the gaunt, lean, flat-sided animals so generally seen in France and Germany. However, if the charge of gluttony be proved against the pig fattening in his sty, it may be equally proved against the ox fattening in his stall. When old, or when oppressed by fat, the hog, it must be confessed, is slug gish and indolent; when young, however, it is lively and energetic, and disposed to indulge in sportive gambols, which, for any thing we can see, are quite as amusing as those of lambs.

Many extraordinary examples of the docility and intelligence of the too much despised hog are on record. Be it remembered, that it belongs to that group of which the sagacious elephant forms a portion—not that we assert the intellectual equality of the two animals; still, we believe that the hog may be trained to various modes of labor, with far less trouble than is generally supposed. It is not, however, needed for any such purposes; consequently, except in a few isolated instances, its education is utterly neglected; all it has to do is to eat and sleep, and become fat—its utility to man commencing at its death, by the knife of the butcher. Yet, even under the disadvantages in which the pig is placed—debarred its liberty, prevented from exercising its natural instincts, and undisciplined in the slightest degree—it manifests both discernment and attachment; it recognizes the voice, and even the footsteps of its feeder, and is evidently pleased with his notice. Instances of the attachment of pigs to particular persons, and even to other animals, are on record. It is not often, however, that porcine familiarity is encouraged. Setting all prejudice aside, it must be confessed that the animal would be more likely to prove troublesome and annoying, than agreeable or welcome. We have, however, heard of persons who have petted pigs, and know many who would abhor to partake of the flesh of one reared upon their own premises—a circumstance not to be wondered at, when we consider that, while alive, the animal not only knew them, but greeted their approach, and displayed unmistakable signs of attachment.

The senses of smell, taste, and hearing, are possessed by the hog in great perfection. It is a common saying that pigs can smell the coming storm; certain it is that they are very sensitive of approaching changes of weather. They become agitated, hurry under shelter, and during the continuance of the storm utter screams, run about with straw in their mouths, or carry it to their sty as if to add to their comfort and defence. This peculiarity has been noticed in ancient times, as well as in the present. Dr. Darwin, in his *Zoonomia*, says, "It is a sure sign of a cold wind when pigs collect straw in their mouths, and run about crying loudly. They would carry it to their beds for warmth, and by their calls invite their companions to do the same, and add to the warmth by numerous bedfellows." At all times pigs are fond of huddling together under the straw, but especially in chilly or windy weather, from which the young in particular appear to suffer much. From this cause, litters of pigs farrowed during a severe winter are often greatly thinned, and the survivors thrive with difficulty.

CHAPTER IV

THE wild boar (*sus scrofa ;* var. *aper*) is generally admitted to be the parent of the stock from which all our domesticated breeds and varieties have sprung. This animal is generally of a dusky brown or iron-gray color, inclining to black, and diversified with black spots or streaks. The body is covered with coarse hairs, intermixed

THE WILD BOAR.

with a downy wool ; these hairs become bristles as they approach the neck and shoulders, and are here so long as to form a species of mane, which the animal erects when irritated. The head is short, the forehead broad and flat, the ears short, rounded at the tips and inclined towards the neck, the jaw armed with sharp crooked tusks which curve slightly upwards, and are capable of inflicting fearful wounds, the eye full, neck thick and muscular, the shoulders high, the loins broad, the tail stiff, and finished off with a tuft of bristles at the tip, the haunch well turned, and the legs strong. A full-grown wild boar in India averages from thirty to forty inches in height at the shoulder. The African wild boar is about twenty-eight or thirty inches high.

The wild boar is a very active and powerful animal, and becomes fiercer as he grows older. When he exists in a state of nature, he will usually be found in moist, shady, and well-wooded situations, not far remote from streams or water. In India, they are found in the thick jungles, in plantations of sugar-canes, rice, or rhur, or in the thick patches of high, long grass.* In England, France, Germany, Italy, and Spain, their resorts have been in the woods and forests. This animal is naturally herbivorous, and appears to feed by choice upon plants, fruits, and roots. He will, however, eat the worms and larvæ which he finds in the ground, also snakes and other such reptiles, and the eggs of birds; and Buffon states that wild boars have been seen to devour the flesh of dead horses, while other authors accuse them of devouring hares, leverets, partridges, and indeed all kinds of small game, and feeding greedily upon carrion; but this has also been asserted to be only the case when they are pressed by hunger. They seldom quit their coverts during the day, but prowl about in search of food during twilight and the night. Their acute sense of smell enables them to detect the presence of roots or fruits deeply imbedded in the soil, and they often do considerable mischief by ploughing up the ground in search of them, particularly as they do not, like the common hog, root up a little spot here and there, but plough long continuous furrows.

The wild boar, properly so called, is neither a solitary nor a gregarious animal. For the first two or three years the whole herd

---

* The wild hog delights in cultivated situations, but will not remain where water is not at hand in which he can quench his thirst and wallow at his ease. nor will he resort a second season to a spot that does not afford ample cover, either of heavy grass or underwood jungle, within a certain distance of him, to fly to in case of molestation, and especially to serve as a retreat during the hot season, as otherwise he would find no shelter. The sugar-cane is his great delight, both as affording his favorite food and yielding a highly impervious, and unfrequented situation. In these the hogs, and the breeding sows especially, commit great devastation, for the latter not only devour but cut the canes for a litter, and to throw up a species of hut, which they do with much art, leaving a small entrance which they can stop up at pleasure. Sows never quit their young pigs without completely shutting them up. This is, however, only requisite for a few days, after which, the little ones may be seen following their mother at a good round pace, though evidently not more than a week or ten days old.—Williamson's *Oriental Field Sports.*

follows the sow, and all unite in defence against any enemies, calling
upon each other with loud cries in case of emergency, and forming
in regular line of battle, the weakest occupying the rear. But when
arrived at maturity, the animals wander alone, as if in perfect con-
sciousness of their strength, and appear as if they neither sought
nor avoided any living creature. They are said to live about thirty
years ; as they grow old the hair becomes gray, and the tusks begin
to show symptoms of decay. Old boars are rarely found associating with a herd, but seem to keep apart from the rest, and from
each other.

The female produces but one litter in the year, and her litters are
much smaller in number than those of the domestic pig ; she carries
her young sixteen or twenty weeks, and generally is only seen with
the male during the rutting season. She suckles her young for
several months, and continues to protect them for some time after
wards ; if attacked then, she will defend herself and them with
exceeding courage and fierceness. Many sows will often be found
herding together, each followed by her litter of young ones, and in
such parties they are exceedingly formidable to man and beast.
Neither they nor the boar, however, appear to want to attack any
thing, but only when roused by aggression, or disturbed in their
retreat, do they turn upon their enemies and manifest their mighty
strength with which nature has endowed them, otherwise they pursue their way in a kind of solitary savage majesty. Occasionally
when two males encounter each other, a fierce and furious battle will
ensue, especially if this happens during the rutting season, when their
passions are inflamed. When attacked by dogs, the wild boar at first
sullenly retreats, turning upon them from time to time, and menacing
them with his tusks ; but gradually his ire rises, and at length he
stands at bay, fights furiously for his life, and tears and rends his
persecutors. He has even been observed to single out the most
tormenting of them, and rush savagely upon him.

Hunting the wild boar has been a favorite sport, in almost all the
countries in which this animal was found, from the earliest ages. In
all the ancient Grecian and Roman classical writers, some allusions
to this animal will be found. Homer, whose vivid portraitures of
the actions and habits of princes and warriors nearly thirty years
ago, are known to almost every scholar, again and again refers to
this savage denizen of the forests, nor can we deny ourselves the
pleasure of extracting the following graphic lines :—

> " Soon as the morn, new roll'd in purple light,
> Pierc'd with her golden shafts the rear of night,
> Ulysses, and his brave maternal race
> The young Antolici, assay the chase ;
> Parnassus, thick perplex'd with horrid shades,
> With deep-mouthed hounds the hunter troop invades ;

What time the sun from ocean's peaceful stream
Darts o'er the lawn his horizontal beam.
The pack impatient snuff the tainted gale ;
The thorny wilds the woodmen fierce assail ;
And foremost of the Train, his cornel spear
Ulysses wav'd to rouse the savage war ;
Deep in the rough recesses of the wood,
A lofty copse, the growth of ages stood ;
Nor winter's boreal blast, nor thund'rous show'r,
Nor solar ray could pierce the shady bower,
With wither'd foliage strew'd, a heavy store!
The warm pavilion of a dreadful boar.
Rous'd by the hounds' and hunters' mingling cries,——
The savage from his leafy shelter flies,
With fiery glare his sanguine eye-balls shine
And bristles high impale his horrid chine.
Young Ithacus advanced, defies the foe,
Poising his lifted lance in act to throw :
The savage renders vain the wound decreed,
And springs impetuous with opponent speed!
His tusks oblique he aim'd, the knee to gore ;
Aslope they glanced, the sinewy fibres tore,
And bar'd the bone : Ulysses undismay'd,
Soon with redoubled force the wound repaid ;
To the right shoulder-joint the spear applied,
His further flank with streaming purple dyed ;
On earth he rush'd with agonizing pain.
With joy, and vast surprise, the applauding train
Viewed his enormous back extended on the plain."

The wild boar formed part of the sports, pageants, and wild-beast shows and fights of the Romans. On the return of Severus from Arabia and Egypt, in the tenth year of his reign, sixty wild boars fought each other ; and in the year that Gordian the First was ædile, he entertained the people of Rome, at his own expense, once a month ; and " on the sixth month there were two hundred stags, thirty wild horses, one hundred wild sheep, twenty elks, one hundred Cyprian bulls, three hundred red Barbary ostriches, thirty wild asses, and one hundred and fifty wild boars," given out to be hunted, and became the property of whosoever was fortunate enough to catch them.

During the middle ages, hunting the wild boar formed one of the chief amusements of the nobility, in most European countries. The dogs provided for this sport were of the slow, heavy kind, anciently known by the name of the "boarhound." None but the largest and oldest boars were hunted, and these afforded a very exciting and often dangerous sport, lasting for many hours ; for when first the animal was "*reared*," he contented himself with slowly going away, just keeping ahead of his pursuers, and apparently caring but little for them, and pausing every half mile to rest himself, and give battle to his assailants, who are, however, too wary to advance upon him until he becomes tired ; then he takes his final stand, and dogs and

3

hunters close around him, and a mortal combat ensues, in which the beast eventually falls a victim.

In treatises on venery and hunting, the technical term for the boar in the first year is "a pig of the sounder;" in the second, "a hog;" in the third, "a hog steer;" and in the fourth, "a boar."

Many of the forests in our own country were infested by wild boars. The Anglo-Saxons seem, from the rude frescoes and prints which are handed down to us, to have hunted this animal on foot with no other weapon but the boar-spear, and attended by powerful dogs; and apparently with such success, that at the Norman conquest William the First thought it necessary to make some strict laws for the preservation of this beast of the chase. The period for hunting the wild boar among the Anglo-Saxons was in September. Howel Dha, the celebrated Welsh lawgiver, gave permission to his chief huntsman to chase the boar from the middle of November until the end of December.

These animals continued to linger in the forests of England and Scotland for several centuries after the Norman conquest, and many tracts of land have derived their name from this occurrence, while instances of valor in their destruction are recorded in the heraldic devices of many a noble family. Fitzstephen, a writer of the twelfth century, informs us that wild boars, stags, fallow-deer, and bulls, abounded in the vast forests which existed on the northern side of London in the time of Henry II. The learned Whittaker informs us that this animal roved at liberty over the woods of the parish of Manchester for many centuries after the Romans departed from that station, and hence the name of Barlow (*boar*-ground) came to be assigned to a district in the south-western portion. In Cumberland, the appellation "Wild Boar's Fell," still points out the haunts of this animal. The forests of Bernwood in Buckinghamshire, of Stainmore in Westmoreland, and those extensive woody districts which once existed in Hertfordshire and over the Chiltern Hills, were formerly peopled with wild boars, wolves, stags, and wild bulls. Many ancient Scottish writers, too, speak of the existence of this animal in the woods of Caledonia. In the county of Fife there exists a tract of country formerly called *Muckross* (which in the Celtic signifies Boar's Promontory); it is said to have been famous as the haunt of wild boars. One part of it was called the Boar Hills, which name has since been corrupted into Byro Hills. It lies in the vicinity of St. Andrew's, and in the cathedral church of that city two enormous boar's tusks were formerly to be seen chained to the high altar, in commemoration of an immense brute slain by the inhabitants after it had long ravaged the surrounding country.

The precise period at which the wild boar became exterminated in England and Scotland cannot be correctly ascertained. Master John

Gifford and William Twety, who lived in the reign of Edward II., composed a book on the craft of hunting, part in verse and part in prose, and among the beasts mentioned in those hunted we find—

> "To venery I cast me fyrst to go ;
> Of whiche foure beasts there be ; that is to say,
> The *hare*, the *herte*, the *wulfhe* the *wild boor* also."

In the time of Charles I. they had evidently been long extinct, for he endeavored to reintroduce them, and was at considerable expense in order to procure a wild boar and his mate from Germany. These are said to have been turned into the New Forest, where they propagated greatly. The breed commonly called "forest pigs," have many of the characteristics of the wild boar.

Throughout the whole of England, the boar's head was formerly a standard Christmas dish, served with many ceremonies, and ushered in by an ancient chorus chanted by all present, the words of which are preserved in " Ritson's Ancient Song :—

> " The bore's heed in hand bring I,
> With " garlands" gay and rosemary,
> I pray you all synge merily,
> *Qui estis in convivio.*
>
> The bore's heed, I understande,
> Is the " chefe" servyce in the lande
> Loke where ever it be founde,
> *Servite cum cantico.*
>
> Be gladde, lordes, bothe more and lasse,
> For this hath ordeyned our stewarde,
> To chere you all this Christmasse,
> The bore's heed with mustarde.'

Queen Margaret, wife of James IV. of Scotland, " at the first course of her wedding dinner," was served with a " wyld bore's head gylt within a fayr platter."

King Henry II. himself bore this ancient dish into the hall, attended with trumpeters and great ceremony, when his son was crowned.

The boar's head is to the present day placed upon the table of the Queen's College, Oxford, on Christmas day, but now it is neatly carved in wood instead of being the actual head of the animal. This ceremony is said to have originated in a tabender belonging to that college having slain a wild boar on Christmas-day, which had long infested the neighborhood of Oxford.

The abbot of St. Germain, in Yorkshire, was bound to send yearly a present of a boar's head to the hangman, which a monk was obliged to carry on his own. This rent was paid yearly, at the feast of St. Vincent, the patron of the Benedictines, and on that day the executioner took precedency in the procession of monks.

France, too, formerly had its trackless forests, through which the grisly boar roved in savage grandeur—its boar hunts—its legends of sanguinary combats with these monsters. The "wild boar of Ardennes" has been the theme of many a lay and romance. But civilization, the increase of population, and the progress of agriculture, have here, too, been at work. Still, however, in the large tracts of forest land which yet exist and supply the towns with fuel, boars are still occasionally to be met with, although they cannot be regarded as so wild or ferocious as the ancient breed. At Chantilly, within forty miles of Paris, the late Prince of Condé, who died in 1830, kept a pack of hounds expressly for the purpose of hunting the boar; and some English gentlemen who visited the hunting palace in the summer of 1830, were informed by the huntsman that a few days previously he had seen no less than fourteen wild hogs at one time. But the good old "wild boar hunt," as once existed with all its perils and excitements, is now extinct in France as well as in Germany. Where any traces of it remain, they resolve themselves into a battue of a most harmless description, which takes place in the parks of the princes or nobles. The drivers beat up the woods, the wild swine run until they come in contact with a fence stretched across the park for the purpose, and about the centre of which, at an opening in the wood, a sort of stage is raised, on which the sportsmen stand and fire at the swine as they run past.

Germany being a country boasting forests of immense extent, was once the most celebrated of all nations for its wild boars and boar-hunts; and in many parts wild hogs are still abundant, and various methods are adopted to destroy them, as well for amusement as to turn their carcasses to account, which furnish those finely-flavored hams called Westphalian.

The most simple and effectual way is to find out the haunts of the boar, and place a matchlock on rests, well charged, and concealed by brambles near it. A rope is attached to the trigger, and carried below the rests to the trunk of a tree at some little distance, so as to intersect the animal's path to the forest. Over this the hog inevitably stumbles, and thus discharges the piece, and receives the ball in the neck or shoulder.

The ordinary method of shooting the hog in Germany is as follows :—

The huntsman, or *jäger*, goes out with an ugly but useful animal, not unlike a shepherd's dog, but smaller, which is in German language called "a sow-finder." The business of this creature is to seek the hog, and so well trained is he that no other animal will turn him from that particular scent. On meeting with the object of his search he gives tongue incessantly, and with active but cautious irritation pursues the boar till he is at bay; then, by continual teasing, he manages to turn him sideways to his master, the shoulder affording the best aim for readily disabling him. In this situation the sagacious dog contrives to keep him until his master fires; then if the wounded boar makes off, the boar-hound (a species of blood-hound) is let loose, who pursues him for miles, giving tongue, nor will he leave him even if other boars come in the way.

At the wild boar park of the Emperor of Austria, which is at Hüttelsdorf, near Vienna, Mr. Howitt states that he saw "numbers of swine of all ages and sizes, from the grisly old boar to the sow and her troop of suckling young ones. Here some grim old fellow as black as jet, or of a sun-burnt and savage gray, lay basking in the deep grass, and at our approach uttered a deep guff, and starting up, bolted into the wood. Others were lying their length under the broad trees, others scampering about with cocked tails. The sows and their young seemed most savage and impatient of our presence. Some were tame enough to come at the whistle of the keeper, and scores ran voraciously when he shook one of the wild cornel-trees, which grew plentifully in the forest. This is a tree as large as an apple-tree, bearing, in autumn, fruit of about the size of cherries, and of a coral red color. The swine are very fond of it, and as the trees were shook, and it pattered to the ground, they came running on all sides, and stood in the thickets eager for our departure, when they rushed ravenously forward and devoured it."

"After all," he continues, "the wild swine here can present but a faint idea of what they were in their ancient wilds. They are all of the true breed, and cannot for a moment be confounded with the tame variety; there is the tusked mouth, the thick fore-quarter, the narrow hind-quarter, the mane, the coarse bristles, the speed of gait, indicative of the wild breed, but they appeared tame and pigmy in comparison with the huge savage monsters bred in the obscure recesses of deep forests, and unacquainted with the sight of man.

"Hunters tell us that, notwithstanding the orders of Government to exterminate swine in the open forests, on account of the mischief they do to cultivated land, there are numbers in the forests in Hanover and Westphalia, huge, gaunt, and ferocious as ever. These will snuff the most distant approach of danger, and with terrific noises rush into the densest woods; or surrounding a solitary and unarmed individual, especially a woman or a child, will scour round and round them, coming nearer and nearer at every circle, until at last, bursting in upon them, they tear them limb from limb and devour them. Tame swine, which are herded in these forests and become mixed in breed with the wild, acquire the same blood-thirsty propensities, and will, in their herds, surround and devour persons in a similar manner."

The wild breed abound in Upper Austria, on the Styrian Alps, and in many parts of Hungary. In the latter country, a recent author speaking of them, says: "These animals have lost some little

of their natural ferocity, but they still fly at the approach of stran
gers, and in their form and habits preserve all the characteristics of
the true wild boar, from which stock they are descended without intermixture of any other breed. I am told, too, that their flesh has
all the peculiar flavor of the wild boar. This animal, in a completely
savage state, is now becoming very scarce in Hungary, and is only
met with in the most secluded forests, and in the recesses of the Car-
pathian mountains.

The forests of Poland, Spain, Russia, and Sweden, still contain
animals of the wild boar tribe, and the inhabitants of these countries
hunt them with hounds, or attack them with fire-arms, or with the
proper boar-spear.

But the most exciting accounts we now have of this sport are furnished by our countrymen in the East, who diversify their other
hunts and field-sports by occasionally chasing the wild hog. Cap-
tain Williamson, in his graphic volume, gives some very animated
accounts of the perils of this chase, as does also Mr. Johnston; and
if any thing could reconcile us to the pursuing, tormenting, and shedding the blood of an animal who only puts forth his strength in self-
defence, it would be the bravery and presence of mind exhibited by
some of the huntsmen. One or two quotations will illustrate the
habits of the wild hogs of India, as well as the mode in which they
are hunted.

"The pace and powers of 'the wild hog' are not to be estimated
by any comparison with those of the tame one. Persons unacquainted with the vigor and speed of the jungle hog will be surprised to learn that it requires a good horse to keep near a moderately-sized hog, and that it is by no means uncommon to see what
is considered as a moderately-sized animal overthrow many horses in
succession. The fact is, that from April to November, during which
period the canes and corn are off the grounds, the wild hogs are
compelled to wander from the copses and long grass jungles in which
they take refuge, to greater distances, in search of food, by which
means they are not only kept low in flesh, but, from their daily
exercises, get confirmed in good wind, and seem rather to attack
the hunter than to run away; and this is not merely during the
space of a few hundred yards, but for a considerable distance. I
recollect being one of four well-mounted riders, who were completely
distanced in a chase of about three miles.

"In crossing the country early in June, about sunrise, we saw at
a considerable distance a hog trotting over a plain to his cover,
which was a large extent of brambles and copse, from which we
could not hope to drive him. As there appeared no chance of over
taking him, we agreed to let him proceed unmolested, and to be at
the place whence he had come by daybreak on the next morning.
We accordingly were up early on the following morning, anticipa-

ting the pleasure of being at his heels, but on arriving at the spot in which we had observed him on the preceding day we found him nearer to his cover than before.

" Knowing that when hogs take the alarm they are apt to change their route and their hours, we were not surprised at this manœuvring.   We were still earlier on the third morning, when we took our positions nearer his place of nightly resort, and had the satisfaction to find that we were in time to bear him company homeward.   Here, however, some delay took place.   The hog on his first breaking from the small jungle where we awaited him, and through which he had to pass, after glutting himself in a swamp among some rye, sown extremely thick for transplanting, found that he was watched.   He, therefore, after trotting out a hundred yards, gave a sort of snort and returned.   This was precisely what we wished for.

" It was not yet day, and the desire to intercept our prey had made us push forward so as to place our people far behind.   They, however, came up to the number of a hundred, and after beating the cover for a short time, our friend took fairly to the plain.

"As we were careful not to dispirit, and had cautiously kept from that side on which we wished him to bolt, he gained upon us a little. He had to go at least three miles, and the whole of the plain was laid out in *paddy*, or rice fields.

" The hog kept a-head the whole way, so that there was no possibility of our throwing a distant spear.

" The swine generally establish themselves in cane or grain plantations, when these are high and afford good shelter, and here they live for several months ; but about the middle of March, or, at the latest, the beginning of April, they are obliged to shift their quarters, as the cane and grains are generally cut about that time.

" Hogs are often found in March with three or four inches of fat on the chines and shoulders.

" It usually requires a great number of persons to drive the hogs out of the sugar-canes, on account of their extent.

" The hog, being forced from his covert, is crowded upon by several horsemen with spears, which they use in the manner of javelins.   They pursue the animal at speed as he makes his way to the nearest covert, darting their spears into his body as they come up to him.

" Many may be seen with scars, evidently the result of wounds received on former occasions, and such are extremely difficult to deal with.   They will break out of the line repeatedly, dash at all they meet with, and eventually create such terror as effectually to discourage the beaters, who thence get into groups, and, though they continue their vociferation, act so timorously as to render it expedient to withdraw them for the purpose of trying a fresh cover.   It is very common to see a plough at work at the very edge of the canes where the villagers are beating for hogs; and as the bullocks employed are extremely skittish and wild, it often happens that they take fright and run off with the plough, which frequently is broken to pieces. The ploughman, alarmed equally with his cattle, also takes to flight, as do all the peasants who may see the bristling animal galloping from his haunt."

Mr. Johnson describes another scene eminently characteristic of the desperate fierceness and strength of the wild hog. He was one of a party of eight persons, on a sporting excursion near Patna on the banks of the Soane. Returning one morning from shooting, they met with a very large boar, which they did not fire at or molest, as, although several of the party were fond of hunting, they had no spears with them. The next morning they all sallied forth in search of him, and just as they had arrived at the spot where they had seen him the day before, they discovered him at some distance galloping off towards a grass jungle on the banks of the river. They pressed their horses as fast as possible, and were nearly up with him when he disappeared all at once.

The horses were then nearly at their full speed, and four of them could not be pulled up in time to prevent their going into a deep branch of the river, the banks of which were at least fourteen or fifteen feet high. Happily, there was no water in, or any thing but fine sand, and no person was hurt. One of the horses, that was exceedingly vicious, got loose, attacked the others, and obliged them and all the rest, to recede.

A few days afterwards they went again, early in the morning, in pursuit of the same hog, and found him farther off from the grass jungle, in a rhur-field, from which with much difficulty they drove him into a plain, where he stood at bay challenging the whole party, and boldly charging every horse that came within fifty yards of him, grunting loudly as he advanced.

"The horse I rode," says Mr Johnston, "would not go near him, and when I was at considerable distance off, he charged another horse with such ferocity that mine reared and plunged in so violent a manner as to throw me off. Two or three others were dismounted at nearly the same time; and though there were many horses present that had been long accustomed to the sport, not one of them would stand his charges. He fairly drove the whole party off the field, and gently trotted on to the grass jungle, foaming and grinding his tusks."

In Morocco the wild boar is the most common and prolific of all the ferocious animals found there; the sow produces several large litters in the year; and were it not that the young form the favorite food of the lion, the country would be overrun with these animals.

In the woods of South America there are abundance of wild swine, possessing all the ferocity of the boar. The following fearful scene occurred in Columbia. A party of six hunters had gone out on a sporting expedition. They fell in with a herd of swine, upon which four of them, less experienced than the others, immediately fired, and the swine advanced fiercely to attack them. The four young men, intimidated, took to flight without warning their companions, or considering the danger to which they were exposed. They climbed up into some trees, but the other two were quickly surrounded by the swine. They made a long and desperate defence with their lances, but were at length dragged down. One of them was torn to pieces, and the other dreadfully lacerated, and left for dead by the swine, who now watched the four fugitives in the trees until sunset. Then, probably yielding to the calls of nature, they retired. The surviving hunters then came down and assisted their wounded companion into the canoe, and carried off the remains of the unfortunate man who had fallen in this horrible encounter. (Cochrane's *Columbia*, vol. i.)

We have entered thus much at length into the history of the wild boar, because no one can for a moment doubt that it is the parent stock from which the domesticated breeds of swine originally sprung; the well-known fact that all kinds breed with the boar, is in itself a sufficient testimony; but to this we can add that the period of gestation is the same in the wild and tame sow; the anatomical structure is identical; the general form bears the same characters; and the habits, so far as they are not altered by domestication, remain the same.

Where individuals of the pure, wild race, have been caught young and subjected to the same treatment as a domestic pig, their fierceness has disappeared, they have become more social and less noctural in their habits, lost their activity, and lived more to eat. In the course of one or two generations even the form undergoes certain modifications; the body becomes larger and heavier; the legs shorter and less adapted for exercise; the formidable tusks of the boar, being no longer needed as weapons of defence, disappear; the shape of the head and neck alters; and in character as well as in form, the animal adapts itself to its position. Nor does it appear that a return to their native wilds restores to them their original appearance; for, in whatever country pigs have escaped from the control of man, and bred in the woods and wildernesses, there does not appear to be a single instance recorded by any naturalist in which they have resumed the habits and form of the wild boar. They become fierce, wild, gaunt, and grisly, and live upon roots and fruits; but they are still merely degenerated swine, and they still associate together in herds, nor " walk the glade in savage solitary grandeur" like their grim ancestors.

3*

We shall now proceed to notice some of the accounts given of the swine found in various parts of the world, previous to entering upon a consideration of the breeds peculiar to our own country.

CHAPTER V.

Swine in America—In large towns—Original breed—Improved breed—Swine in Canada—In Ohio—In Mexico—Hebrides—In Columbia—In the South Sea Islands—Swine in Asia—in China and Japan—Ceylon—Hindostan—Turkey and Arabia—Swine in Africa—Guinea—New Holland—Caffraria—Swine in Europe—In Malta—In Italy—In Germany—In Hungary—In Russia—In Sweden—In France—Swine indigenous to the Channel Islands—In Jersey—In Guernsey—In Sark—In Alderney—The Isle of Man—In the Hebrides—In the Shetland Isles —In the Orkneys.

AMERICA.

THROUGHOUT the whole of this quarter of the globe swine appear to abound. They are not, however, indigenous, but were doubtless originally carried thither by the early English settlers, and the breed thus introduced still may be distinguished by the traces they retain of their parent stock; but France, Spain, and, during the slave-trade, Africa, have also combined to supply America with varieties of this animal, so useful to the settler in the wilds and woods, and so much esteemed throughout the whole of the country, as furnishing a valuable article of food.

"It appears that the American zoologists describe no fewer than six species of the hog, some of them so entirely distinct in their general habits and appearance as to prevent their ever breeding or even associating together. Five of these species need only be regarded as objects of curiosity; the sixth is the common wild hog of the eastern continent, which we will describe, in order to illustrate the difference between a good and a bad animal of the same variety; they have long-peaked snouts, coarse heads, thin chests, narrow shoulders, sharp backs, slab sides, meagre, diminutive hams, big legs, clumped feet, the hide of a rhinoceros, the hair and bristles of a porcupine, and as thick and shaggy as a bear's; they have no capacity for digesting and concocting their food in the stomach for nourishment; there is nothing but offal, bones, rind, bristles, and hair, with a narrow streak of gristle underneath, and a still narrower line of lean, as tough and as rank as white leather—their snouts against every man, and every man's hand against them. No reasonable fence can stop them, but, ever restive and uneasy, they rove about seeking for plunder; swilling, grunting, rooting, pawing, always in mischief and always destroying. The more a man possesses of such stock the worse he is off; and he had far better sell his produce at any price, than to put it into such totally worthless creatures."—A. B. Allen.

Stuart says—" Hogs are universal in this part of the world, and are well and frequently fed. At first they are kept in the woods, and nurtured on chestnuts and apples; before being killed, they have good rations of Indian corn or barley-meal, and in many cases are likewise well supplied with steamed food. In South Carolina the climate is so mild that they are allowed to wander about the woods during the whole year, feeding on the nuts, acorns, &c., which are there so abundant, and occasionally eating the fallen fruit they meet with. They are very useful in destroying snakes."—Stuart's *North America.*

In large towns, too, they are apparently as much at home and as common as in the forests, pacing the streets, instead of the glades, and feeding upon the offal and filth rejected by man, instead of the fresh and wholesome fruits supplied by the hand of nature. One of our countrymen gives an amusing graphic account of the swinish multitude, in some of the large towns through which he passed.

" We are going to cross here. Take care of the pigs. Two portly sows are trotting up behind this carriage, and a select party of half-a-dozen gentlemen hogs have just now turned the corner. Here is a solitary swine, lounging homewards by himself; he has only one ear, having parted with the other to vagrant dogs in the course of his city rambles; but he gets on very well without it, and leads a roving, gentlemanly, vagabond kind of a life, somewhat answering to that of our clubmen at home. He leaves his lodgings every morning at a certain hour, throws himself upon the town, gets through his day in some manner quite satisfactory to himself, and regularly appears at the door of his own house again at night, like the mysterious master of Gil Blas; he is a free-and-easy, careless, indifferent kind of pig, having a very large acquaintance among other pigs of the same character, whom he rather knows by sight than conversation, as he seldom troubles himself to stop and exchange civilities, but goes grunting down the kennel, turning up the news and small-talk of the city, in the shape of cabbage-stalks and offal, and bearing no tails but his own, which is a very short one, for his old enemies the dogs have been at that too, and have left him hardly enough to swear by; he is in every respect a republican pig, going wherever he pleases, and mingling with the best society, on an equal, if not superior footing, for every one makes way when he appears, and the haughtiest give him the wall if he prefer it; he is a great philosopher, and seldom moved unless by the dogs before-mentioned; sometimes, indeed, you may see his

small eye twinkling on a slaughtered friend, whose carcass gar
nishes a butcher's door-post, but he grunts out "Such is life; all
flesh is pork!" buries his nose in the mire again, and waddles
down the gutter, comforting himself with the reflection that there
is one snout the less to anticipate stray cabbage-stalks, at any rate.

"They are the city scavengers, these pigs, ugly brutes they are;
having for the most part scanty brown backs, like the lids of old
horse-hair trunks, spotted with unwholesome black blotches; they
have long, gaunt legs too, and such peaked snouts that if one of them
could be persuaded to sit for his profile, nobody would recognize it
for a pig's likeness; they are never attended upon, or fed, or driven,
or caught, but are thrown upon their own resources in early life,
and become preternaturally knowing in consequence; every pig
knows where he lives much better than any body could tell him.
At this hour, just as evening is closing in, you will see them roam-
ing towards bed by scores, eating their way to the last. Occasionally some youth among them who has overeaten himself, or has
been worried by dogs, trots shrinkingly homeward, like a prodigal
son; but this is a rare case; perfect self-possession and self-reliance,
and immovable composure, being their foremost attributes. (Dick-
ens' *American Notes*.)

And Mrs. Trollope piteously exclaims—"I am sure I should have
liked Cincinnati much better if the people had not dealt so very
largely in hogs! The immense quantity of business done in this
line would hardly be believed by those who had not witnessed it.
I never saw a newspaper without remarking such advertisements as
the following: "Wanted immediately, 4000 fat hogs;" "For sale,
2000 barrels of prime pork." But the annoyance came nearer
than this. If I determined upon a walk up Main Street, the chances
were five hundred to one against my reaching the shady side without brushing by a snout or two, fresh dripping from the kennel.
When we had screwed up our courage to the enterprise of mount-
ing a certain noble-looking sugar-loaf hill, that promised pure air
and a fine view, we found the brook we had to cross at its foot, red
with the blood from a pig slaughter-house; while our noses, instead
of meeting "the thyme that loves the green hill's breast," were
greeted by odors that I will not describe, and which I heartily hope
my readers cannot imagine; our feet, that on leaving the city had
expected to press the flowery sod, literally got entangled in pigs'
tails and jaw-bones; and thus the prettiest walk in the neighborhood
was interdicted for ever."

The common breed may for the most part be described as large,
rough, long-nosed, big-boned, thin-backed, slab-sided, long-legged,
ravenous, ugly animals. But latterly great improvements have been
made in it by judicious crossing with the Chinese and Berkshire pigs,
by crossing these two breeds with each other, and by careful breed
ing from these two stocks without intermixture.

Mr. Bement of Albany, who has devoted great attention to the rearing and breeding of swine, speaks in the highest terms of praise of the cross between the pure Chinese breed and the original breed of the country, or, "*land-shads*," as he termed them. He says that the Chinese breed was first introduced about twenty years ago, but that from their size, seldom attaining more than 250 lbs., and from their delicacy, they were not adapted for "a farmer's hog." But with the just-mentioned cross they become all that could be wished. He thus describes the "improved China hogs:"—"In color they are various—white, black and white, spotted, and gray and white; they are longer in the body than the pure Chinese breed; small in the head and legs; broad in the back; round in the body; the hams well let down; skin thin; and flesh delicate and finely flavored. They are easy keepers, small consumers, quiet in disposition, not given to roam or commit depredations; and when in condition may be maintained so upon grass only."—*The Cultivator*, vol. ii.

The best Berkshire breeds, as imported into America, vary somewhat in size and appearance; that from which most of the present stock have been raised was taken to America in 1832. This breed has spread rapidly over the country, and fetches a high price from its peculiar aptitude to fatten. Its prevailing characteristics are—a fine head, a dished face, rather upright ears, close shoulders and hams, and a short body; animals of this kind mature very rapidly, and produce most delicate meat.

There are now various improved breeds, known for the most part under the names of the improvers, or of the localities in which they are found, arising from crosses of the original American hog with the above-mentioned breeds, or others which may have been imported from England and other countries. The establishment of agricultural societies and cattle-shows, has contributed in the New as well as in the Old World to direct the attention of farmers and breeders to all kinds of domesticated animals, and the advantages which have been obtained in swine alone are sufficiently great to prove incentives to increased care and study on the all-important principles of breeding.

Head, in his journey from Halifax to Upper Canada, again and again alludes to the fine pigs he saw, and the delicious pork with which he was regaled by the settlers he met with in various parts. He says that bears are very fond of pork, for they often get into the farm-yards and carry off a squeaking, struggling victim to regale themselves upon

INDIANA.

In Indiana the breed of swine furnishes the principal supply for food and exportation; great quantities of pork being sent to New Orleans. Great numbers of swine roam in the woods of Indiana, far from all human dwellings, where they grow very fat upon the abundance of oak and beech mast. In some parts where great numbers of swine are allowed to run almost wild, a triangular yoke is fixed round their necks to prevent them from breaking through fences. —Weld's *Travels in North America.* They are of a reddish-brown color, with round black spots; there are some quite wild, which any body is at liberty to shoot. These animals are never housed, even in the vicinity of Harmony. In the depth of winter the young ones often perish with cold, or are devoured by the mothers; and then dead swine will be seen lying about in all directions, some partly devoured by others. The negligence and want of feeling with which these animals are treated is very great, and consequently they can never be expected to prosper, or yield those advantages which might be derived from them under proper treatment.

OHIO.

Professor Silliman, in his account of Ohio, says that large numbers of hogs pass the winter in the woods quite independent of the assistance of man, subsisting on nuts and acorns. Single individuals of these are occasionally destroyed by bears and wolves, but a herd of ten or twenty hogs are more than a match for a wolf or panther. Indeed an old hunter once saw a panther spring from a tree into a drove of wood hogs, and scarcely had he touched the ground than the larger ones fell upon him with their tusks and the weight of their bodies, and killed and tore him in pieces in a few moments. *Arcana of Science,* 1828.

MEXICO.

In Mexico fine breeds of pigs are kept by many persons of wealth as an article of trade as well as of consumption, and the greatest possible care and attention are paid to the cleanliness and comfort of these animals; nay, more, the Mexican pigs may be said to possess the luxuries of life, for two Indian lads are kept to sing the grunting herd to sleep. These boys are chosen for the strength of their lungs and their taste and judgment in delighting the ears and lulling the senses of the porcine harmonists, and they take it by turns to chant throughout the whole day; nor does their performance appear to be unappreciated by their strange audience, but rather to afford exceeding delight and gratification.

HEBRIDES.

The New Hebrides, the Marquesas, the Friendly and Society Islands, and New Guinea, abound with a breed of swine closely resembling the Chinese, and these being almost the only domestic animals which the natives of these islands possess, they accordingly receive great care and attention. This race is small, the belly hanging, the legs short, the tail almost imperceptible, and the color gray. Its flesh is very white and delicate.

COLUMBIA.

In the woods of Columbia there are numbers of swine, but for the most part wild; and the flesh of these wild ones is far superior to that of the few that are domesticated, as that of the latter, from the animals being often fed on stale fish and all kinds of abominations, acquires a rancid and unpleasant flavor. Some of the settlers chiefly live by the sale of the flesh of wild swine, which they obtain by hunting, and then cure or dry it.

Experienced hunters will kill their fourteen or fifteen swine a-day, and a well-trained dog will often destroy two or three of these animals a-day by himself. The mode of proceeding is for the dog to keep the hog at bay while the hunter creeps up, and watching his opportunity, throws his lance with such vigor as to pin the animal to the ground. This done, he rushes upon him, seizes the lance firmly with one hand, and with the other dispatches the game with his knife.

In Paraguay and Brazil, swine are likewise abundant, and for the most part wild.

The Falkland Islands were stocked with swine by the French and Spaniards, but little, if any, trace of the original breeds can now be discovered in the fierce, bristly, tusked animals now found there, some of the older ones of which rival the grisly boar in appearance and wildness.

SOUTH-SEA ISLANDS.

The South-Sea Islands, on their discovery by Europeans, were found to be well stocked with a small, black, short-legged hog; the traditionary belief of the natives was, that these animals were as anciently descended as themselves. The hog, in fact, is in these islands the principal quadruped, and is of all others the most carefully cultivated. The bread-fruit tree, either in the form of a sour paste or in its natural condition, constitutes its favorite food, and its additional choice of yams, eddoes, and other nutritive vegetables, renders its flesh most juicy and delicious; its fat, though rich, being at the same time (so says Foster) not less delicate and agreeable than the finest butter. Before our missionary labors had proved so successful in these once benighted regions, by substituting the mild spirit of Christianity for the sanguinary forms of a delusive and degrading worship, the Otaheitans and other South-Sea Islanders were in the habit of presenting roasted pigs at the *morais*, as the most savory and acceptable offering to their deities which they could bestow.

Throughout the greater part of Asia, swine are to be found. The extensive and magnificent forests which cover much of the Birmese Empire, Siam, Cochin China, and other kingdoms of the south-east, abound with hogs, as well as other pachydermatous animals.

Here are found the celebrated Siamese or Chinese breed, so much esteemed throughout all parts of the world to which they have been exported: distinguished for their small size, fine head and snout, compact deep carcass, large hams and shoulders, short limbs, delicate feet, fine hair and skin, aptitude to fatten and grow, and the sweet, delicate meat they yield.

The Chinese and Japanese are great pig-breeders, and make the art of crossing, breeding, and rearing swine, which furnishes them with their principal animal food, an object of peculiar attention and study. Merchants who have resided for some time in China, and even travellers who have merely been able to bestow a superficial glance on matters, speak of the great care bestowed on this point; but no author appears to have given any details as to the course of practice adopted. Perhaps from the naturally jealous and uncommunicative disposition of the Chinese, they have been unable to acquire any; and, perhaps, few have thought it worth while to trouble themselves about so degraded an animal as the hog. However this may be, it is much to be regretted that the information is so very scanty, for many valuable hints might probably have been thus obtained.

Tradescent Lay, the naturalist in Beechy's expedition, in his interesting work on China, thus amusingly speaks of the natives and their swine:—"There is a striking analogy between these two. A Chinese admires a round face and the smooth curvatures of a tunbelly, and where opportunity serves, cultivates these additions to personal beauty in himself. The Chinese pig is fashioned on the same model. At an early period the back becomes convex, the belly protuberant, and the visage shows a remarkable disposition to rotundity. Nor is the resemblance merely personal; in the moral character there is an amusing similitude, contrariety and obstinacy being the prevailing characteristics of both men and brutes."

The same author informs us that swine are rarely driven or made to walk in China, but conveyed from place to place in a species of cradle suspended upon a pole, carried by two men. But he says, "the difficulty is to get the animal into this conveyance, and this is accomplished by the cradle being placed in front of the pig, and the owner then vigorously pulling at 'porky's tail,' and in the spirit of opposition the animal darts into the place they have prepared for him. At the journey's end, the bearers dislodge him by spitting in his face."

Mr. Lay states that "pork is very plentiful in China, but never agreeable to the European eye, from its shining, flabby appearance; it does not taste either like our pork, and is only tolerable when cut into thin slices and fried in soy to correct the grossness of its natural juices. The natives cut it in long slices or rashers, and dry it in the sun, and thus prepared it is not unpleasant in flavor, although it is then by no means easy to distinguish it from dogs' or cats' flesh similarly prepared."

CEYLON.

In speaking of Ceylon, and its neighborhood, an intelligent traveller says:—"The swine here are a long-legged, ugly breed, allowed to run wild and pick up whatever food they can get. I never saw, at any native cottage or farm, a pig penned up or put to fatten, and yet the natives are very fond of hog's flesh, and never hold any feast or festival without this meat constituting the chief and most approved dishes."

HINDOSTAN.

The existence of a breed of swine in Hindostan and the Birmese empire is mentioned by several travellers, but scarcely one gives any account of them. It would seem, however, that they are identical with the Siamese breed. Hogs are also enumerated as among the wild beasts of Central India. Some of the Hindoo tribes use hog's blood for all the purposes to which other nations apply holy water; but pork is not eaten, excepting by Europeans and the lowest caste of Hindoos. In the Eastern Archipelago and the Moluccas, a breed of wild swine exists bearing great resemblance to the Chinese, but rather longer in the legs and lighter in the body, and affording delicious meat.

TURKEY AND ARABIA.

In Turkey, Syria, Persia, Arabia, and the north-eastern parts of Asia, comparatively few pigs are found, and these are of an iron-gray, black, and occasionally brown hue; short-legged, small, round in the body, very apt to fatten, and attaining the weight of from 350 to 400 lbs. And there are two ways of accounting for this, viz.; the prevalence of the Mohammedan religion, and the sandy, open nature of the country; for it is chiefly in well-wooded if not cultivated districts that we find swine, their nature and habits alike unfitting them for dry sandy deserts.

AFRICA.

In this quarter of the globe again, we meet with but few swine, until we approach the south-eastern parts, and for the same reasons which we have just given. In Abyssinia they are to be found, but they are not held in much estimation. They have been imported into New Holland, Caffraria, and the Cape of Good Hope, but are not kept to any extent, on account of the difficulty of feeding them. In most of these places pork is chiefly used as food for the lower classes, and but little care or attention is bestowed upon the animals; and the breeds greatly resemble the Chinese variety, but are somewhat less, being short-legged, round-bodied animals, of a black or dark brown color, the bristles few and almost as fine as hairs, and the tail terminated by a tuft.

The Coast of Guinea used to possess a breed of swine which have been exported thence as an article of commerce, especially to the new settlements in America and to some parts of the East Indies, and were held in high estimation at that time. But the cessation of the intercourse induced by the slave-trade, and the discovery of more valuable breeds, have rendered these almost forgotten. These animals were large in size, square in form, of a reddish color, the body covered with short, bristly hair, and smoother and more shiny than almost any other variety of the porcine race; the tail very long, and the ears long, narrow, and terminating in a point. This variety is also found in Brazil.

EUROPE.

We now find swine almost universal, and every where, more or less, an object of special care and attention, both as furnishing a valuable kind of animal food, and an article of commerce.

MALTA.

Coming up the Mediterranean Sea we find the small black Maltese breed, the bodies of which are almost bare and smooth, and which fatten so aptly and afford such delicate pork. Spain then offers its breeds, none of which are, however, held in great estimation out of their native country. The chief of these is a short-headed, long, yet round-bodied, dumpty-legged variety, of a reddish-brown or copper color; the skin fine and the bristles slender; it is small in size, very prolific, and may easily be fattened to an enormous weight. This breed is also found in Portugal and some parts of the south of Italy ; it closely resembles the Siamese pigs, and has doubtless originally sprung from them. The far-famed Bologna sausages are made from the flesh of this animal.

ITALY.

Italy too is in some degree celebrated for its pigs, the best breeds of which, like the Maltese, are small, black, destitute of bristles, and delicate in flesh. The Neapolitan breed has been extensively exported, for the purpose of crossing with other kinds, and has found considerable favor in many parts of England. In themselves these pigs are not sufficiently hardy for general use, but, crossed with rougher breeds, they yield a valuable progeny, fine in form, delicate in flesh, and easy to fatten. There is a much larger race of swine bred in the Duchy of Parma, and generally considered to be the finest breed in Italy, in every point of view.

In Palermo, Bosco, the environs of Rome, and the neighborhood of Bologna, Count Chateauvieux tells us pigs are kept. Those at Bosco, on the Apennines, he describes as a good breed, which the farmers fatten on chestnuts and milk, housing them in the winter and suffering them to run over the mountains during the summer. At the farm of Campo Morto he found a herd of 2000, of the domestic breed, and black. They run all the year on the immense tract of land which extends towards the sea, are fattened on nuts and acorns, and yield excellent meat. They are not indigenous, but have been brought thither to stock the woods, and they are regarded by the proprietor of that farm as the most valuable part of his stock, for their keep costs him little or nothing, and they yield a very good profit.

The pigs he found on the marshy plains of Polesimo, between Bologna and Ferrara, he describes as large, lean, thin-flanked, and long-limbed animals. (Chateauvieux's *Letters from Italy.*)

GERMANY.

Pursuing our way to Germany we meet with totally different animals, submitted for the most part to an entirely different management. The common breeds of the country are every where described as huge, gaunt, long-legged, lean-bodied, greyhound-like animals, with exceedingly long snouts and coarse bristles, forming almost as much of a mane on the neck and shoulders as those of the wild boar.

In Prussia and many parts of Poland a rather smaller but scarcely less uncouth race are met with, of a yellow or redd'sh-brown color.

Thäer informs us, that "the chief breeds of pigs known in the north of Germany and crossed in various different ways, are,—the Moldavian, Wallachian, and Bothnian, remarkable for their enormous size, iron-gray color, and large lapping ears; and the Polish, or, properly speaking, the Podolian, which are also very large, but are of a yellow color, and have a broad brown stripe along the spine." These two breeds, he says, furnish the large pigs for fattening, but they require a proportionably large quantity of food, and besides are not very productive, the sows seldom bringing forth more than four or five at the most at a birth.

The Bavarian pigs, he states, are much esteemed for their smallness of bone and aptitude to fatten; but the flesh is not liked, it being too flabby and soft. This breed is usually marked with reddish-brown spots.

The Westphalian is another breed very generally met with; these animals are large in size and very prolific, bringing forth ten or twelve at a litter.

The next variety mentioned he designates "the English pig," and describes it as being large, full, and deep in the body, and requiring very substantial food. A cross between this breed and the Westphalian is stated to produce an excellent animal.

To these he adds the Chinese breed, the Spanish or African black pig, which he estimates very highly from its aptitude to fatten on indifferent or scanty food, its rapid growth, delicate flesh, excellent hams, and the advantages derived from crossing the larger breeds with it; and lastly, the German pig, properly so called. But it appears that this can scarcely be regarded as a distinct breed, but rather as the result of numerous and various crosses, for he says: "This breed is different in its characteristics in different provinces; the color is white, black, gray, or spotted. It is of a middling size and can be supported on a moderate quantity of nourishment. There is no doubt but that by more attention being bestowed upon the breeding, rearing, and feeding of this race, they might be materially improved, but most of the persons who undertake the management of pigs on an extensive scale, seem rather anxious to try the effect of different and new crosses than to improve the old breed."

HUNGARY.

In Hungary, Croatia, and Servia a race of swine resembling that found in Turkey are met with; small, of a dark gray color, and short-legged, yet not apparently deriving their origin from the Chinese. The flesh of the swine reared in Servia is said to be more delicate than will be met with any where throughout the whole of Europe.

In Poland, Russia, Sweden, and the northern parts of Europe, the swine yet retain all the characteristics of their ancestor the wild boar. They are mostly of a red, or dirty brown, or yellow color; long in the body, light and active in make, having long legs, a broad flat head, erect ears, and a nervous, slightly up-turned snout. They are wild in their habits, fierce, not apt fatteners, or producing delicate meat.

In Holland and Belgium we find numerous varieties and crosses, but the original breeds have large bodies and long lopping ears; the sows are prolific, and if properly attended to, the animals fatten very kindly. There is a variety often met with,—and much esteemed for its productive powers, its disposition to fatten, and the delicacy of its flesh,—which most probably derives its origin from a cross between a native pig and one of the Siamese breed. This animal is of a medium size, rather short on the legs, with a full round body, straight back, broad flanks, and small head. The bristles are white and thinly scattered over the back, but growing rather closer upon the neck and towards the head.

FRANCE.

The original breeds of France are mostly coarse ungainly animals, for the most part white, excepting towards the south, and there we find the native breeds very much to resemble those of Italy. "In the time of Buffon, the greater proportion of the hogs in the north of France were white, as were likewise those of Vivarais; while in Dauphiny, which is not far distant, they were all black. Those of Languedoc and Provence were also of the latter color. Black pigs still prevail both in Italy and Spain. According to the great French naturalist, one of the most evident marks of degeneration (an ill-applied term) is furnished by the ears, which become more supple and pendent as the animal changes into the domestic state. He regards the wild boar as the model of the species erroneously, for it can only be looked upon as formed on the model best adapted to the haunts and habits of a wild animal, the welfare of which requires either the instinct of a cunning concealment or the possession of strength or swiftness. Now concealment in a pigsty is of little avail when the day of terror comes, and the obesity of a well-fed porker is, and must ever continue, entirely inconsistent either with speed of foot or vigor of limb; therefore the proper attributes of the animal in its unreclaimed and domesticated conditions being incompatible with each other, those of the former ought not in any way to be set up or assumed as a model by which the latter should be altered or improved."—*Quarterly Journal of Agriculture*, vol. iii. Of late years French agriculturists have seen the advantages small breeds possess over large ones, and endeavored by judicious crosses to reduce the size of their pigs, and at the same time give to the breeds all the value arising from early maturity, a kindly disposition, and productiveness. M. Magne says, " Our breeds of pigs are in general very defective; they are long-limbed, thin-necked, narrow-chested, and have high curved backs; they are hardy, but far from precocious, fatten with difficulty, and consume an immense quantity of food compared with the flesh they yield."

We are partly indebted to Mr. Wilson's valuable " Essay on Domestic Animals" for the following account of the present chief breeds of swine in France. The most distinguishable of the present races of France are the following :—

" 1. *The race of the Pays d'Auge*, (by some authors called the Normandy breed,) which has the head small and sharp-pointed; the ears narrow and pointed; the body lengthened; the legs broad and strong; the hair coarse, spare, and of a white color; and the bones small. It attains to the weight of 600 lbs." M. Bella considers that this breed are great eaters, but do not fatten kindly.

2. *The race of Poitu,* of which the head is long and thick, the point projecting; the ears large and pendulous; the body lengthened; the bristles white and coarse; the feet broad and strong; and the bones large. Its weight does not exceed 500 lbs.

3. *The race of Périgord,* of which the neck is thick and short, the body broad and compact, and the hair black, short, and rough. This race, when crossed with the Poitou pigs, produces very good animals; and it is probable that the pied swine, so common in the south of France, are descended from this cross.

4. *The race of Boulogne.* Of considerable dimensions, and well inclined to fatten quickly; ears very broad; general color white. This breed has sprung from a cross between the large English breed and one of the common races of France.

Of other continental races we shall mention the *Jutland swine.* Of these the ears are large and pendent, the body elongated, the back somewhat curved, the legs long. The size of this breed is considerable, as from 200 lbs. to 300 lbs. (French livres) of lard are got from them in their second year. They form an important branch of commerce.

The race known abroad under the name of *Cochon de Siam* is the representative of our Chinese breed. Its ears are short, straight, and flexible; its body is covered with soft and somewhat silky hair, which is stiff and thick on the head and back of the neck, and frizzly on the cheeks and under jaw; on the other parts it is thin, and for the most part hard and black. The skin is also black, except on the belly; the eyes are surrounded by a slight tinge of flame-color; their tails measure nine inches in length; their bodies three feet three inches; their height at the shoulder is one foot eight inches (French.) This breed appears to have spread extensively over most of the southern shores of the old continent.

To these he adds the Turkish hog, the New Guinea hog, De Witt's hog, and the smooth or short-legged swine, the two latter of which evidently derive their origin from a cross with the Siamese and some other breed, and all of which fatten easily and to a great weight, and are good breeders.

The swine in Normandy are, even to the present day, of the large, gaunt, grizzly race, common in some of the south-eastern counties of England and Germany. Mr. Wilson informs us that in the time of Buffon, by far the greater proportion of the swine in the north of France were perfectly white, as were also those of Vivarais; while in Dauphiny, which is not far distant, they were all black. Those of Languedoc and Provence were likewise black. This is a curious fact, and seems to prove, beyond a doubt, that the parent stock of these two opposite colors was totally different, and also that there was little intermixture or crossing among the breeds of these places, but that the races were preserved pure and distinct. He also mentions that latterly a new variety of the porcine race has been introduced under the name of "*Le Porc de Nobles*," which appears to have been derived from the improved English breed, which originated from a cross between an Anglo-Chinese sow, and an emancipated wild boar. This answers very well, and is much esteemed on account of the delicate flavor of its flesh.

In Champagne the breed of pigs are white, long-limbed, flat-sided, hollow in the flanks, and having large ears.

In Quercy the breed is of a moderate size, has a small short head, little ears, and a curved back; most of these pigs are spotted, but there is more of black than white in them.

In the department of Mayenne, and along the Oudon, some very valuable kinds are found, which have been carefully bred, and reared expressly for the purpose of improving the French breeds of pigs. There are two distinct varieties, the one called the "Craon Breed," which has a long body, short legs, and a back so broad that even when the animals are lean the spine does not project. These fatten well and easily, but do not begin to make much flesh until they are eleven or twelve months old, after which they rapidly develop themselves, and attain an immense weight.

The other variety is designated the "Valley Breed"; here, too, the legs are short, the body of a medium length, the back extremely broad, the ears large and falling to the tip of the snout, which is short and wide; the back is covered with bristles, the tail finished with a tuft of the same, and from the under-jaw two hairy appendages similar to those of a goat depend. Pigs of this breed fatten well, and may be killed at any age.

In the province of Bresse, in the neighborhood of Lyons, of the

Dombes, and Carolais, and prevalent through the department of Aisne, is a breed called the Bressane race. These animals are of a moderate size, long in the body, round in form, short-legged, with long, pendulous ears, and of a dark or blackish color, with a broad stripe of white encircling the body : their flesh is delicate, and of a fine flavor.

An attempt was made to introduce some of the English breed of swine into France by an agriculturist, and he thus narrates the results :—" I began with the large Shropshire pigs. They pleased my eye, and for some little time I was perfectly satisfied; but presently I began to remark, that, although they devoured an amazing quantity of food, they fattened but very slowly, and seemed to derive no advantage whatever from the herbage and vegetables which they found in the fields.

" When killed, the flesh, and especially the fat, was exceedingly coarse. The sows, nevertheless, yielded many pigs at each farrow, which, from their size when young, sold well to persons who were tolerably rich, and knew little or nothing about the breeding of pigs.

" I next tried the small Berkshire pigs, and immediately perceived a very sensible improvement. They fattened quickly, procured most of their nourishment from the fields, and their flesh was very superior to that of the last-named breed. But as they were large, I thought to effect a still greater improvement by exchanging them for the Chinese; but here I fell into the opposite extreme. The Chinese were prolific, fattened speedily, and almost obtained their own subsistence; but they were faulty in form, their flesh was not firm, but loose in fibre, as if they had died of disease." And, accordingly, the experimenter returned to some of his best native breeds.

In FLANDERS and the NETHERLANDS the indigenous swine are long-legged, narrow-backed, flat-sided, ugly, gaunt animals, difficult to fatten ; but when in good condition making fine-flavored, excellent pork and bacon.

THE CHANNEL ISLANDS.

JERSEY.—Great attention has here been paid to the breed of pigs, which have improved by crosses and admixture with the best English and French varieties. The pork is excellent; many declare it to be finer and more delicate in flavor than any English pork. It forms one of the chief articles of consumption during the winter months.

GUERNSEY.—The swine here have latterly been considerably improved by the exertions and encouragements of the Guernsey Agricultural Society. The original breed resembled the native French and Irish pigs, and were large, coarse, ungainly, and unprofitable, evidently descended from the wild long-legged, flat-sided race; but judicious crosses with the Hampshire and Berkshire breeds, have now made it a well-shaped, profitable animal. The Guernsey pigs of the present day fatten readily and cheaply, and often attain to an enormous size. One was killed not long since weighing 640 pounds, offal not included. The pig here forms part of the establishment of every cottager, and is kept a close prisoner in his sty, where he is well supplied with buttermilk, bran, potatoes, cabbages, and all kinds of vegetables during the spring and summer, and fed almost exclusively on parsnips from September. They are generally killed at about twenty months old, and weigh then from 300 to 400 or 450 pounds. Pork forms the staple food of the Guernsey farmers and cottagers. The author has here to acknowledge his obligation to Colonel Lake, of Woodlands, Guernsey, for the information so kindly contributed by him.

SARK.—The swine here are very similar to those of Guernsey; if there is any difference, it is that they are somewhat larger. They are managed in a similar manner, fatten well, and are profitable animals.

ALDERNEY.—Here, too, the original large breed have been improved by judicious crosses. The fat hogs reach an enormous size, sometimes even outweighing a tolerably fed cow; but 500 pounds is no uncommon weight.

THE ISLE OF MAN.—Here the original breed of swine are small, wild, apt to fatten, and that without much care or attention, and yielding excellent meat. Crosses have been introduced, which perhaps have better adapted the animals to the system of sty-feeding; but we question whether they can be said to be improved by having been rendered more dependent upon the care of man.

The HEBRIDES, or WESTERN ISLES.—The most common breeds of these islands are generally considered to be aboriginal, and lineally descended from the wild boar. These swine are described as being very small, active, and shaggy, of a grayish or dirty yellow color, grazing wild upon the hills like sheep, their sole food herbage and roots, and receiving no other sustenance or shelter all the year round but what is furnished them by nature, yet being in good condition, and affording excellent meat. When artificially fed, and carefully sheltered and tended, they will attain to a very considerable bulk, without any deterioration of the quality and flavor of their flesh.

The SHETLAND ISLANDS.—The breed of swine here, very much resemble those we have just been describing. They are small, of a dirty white or yellowish brown color, remarkably strong in the snout, with sharp-pointed ears, and arched back, from which rises a forest of stiff bristles When poor, the flesh of these animals is coarse; but those which are properly fattened yield sweet and deli-

4

cate meat, and the hams, when cured, are pronounced by connois-
seurs to be excellent. The Shetland pigs are generally suffered to
roam about and forage for themselves at will, and the mischief they
do is by no means inconsiderable; for with their muscular snouts
they plough up the soil, and root out potatoes, carrots, and turnips,
and even upturn the growing corn; and, far from being a source
of profit, are, from the mischief they do, an absolute loss to the
country.

Dr. Hibbert, (*Account of the Shetland Isles,*) describes the original Shetland pig as "a little brindle monster, the very epitome of a
wild boar, yet scarcely larger in size than a terrier dog :—

> "His bristled back a trench impaled appears,
> And stands erected like a field of spears."

According to his account, "this lordling of the seat-holds and
arable lands ranges undisturbed over his free demesnes, and, in quest
of the earthworms and the roots of plants, furrows up the pastures
or corn-fields in deep trenches, destroying in his progress all the
plovers', curlews', and other birds' nests he meets with. He bivouacs
in some potato-field, which he rarely quits until he has excavated
a ditch large enough to bury within it a dozen fellow-commoners
of his own weight and size. Nor is the reign of this petty tyrant
wholly bloodless; young lambs just dropped often fall victims to
his ferocity or thirst for blood."

The ORKNEYS.—To describe the swine found here would be but
a repetition of what we have already said. They are small, of roving habits, do much mischief, yield but poor meat unless carefully
fattened, and seldom reach a weight of more than sixty or seventy
pounds. Low informs us that the pork rarely fetches more than
2*d*. per pound, and a butcher never thinks of giving more than 4*s*. or
5*s*. a-head for the pigs. Ropes are fabricated from the bristles of these
animals, by which the natives suspend themselves over the most
fearful precipices in search of sea-fowls' eggs; and, short as the hair
or bristles are, the ropes manufactured from them are said to answer
better for this perilous purpose than hempen ones would, being less
liable to be frayed by the sharp and rugged rocks.

It is in these northern islands that several authors have spoken of
swine being used as beasts of draught, but it could not have been
these aboriginal and diminutive breeds, we should conceive, but
some of the large, heavy kinds imported from England or Ireland.

CHAPTER VI.

SCOTLAND.

THERE can be little doubt but that the aboriginal breed of Highland swine are, like those found in the Hebrides, descended from the wild boar, for until within the last half-century, they retained much of the form, and many of the habits and characteristics, of the wild breed. They also are small, shaggy, bristled, and wild; wandering about the hills, grazing and seeking out roots and other favorite food, and requiring no care or sustenance at the hand of man, yet keeping in condition, and making excellent pork or bacon. The latter end of the autumn is the best time to kill them, as they are then in good flesh.

Those which have been brought into the low country and artificially fed, have fattened to a considerable size, and yielded fine-grained, firm, and well-flavored meat.

Formerly immense herds of these small swine were reared in the Highlands of Scotland, and brought down to the Lowland markets for sale; the practice of keeping these animals gradually declined some fifty or sixty years ago, but has latterly been revived since the cultivation of the potato has become more extensive. There cannot, however, be a doubt that a great number of this breed of pigs might be advantageously fattened upon every Highland farm where the land and crop is inclosed, both on account of the little artificial food they require, and the roots and various substances they will consume which no other kind of stock would touch.

But although the practice of keeping swine in the Highlands and north of Scotland is of very ancient date, there are no records which speak of their existence in the more southern parts of Caledonia; indeed, if we may give credence to several anecdotes related by Mr. Henderson, they were absolutely unknown animals in several parts. *Treatise on Breeding Swine.*

It would seem that, some hundred and twenty years since, a person residing in the parish of Ruthwell, in Dumfriesshire, received a present of a young pig, which is said to be the first which had ever appeared in that part of the country. This pig strayed from his new home one day into the adjoining parish of Carlavroc, and wandering along the seaside came upon a woman who was keeping cattle. She screamed at the sight of the " strange beast," and ran off to her village, and the pig after her. There she declared she had seen " the deil come out of the sea, and that he had chased her, roaring and gaping at her heels." One of the bravest of the villagers got a Bible and an old sword to "cunger the deil;" but while he was uttering his threats, along came the creature with such a loud "grumph," that the poor man fell down half dead with fright, and all the rest fled, and then from windows and house-tops peeped at the "monster," until one fellow cried out that it was "the gude man o' the brow's grumphy," and gradually the alarm subsided.

This same pig seems to have frightened many persons at different times, as did another which escaped by some means from a vessel which put into Glencaple Quay, just below Dumfriesshire, and was hunted as a wild beast, and at last slain with a pitchfork by a man, who was termed "stout-hearted Geordy" all the rest of his life for the performance of this valorous exploit.

In 1760 there was scarcely a parish in Dumfriesshire which could muster twenty swine, but within ten years of that time they gradually began to increase, and each farmer took to keeping one or two, and from 1775 to 1780 the trade became pretty considerable. This increase was chiefly owing to the exertions of Lord Graham, of Netherby, who encouraged the breeding and rearing of swine among his tenants by every means in his power, and was the chief institutor and supporter of a market at Longtown, in Cumberland, for the sale of swine and pork.

The next step were the establishments of pig-markets in several other principal towns in the southern parts of Scotland, and small premiums offered on every market-day to the owners of the finest pig or the largest number of good swine brought to the market.

Where thirty or forty years ago there was not a pig to be seen, as much as 400*l.* or 500*l.* worth of hogs and bacon, or pork, are now sold every market-day. This alteration is ascribed by some persons to the extension of the cultivation of the potato, and the consequent increased facility for feeding and fattening swine; but it may, doubtless, be also attributed to the increasing demand for animal food, the more extended views of farmers and agriculturists of the present day, and an appreciation of the profit and advantage arising from the keeping of these valuable animals.

There is a very good kind which are well made, white in color, have short upright ears, fatten quickly and on little food, and come early to maturity. Crosses with the Chinese have been tried, but they produce too delicate an animal, and consequently have fallen into disrepute. It would, however, be needless to enter into an account of all the varieties of swine now existing in Scotland, as, in describing the English breeds, we shall have to speak of all those which of late years have been introduced into Scotland, and either crossed with the original small, dark, prick-eared Scottish pig or with each other, or retained in their natural state. Henderson says that hundreds of pigs and shots (pigs from six to eight months old) are brought over from England every year, and fattened in Scotland.

ENGLAND.

The original breeds of this country are now rapidly losing all traces of individuality under the varied systems of crossing to which they are subjected. Formerly they might have been divided into two principal classes, the small and the large breeds: the former having ears tending to the upright, being dusky in hue, and greatly resembling the wild boar in form; and the latter being long-bodied,

THE OLD ENGLISH HOG.

long-eared animals, mostly white or spotted. The former were chiefly found in Scotland, and on the northern hills; and the latter in the lower and more midland counties of England, where the hog had been more domesticated.

Where individuals of the pure old breed are met with, they will be found long in limb, narrow in the back, which is somewhat curved, low in the shoulders, and large in bone; in a word, uniting all those characteristics which are now deemed most objectionable, and totally devoid of any approach to symmetry. The form is uncouth, and the face long and almost hidden by the pendulous ears. They nevertheless have their good qualities, although aptitude to fatten does not rank among the number, for they consume a proportionally much larger quantity of food than they repay; but the females produce large litters, and are far better nurses than those of the smaller breeds. They are, however, now nearly extinct, disappearing before the present rage for diminishing the size of the hog and rendering his flesh more delicate; points which, however desirable to a certain extent, may easily be carried too far. Low judiciously observes: " While we should *improve* the larger breeds that are left us, by every means in our power, we ought to take care that we do not sacrifice them altogether. We should remember that an ample supply of pork is of immense importance to the support of the inhabitants of this country. England may one day have cause to regret that this over-refinement has been practised, and future improvers vainly exert themselves to recover those fine old races which the present breeders seem aiming to efface."

It would be vain to attempt to particularize the breeds of swine at present kept in this country, for they are daily altering their characteristics, under the influence of some fresh cross; we will therefore content ourselves with enumerating those which are allowed to have been the chief and best breeds, and pointing out some of the alterations which have latterly taken place in them.

YORKSHIRE.

The old Yorkshire breed was one of the very large varieties, and one of the most unprofitable for a farmer, being greedy feeders, difficult to fatten, and unsound in constitution. They were of a dirty white or yellow color, spotted with black, had long legs, flat sides, narrow backs, weak loins, and large bones. Their hair was short and wiry, and intermingled with numerous bristles about the head and neck, and their ears long. When full grown and fat they seldom weighed more than from 350 to 400 lbs.

These have of late years been crossed with pigs of the new Leicester breed; and where the crossings have been judiciously managed and not carried too far, a fine race of deep-sided, short-legged, thin-haired animals have been obtained, fattening kindly, and rising to a weight of from 250 to 400 lbs., when killed between one and two years old, and when kept over two years reaching even 500 to 700 lbs.

Mr. Samuel Wiley, of Bransby, to whose courtesy we are indebted for the information, and who has paid much attention to the breeding of swine, keeps only the pure improved Leicester breed, which with ordinary feeding will, at sixteen or eighteen months old, weigh from 250 to 300 lbs.; and, when put up to fatten, attain the weight of 400 lbs. He considers them far superior to, and more profitable than the larger breeds.

Other breeders have crossed with the Chinese and Neapolitan breeds, and with some considerable success—the extremes of the large and small kinds happily correcting each other. The Berkshire pigs have also been employed as a cross, and hardy, profitable, well-proportioned animals obtained. The original breed, in its purity, size, and defectiveness, is now hardly to be met with, having shared the fate of the other large old breeds, and given place to smaller and more symmetrical animals. Mr. Smith, of Hoyland Hall, Sheffield, whose kind replies to our queries we have to acknowledge, is another great pig-breeder, and his swine have carried off numerous prizes ; they appear to be descended from a cross between a Yorkshire and Lord Western's improved Essex pigs. Their chief characteristics are : smallness of bone, great development of the fleshy parts, symmetry of form, and a strong propensity to fatten. Although hearty feeders, a small quantity of food suffices for them. When matured they readily attain the weight of from 400 to 500 lbs.

LINCOLNSHIRE.

The true Lincolnshire pigs are white, with long, straight bodies, round carcasses, fine skins, and few bristles ; the heads are well formed and of moderate size, and the ears erect, pointing somewhat forward, and curling slightly at the tips ; the hair is long and fine, but scanty. This breed was formerly considered as superior to any but the Berkshire in point of form and value, they being easily fattened, and the flesh being tender, and of a fine flavor ; with care they will reach 600 to 700 lbs. ; and many, at a year and a-half old, will weigh 350 to 400 lbs. They certainly do not attain to their maturity as early as some of the smaller breeds, but are, notwithstanding this, profitable animals, and good, sound, handsome stock. A cross between the Lincoln and Chinese pig is productive of an animal presenting great tendency to fatten, and a small eater.

The old breed of this county are long-legged, narrow-backed, ungainly animals, with thick skins, covered with short, thick hair ; the head is large, the forehead wide, and the ears set far apart. They are far from profitable animals, being enormous eaters, and fattening but poorly ; few attain a greater weight than 250 to 280 lbs.

DERBYSHIRE.

Here there is no prevailing breed. The greater part of the pigs kept in this county come from Cheshire and Shropshire, and these are either left in their pure state, or crossed with some of the small

English or foreign breeds, according as the taste or circumstances of the farmer or breeder leads him to prefer large or small animals.

LEICESTERSHIRE.

The old Leicestershire breed was a perfect type of the original hogs of the midland counties; large, ungainly, slab-sided animals, of a light color, and spotted with brown or black. The only good parts about them were their head and ears, which showed greater traces of breeding than any other parts. Mr. Bakewell improved them, and the variety thus obtained was called after him, and was superior in value and beauty to the old stock. Within the last few years various crosses have been tried, and the original breed is now fast losing all its peculiarities and defects.

ESSEX.

The Essex pigs, too, have been indebted for their improvement to crosses with the foreign breeds, and especially the Neapolitan, and

LORD WESTERN'S ESSEX BREED.

with the Berkshire swine. They are mostly black and white, the head and hinder parts being black, and the back and belly white;

they have smaller heads than the Berkshire pigs, and long thin upright ears, short hair, a fine skin, good hind quarters, and a deep round carcass; they are also small-boned, and the flesh is delicate and well-flavored. They produce large litters, but are bad nurses.

The most esteemed Essex breeds are entirely black, and are distinguished by having small teat-like appendages of the skin depending from the under part of the neck, which are commonly termed *wattles*. Some of these animals will attain the weight of 480 lbs., but they are not, according to some breeders, quick fatteners; while others prize them for their rapid growth and aptitude to lay on flesh, as well as for its excellence; it forms small and delicately-flavored pork. Lord Western has been the great improver of the Essex pigs, and his breed is highly esteemed throughout the kingdom.

Some Essex pigs, at only 23 weeks old, carried off one of the prizes at the Smithfield Club Cattle Show of 1846.

SUFFOLK.

The old pigs of this county are white in color, long-legged, long bodied, and narrow back, with broad foreheads, short hams, and an

A SUFFOLK BOAR, THE PROPERTY OF HIS LATE MAJESTY WILLIAM IV.

abundance of bristles. They are by no means profitable animals.

4*

Lord Western's improved Essex breed is much esteemed in Suffolk, and so are the Lincolnshire hogs.

A cross between the Suffolk and Lincoln has produced a hardy animal, which fattens kindly, and will attain the weight of from 400 to 550 and even 700 pounds. Another cross, much approved by farmers, is that of the Suffolk and Berkshire. On the whole, there are few better breeds to be found in the kingdom, perhaps, than the improved Suffolk pigs; they are well-formed, compact, short-legged, hardy animals, equal in point of value to the best of the Essex, and superior in constitution, and consequently better adapted for general keep, and especially for the cottager. The greater part of the pigs at Prince Albert's farm, near Windsor, are of the improved Suffolk breed; that is to say, the Suffolk crossed with the Chinese. They are medium in size, with round, bulky bodies, short legs, small heads, and fat cheeks. Those arising from the Berkshire and Suffolk are not so well shaped as those derived from the Chinese and Suffolk, being coarser, longer-legged, and more prominent about the hips. They are mostly white, with thin, fine hair; some few are spotted, and are easily kept in fine condition; they have a decided aptitude to fatten early, and are likewise valuable as store-pigs.

Many of the improved Suffolk breed will, at a year or fifteen months old, weigh from 250 to 320 pounds; at this age they make fine bacon hogs. The sucking pigs and porkers are also very delicate and delicious.

BEDFORDSHIRE.

There is no distinct breed in this county; the animals are mostly Suffolk or Berkshire pigs, variously crossed. Some of the best kinds are distinguished for their aptitude to fatten early, and on a small quantity of food.

NORFOLK.

The pigs of this county do not materially differ from those of Lincolnshire, but are rather smaller. They, too, are white, fine boned, long-eared, and well-formed, good feeders, and yielding fine meat. This is especially the case in that part of the county which approaches Lincoln. Various breeds and varieties, are, however, to be met with in Norfolk, and among them some very inferior animals. There is a small variety resembling the Chinese, and probably descended from that breed, which is peculiar to this county, and much esteemed for its aptitude to fatten on a small quantity of food. A cross between the Norfolk and Suffolk pigs produces a fine, hardy animal.

NORTHAMPTONSHIRE.

The old breed of Northamptonshire were large-bodied, large-boned, bristly animals, covered with white, coarse hair. Their legs were short and their ears very long, so much so as often to trail upon the ground. They were capable of being fattened to a considerable size, but not without great trouble and expense. These gave place to a lighter-made animal, equally large, but with small bones, small ears, and greater aptitude to fatten. The Bakewell Leicester pigs are highly esteemed by some of the breeders and farmers of this county.

SHROPSHIRE.

This seems to have been only another variety of the Northamptonshire pigs; they are coarse, ungainly animals, with long heads, pendent ears, arched loins, large bones, flat sides, many bristles, and coarse wiry hair; they are brindled, or of a dirty white-gray, or drab color, with spots of black. They were capable of being fattened to a considerable size, and might be made at two years old to weigh 560 or 575 pounds; but to accomplish this an abundance of food was required. They are by no means adapted for farm stock; but brewers, distillers, and those who have large quantities of refuse wash and grains, hold them in some estimation. Latterly the breed has been very much improved, and rendered more profitable, by crossing it with the Berkshire, Chinese, and other esteemed breeds, under the influence of which the most salient and objectionable points have disappeared, and the animals are now short-legged, fine-haired, straight-backed, and thin-skinned, white in color, and weighing 200 pounds at two years old. Lord Forester of Willy Park, and Sir F. Lawly of Monkhopton, are in possession of the best breeds.

CHESHIRE.

The old breed of this county were some of the largest swine in England, standing from three and a half to four and a half feet high. They were black and white, white, and blue and white; long-bodied, narrow-backed, slab-sided, large-boned, long-limbed animals, having large heads, drooping ears, of such a size as scarcely to permit them to see out of their eyes, and loose coarse-looking skins. Nevertheless they fatten to an enormous weight, and without consuming a comparatively larger amount of food than many of the much more esteemed English breeds. One excellent variety has been obtained by a cross with a Berkshire boar.

Of late years, however, the old Cheshire breed has almost entirely disappeared, and been replaced by a fine-boned round-bodied animal, longer from head to tail and wider across the shoulders, coming earlier to maturity and easily fatten ; the form of the head, too, is improved, and the ears are smaller and more shapely. These animals are chiefly derived from the old Berkshire and Cheshire breeds with an occasional and judicious cross with the Chinese. There is, too, a slight admixture here and there of the Leicestershire blood. They never attain to the size or weight of the old breeds, but their forms are more compact, their flesh finer grained, and their bones smaller. They are considered by many persons to be equal in value in all points to any breed in Europe.

GLOUCESTERSHIRE.

The Gloucestershire is another of the large old breeds, gaunt, long legged, and unprofitable, of a dirty white color, and having *wattles* depending from the neck. It has been supposed to have once been the prevailing breed in England, but is now rapidly disappearing before the alterations produced by the present prevailing system of crossing from small breeds.

HEREFORDSHIRE.

The pigs of this county are of the large class, similar in many respects to the Shropshire swine, and in all probability produced by a cross between those and some one or more of the smaller breeds ; for they are smaller, finer-boned animals than the Shropshire pigs, have better-shaped heads and ears, are more compact in form, and have greater aptitude for fattening. They may, in fact, be fed to an enormous size ; and with proper management will, at two years old, weigh two or three times as much as most hogs of other breeds at the same age. No farmer need wish to possess finer and more profitable animals than may be found among the Herefordshire pigs ; the bacon made of their flesh yields in excellence to none.

Latterly this breed has been crossed with the Berkshire, and the result has been a fine, useful animal, possessing numerous good points, but not much superior to the good old stock.

WILTSHIRE.

Here the old breed was one of the larger class. The Wiltshire swine were long in the body, round in carcass, hollow about the shoulders, and high on the rump; short-legged, large-boned, light-colored, and the ears were large and pointed. They were, like most of this kind of pigs, large eaters and slow to fatten ; but when fat attained a fair average weight, and their flesh was fine-grained and highly esteemed, especially as bacon. Crosses with the Chinese and Neapolitan breeds have, however, much improved the original race; they are now smaller boned, not so large in size, and fatten earlier and more readily.

CORNWALL.

The CORNISH BREED.—Here again, the march of improvement is decidedly evident; the old Cornish hog, a large, white, long-sided, heavy-boned, razor-backed animal, possessing but little aptitute to fatten, is nearly extinct; and in its place we see a compact, well-made pig, fattening kindly, coming early to maturity, and yielding in excellence and value to few. This variety has been produced by crossing the old breed with the Berkshire, Chinese, Essex, Leicester, and Neapolitan pigs. These animals require little food beyond vegetables and the farm-house wash, excepting at the period of fattening, when about 3 bushels of barley will suffice to bring them, at nine months old, to the weight of from 350 to 400 pounds.

BERKSHIRE.

The Berkshire pigs belong to the large class, and are distinguished by their color, which is a sandy or whitish brown, spotted regularly with dark brown or black spots, and by their having no bristles. The hair is long, thin, somewhat curly, and looks rough; the ears are fringed with long hair round the outer edge, which gives them a ragged or feathery appearance; the body is thick, compact, and well-formed; the legs short, the sides broad, the head well set on, the snout short, the jowl thick, the ears erect, the skin exceedingly thin in texture, the flesh firm and well-flavored, and the bacon very superior. This breed of pigs has been generally considered to be one of the best in England, on account of its smallness of bone, early maturity, aptitude to fatten on little food, hardihood, and the females being such good breeders. Although termed the Berkshire breed, these pigs have been reared in various parts of the kingdom; and some of the very best have come from Staffordshire, from the progeny of the celebrated *Tamworth boar*. In Leicestershire, also, is a very fine race of them, descending from the stock of Richard Astley, Esq., who devoted much care to the improvement of the Berkshire pigs. Hogs of the pure original breed have been known to attain to an immense size, and weigh as much as 800 to 950 pounds.

One bred at Petworth measured seven feet seven inches from the tip of his snout to the root of his tail, and seven feet ten inches in girth round the centre; five feet round the neck, ten inches round the thinnest part of the hind leg, and two feet across the widest part of the back. He stood three feet nine inches high; and, what was most remarkable in this monstrous animal, he did not consume more

than two bushels and three pecks of ground oats, peas, and barley
per week.

Parkinson, in his *Live Stock*, vol. ii., gives some extraordinary
accounts of the size and weight attained by individuals of this breed,
and the profit yielded by them, and also of their aptitude to fatten
at grass.

They are not, however, generally of an enormous size, being much
smaller than several of the older breeds; their ordinary weight
averages from 250 to 300 pounds, and some will at two years old
weigh 400 pounds.

BERKSHIRE SOW.

It would be impossible to give an account of the numerous crosses
from this breed; the principal foreign ones are those with the Chinese and Neapolitan swine, made with the view of decreasing the
size of the animal, and improving the flavor of the flesh, and rendering it more delicate; and the animals thus obtained are superior
to almost any others in their aptitude to fatten, but are very susceptible of cold from being almost entirely without hair. A cross
of the Berkshire with the Suffolk and Norfolk pigs also is much
approved in some parts of the country. A hardy kind is thus produced, which yields well when sent to the butcher; but even the
advocates of this cross allow that, under most circumstances, the
pure Berkshire is the best.

HAMPSHIRE.

Here there are two varieties, the one larger than the other, in color they are either white or black and white, with long necks and bodies, flat sides, and large bones. The smaller variety are more easily fattened to a considerable size and weight, and make excellent bacon, but the larger kind require an extra amount of food to bring them to perfection, although when this object is attained they will often weigh from 600 to 800 lbs.

Considerable improvement has however been latterly effected by crosses of the Berkshire, Chinese, Essex, and Suffolk pigs, with the large old Hampshire hog. The animals resulting from these intermixtures are better shaped and more profitable; in fact, they bear about them the characteristics of the breed from which they were obtained. There is also a third variety of swine found in Hampshire, called the "Forest pigs," differing materially from the true Hampshire breeds, and in many points strongly resembling the wild boar, from which it is not improbable they derived their descent, for the last wild boars known to be at liberty in England were those turned into the New Forest by Charles I., and which he obtained from Germany with a view to the reintroduction of the fine old sport of boar-hunting. The Forest pig is broad-shouldered and high-crested; light and lean in the hinder quarters; has a bristly mane and erect ears; is of a dark or blackish color; and lives chiefly on beech-mast and acorns. This breed is no favorite in Hampshire; the animals are wild, fierce, not apt to fatten, and, from their peculiar make, do not cut up to advantage when killed; it is, however, now losing its distinctive characteristics, and becoming, as it were, more civilized or domesticated.

SUSSEX.

The breed of this county are by some authors supposed to have descended from the large spotted Berkshire swine; while others assert them to be a variety of the black and white Essex pig, if not the original stock. They are of a moderate size, handsomely formed, thin-skinned, and black and white; not, however, spotted, but white at one extremity and black at the other. The hair is fine and long, but spare; the head long and tapering; the ears well set on, and pointing forwards; the eyes quick and vivacious; and the snout fine. The chief fault in their make is, that the bones are somewhat too large. They grow quickly, feed well, fatten kindly, and will, when full-sized, weigh from 250 to 350 lbs.

Some of the finest pigs of this kind ever reared were in the possession of the Western family, at Felix Hall, Essex.

In speaking of the breeds of pigs belonging to this county, we must not omit the now extinct Rudgwick swine, which derived their name from a village in Sussex, and were some of the largest hogs produced in England. They fattened but slowly, and were consequently deemed unprofitable, but yielded excellent meat and in considerable quantities. They have, however, passed away before the alterations produced by the general aim of the present system of breeding.

THE CHINESE SWINE

Although these have been already noticed when speaking of Asia, we cannot now pass them over, as they actually form one of the recognized stock breeds of England. There are two distinct varie-

CHINESE PIG.
From a Sow sent direct from China to William Ogilvy, Esq., Hon. Sec. Zool. Soc.

ties, the *white* and the *black ;* both fatten readily, but from their diminutive size attain no great weight. They are small in limb, round in body, short in the head, wide in the cheek, and high in the chine ; covered with very fine bristles growing from an exceedingly thin skin ; and not peculiarly symmetrical, for, when fat, the head is so buried in the neck that little more than the tip of the snout is visible. The pure Chinese hog is too delicate and susceptible of cold ever to become a really profitable animal in this country; it is difficult to rear, and the sows are not good nurses; but one or two judicious crosses have in a manner naturalized it.

This breed will fatten readily, and on a comparatively small quantity of food; and the flesh is exceedingly delicate, but does not make good bacon, and is often too fat and oily to be generally esteemed as pork. They are chiefly kept by those who rear sucking-pigs for the market, as they make excellent roasters at three weeks or a month old. Some authors point out five, some seven varieties of the Chinese breed, but these are doubtless the results of different crosses with our native kinds; among these are black, white, black and white, spotted, and blue and white, or sandy. Many valuable crosses have been made with these animals; for the prevalent fault of the old English breeds having been coarseness of flesh, unwieldiness of form, and want of aptitude to fatten, an admixture of the Chinese breed has materially corrected these defects. Most of our smaller breeds are more or less indebted to the Asiatic swine for their present compactness of form, the readiness with which they fatten on a small quantity of food, and their early maturity; but these advantages are not considered by some persons as sufficiently great to compensate for the diminution in size, the increased delicacy of the animals, and the decrease of number in the litters. The best cross is between the Berkshire and the Chinese.
mmm

IRELAND.

Here the hog is, in the fullest sense of the word, a *domesticated* animal. The Irish pig is born in the warmest nook of his master's cabin, reared among the children, and often far better fed and more carefully tended than the ragged urchins who play around him, for the peasant will half starve himself and children in order to have more food for his pig; and while the former have only potatoes, and few enough of them, the porker frequently gets not only a good meal of potatoes, but some porridge, or bran, or refuse vegetables in addition. He is in fact the chief person in the household; on him the poor man reckons for the payment of his rent or the purchase of the necessaries of life. Swine abound in all parts of Ireland; scarcely a peasant's cot but numbers a pig among the family; and the roads, lanes, and fields in the neighborhood of every village, and the suburbs of every large town, are infested with a grunting multitude.

Until lately, however, notwithstanding the value set on these animals, the real Irish pig was a huge, gaunt, long-legged, slab-sided, roach-backed, coarse-boned, grisly brute; with large flapping ears which almost wholly shrouded the face; of a dirty white, or black and white color with harsh coarse hair, and bristles that almost stood erect. It was also far from being a profitable animal, requiring a very considerable quantity of food, and when fat producing only coarse-grained meat. But since the facility of export has become greater, considerable improvement has been effected by the introduction of Berkshire and Chinese boars and sows, and crossing the old breed pretty extensively with these. Thus the unwieldiness of size and coarseness of bone have been diminished, and greater aptitude for fattening communicated, which latter qualification is invaluable to the poor peasant. There is, however, great room for still further improvement, and we trust that before long some enterprising individuals will devote their energies to the task, and thus become the means of bestowing a great benefit on the peasantry of the "sister isle."

Steam navigation has wonderfully increased the trade in pigs between England and Ireland, for we find that in 1821 only 104,501 of these animals were brought into Liverpool; while in 1837, 595,422 were imported. The cost of conveyance has been so materially decreased by the facility of steamboat and railway conveyance, that this is not at all to be wondered at.

Irish pork or bacon is not so fine-grained or so finely flavored as the English; and although imported in considerable quantities, sells for a much lower price than our own. This has been attributed by some to the pigs being entirely fattened on potatoes, but it is also referable to the innate coarseness of the animals themselves.

Martin says :* The improvement in our breeds of domestic swine during the last few years has been very decided. And not only so; the general system of crossing now pursued, tends to the establishment of a uniform race throughout every county, that is, a race presenting the same outstanding characteristics. Changes are rapidly taking place, and the fear is, that the improvements may be carried so far as to result in the formation of a stock of animals smaller in size than comports with utility, and delicate in constitution. We say there is a fear of this: at the same time, we well know that the farmer will not lose sight of his own interests. It cannot be denied that our breeds, for ages occupiers of the land once tenanted by their wild and fierce progenitors, needed great alteration. They were large, coarse, unthrifty animals, with a long broad snout, large flapping ears, low in the shoulders, long in the back, flat-sided, long in the limbs, and large-boned, with a thick hide covered with coarse bristles. Their color was generally white or yellowish, sometimes more or less spotted with black. They were enormous feeders, but slow fatteners, consuming more food than was repaid by their flesh. At the same time, the females were peculiarly fertile, and this is almost the only thing that can be said in their praise.

Such, then, was the old, coarse, uncouth breed, spread, with trifling

* What follows, to page 100, is by Martin.

degrees of difference, over the greater part of England. In the northern counties, and especially in the north of Scotland, a smaller race, with sharp and almost erect ears, greatly resembling the wild boar in form, long existed, and is yet extant. These animals were dusky or brownish-black, wild in their habits, and very hardy. We say *were*, but in fact such is still the race in the Orkneys and Hebrides. They are small, rough, semi-wild beasts, depending principally upon their own means of gaining a subsistence, and are evidently the descendants of a wild stock. Their degeneracy in size may be attributed to climate and deficiency of nutrition while young; for when brought into more southern districts, and fed in the ordinary way, they rapidly acquire an increase in size, fatten kindly, and return excellent meat.

These mountain hogs are in tolerable condition after their summer fare, and should be killed in autumn. During the long rigorous winter these animals must suffer extremely, and in some islands many probably perish.

This breed, which not a century since was common in the Highlands, where vast herds were kept for the sake of sale in the Lowlands, is less thoroughly reclaimed than were the old gaunt flap-eared breeds of England. The latter had undergone a certain degree of modification long before the improvements effected in modern days. Among these old breeds was one described by Mr. George Culley; it prevailed in Yorkshire and Lancashire; the animals were of large size, and white, with huge ears hanging over their eyes. "They were very plain, thin, awkward hogs, with very long legs; but what distinguished them most was two wattles or dugs, not unlike the teats of a cow's udder, which hung down from their throats, one on each side." This breed appears to be altogether extinct in our island.

It is not often that we now hear of hogs of enormous size being slaughtered; formerly such overgrown monsters were not uncommon. The old Berkshire breed, which in its improved state still belongs to the class of large swine, not unfrequently produced huge specimens. The surprising weight that some of these hogs have been fed to, would be altogether incredible, if we had it not so well attested. Mr. Young, in one of his Tours, gives an account of a hog in Berkshire which was fed to 1130 lbs.; but a still more extraordinary pig was, some years since, killed in Cheshire :—"On Monday, the 24th of January, 1774, a pig (fed by Mr. Joseph Lawton, of Cheshire) was killed, which measured from the end of the nose to the end of the tail, 3 yards 8 inches, and in height 4 feet 5½ inches; it weighed 12 cwt. 2 qrs. and 10 lbs. when alive (1410 lbs.); when killed and dressed. it weighed 10 cwt. 3 qrs. and 11 lbs. avoirdupois (1215 lbs) This pig was killed by James Washington, butcher in Congleton, in Cheshire."—*Culley, on Live Stock.*

In the month of December, 1846, a large hog was slaughtered at

Buxton. It was white, and two years and two months old. Its
height was 3 feet 9 inches, the carcass when dressed weighed 660
pounds, exclusive of fat to the amount of 98 pounds. It was fattened
upon Indian meal, pea-meal, &c. It was of the improved old Cheshire breed.

In taking a survey of our improved breeds, we can do little more
than generalize, although a few breeds may require a somewhat
particular notice; we mean those to which other strains owe their
improvement.

Among the early improvers of swine must be enumerated Mr.
Bakewell. Before his time the Leicestershire hogs were of the same
coarse ungainly kind which prevailed generally throughout the midland counties. He commenced by a judicious selection of stock
destined for breeding, and by persevering in this system greatly
modified the characters of the old race; in due time the Bakewell
breed extended into other counties, superseding or influencing the
ordinary races. This was the case in Yorkshire, the old breed of
which county was of large size, gaunt, greedy, and unthrifty, coarse
in the quality of the meat, flat-sided and huge-boned. By crossing
with the new Leicester stock great improvement was soon effected;
the cross-breed lost in size but gained in every good quality; it
became deep-sided, short-limbed, small-boned, and fattened readily.
The coarse wiry bristles were exchanged for fine thin hair, and the
whole aspect of the animal underwent a transformation. The hogs
at about two years old averaged from 420 to 840 lbs., younger
animals weighing in proportion.

Some of the Yorkshire breeders preferred the pure new Leicesters, and these are still reared by judicious farmers, who esteem them
as superior to most others, and certainly more profitable than most
of the larger kinds. They fatten kindly, often attaining the weight
of upwards of 420 lbs., at the age of sixteen or eighteen months.
Other breeds, however, besides the new Leicester, have found advocates in Yorkshire: among these are the Berkshire, crosses between
which and the Yorkshire are deservedly esteemed, as are also crosses
between the Yorkshire and Lord Western's improved Essex variety.
The latter cross is remarkable for smallness of bone, rotundity of
figure, and aptitude for fattening. The hogs when fat average 420
lbs. The Chinese and the Neapolitan pigs have been tried by several
breeders, and judicious crosses between these and the Yorkshire race
are excellent, both as regards good symmetry and fattening qualities. In fact, the large old Yorkshire stock may be regarded as
extinct.

The new Leicesters, even in their own county, have undergone
modification since the time of Mr. Bakewell. Excellent crosses
have been made between them and the Berkshire and Essex breeds.

The improved Berkshire hog belongs to the tribe of large swine, or, perhaps, rather did. Formerly, hogs of the pure breed were often found to weigh from 800 to 960 lbs.; and it is recorded that one bred at Petworth, in Sussex, measured 7 feet 7 inches from the tip of the snout to the root of the tail, 7 feet 10 inches in girth round - the centre, 5 feet round the neck, and 2 feet across the span of the back. Height 3 feet 9 inches. It was remarkable that this huge animal was a moderate consumer of food; his allowance being about two bushels and three pecks of ground oats, peas, and barley, per week.

The present Berkshire breed are moderate-sized beasts, roundly made, short in the limb, and with a short arched neck, with heavy cheeks, sharp ears, an abruptly-rising forehead, short in the snout, well-barrelled, broad-backed, and clean in the limbs; some are sandy-colored or whitish, spotted with black, but most are either white or black, or half white and half black, a coloring indicative of a mixture of the Neapolitan and the Chinese, as well as of the Suffolk strain.

We believe that rather small (not too small) and quickly fattening breeds are, from first to last, the most profitable; indisputably they afford the best meat, in whatever way it is prepared.

The new breeds now to be seen in Berkshire are but thinly clothed, and are said to be somewhat tender, a circumstance in that sunny county of little consequence, for the farmer's straw-yard supplies abundant shelter and comfort.

Around Henley in Oxfordsire, on the banks of the Thames, and about Dorking in Surrey, cross breeds of the Berkshire strain prevail; although in the latter county the improved Essex breed is held in great estimation.

There are few counties in England into which the Berkshire breed of pigs has not penetrated; it is everywhere valued for its excellent qualities, its fair, moderate size, its small bones, its thin skin, its fattening qualities, and excellence of its flesh. First-rate hogs of this breed have been reared in distant counties. Through Middlesex, Hartfordshire, Bedfordshire, and Leicestershire, the Berkshire breed has extended itself, modifying the old races, not without other crossings; indeed, it must be confessed that the modern system of interbreeding renders it difficult to tell the original stock on which the grafts have been made; or rather, what strain shows itself the most prominently.

In Berkshire it is the general custom to singe the hogs after being killed, and not to remove the bristles by means of hot water and scraping; nor do they as a rule smoke the flitches after salting, but merely dry them. The same remark applies more or less to the adjacent counties; for example, the bacon sold in Henley is unsmoked. In fact, the taste for smoked bacon and hams seems to a certain degree to be confined to London, as far as England is concerned. In Derbyshire, Cheshire, Lancashire, and some of the neighboring counties, smoked bacon is a rarity. However, the *porky* or the *smoky* flavor is a matter of taste.

Wiltshire is celebrated, and deservedly, for bacon, as Yorkshire for hams. The old Wiltshire hog was of large size, short-limbed, but heavily-boned, long in the body, but round and high on the croup. The ears, though large, were pointed. These animals were slow feeders, and great consumers of food; nevertheless, when at some cost they were fattened, they produced meat of excellent quality, especially fitted for converting into bacon. They were probably a mere variety of the Berkshire strain, and certainly possessed good qualities; but they are greatly improved, owing to the judicious crossings with the Chinese and Neapolitan stocks; and though, as might be anticipated, they are smaller in stature than formerly, they are finer-boned, more compact in contour, far quicker fatteners, and consequently ready for the butcher earlier. At the same time, the superior quality of the meat has suffered no decline, indeed quite the contrary. Wiltshire bacon commands a high price.

The Hampshire are excellent hogs, generally black, and middle-sized, with rather a long snout, but compactly made; are a modification of the old large-sized Hampshire stock, individuals of which in former days were of huge magnitude, and some carried about for show. This colossal breed is now seldom to be seen, but it had its good points: when fattened (and time and much food were required to effect this) it returned by the way of payment a weighty carcase. As in all such cases, however. the question comes in, Was it profitable? Was the repayment for food and time in a just ratio? The answer must be, quick fattening, even with a smaller carcass, a gain of time and of provision being included, is one of the points in which the farmer finds himself the best remunerated. Slow feeders, however weighty their carcass at last, will not be found profitable when all expenses are calculated. The present Hampshire hog is compounded of the old race, and the Essex, the Chinese, and the Neapolitan, with an admixture also of the improved Berkshire.

A semi-wild breed of pigs are peculiar to the New Forest; they are termed Forest pigs, and differ materially from the ordinary stock cultivated by the Hampshire farmers. Though far inferior in size to the true wild hog, these animals exhibit much of the characteristics of that animal, and probably owe their origin to a cross between the wild hogs introduced into the forest by Charles I., and some of the ordinary breeds of his period. These animals are heavy in the fore quarters, but light and meagre behind; the withers are high, the ears short, the mane thick and bristly, the color black or brindled; the disposition is fierce and distrustful, and they display extraordinary activity and acuteness. The troops are headed by leaders, which take alarm at the slightest appearance of danger, and are ready on an emergency to act on the defensive. This Forest breed, however, is now rarely to be seen in its purity—in fact, it is passing away, or perhaps rather merging into a more domestic and mingled stock, thereby losing its pristine characteristics.

Lincolnshire is one of the counties noted for an excellent breed of pigs. The old race were gaunt, slow-feeding, unprofitable animals, with heavy heads and flat sides; but the improved breed of the present day are well-formed, of moderate size, easily fattened, and produce excellent flesh; they are white, with fine skins, and sparingly covered with bristles, which are slender; the ears are erect and pointed, the body long, straight, and round. These pigs, deservedly esteemed, may be fatted to about 630 lbs., and when at the age of a year and a half, many are found to range between 280 and 420 lbs. A cross between the Lincoln and Chinese breed—though of diminished size—is found to attain more rapidly to maturity than the pure Lincoln, and fattens quickly upon a very moderate allowance of food.

Norfolk produces excellent pigs, somewhat smaller than those of Lincolnshire, but closely agreeing with them in characters; they are well-formed, fatten quickly, and yield fine meat. Besides this breed, a smaller race prevails in many parts of Norfolk, descended, as it would appear, from the Chinese, which it greatly resembles. These pigs are in great estimation; they fatten readily on a small quantity of food, and their flesh is delicate.

Suffolk, now noted for its improved breed, formerly possessed only a coarse, lank, and thriftless stock; but this has given place to a mixed race, admirable for symmetry, and quick and early fattening. The most generally approved breed is a cross between the Suffolk, Berkshire, and Chinese. These animals are rather small, but compact, short-legged, and small-headed; the body is round, and they fatten readily. At the age of a year, or a year and a half, many are found to weigh from 240 to 300 lbs., and produce first-rate bacon. The flesh of the sucking-pigs and of the porkers is esteemed for its peculiar delicacy.

Besides this breed, which stands first, there is an excellent cross between the Suffolk and Lincoln; the pigs attain to a considerable weight, ranging from 420 to 560 lbs. and upwards; they are hardy, and fatten readily. Another breed is between the Berkshire and Suffolk, and this has its admirers; it is easily kept in good condition, fattens quickly, and makes excellent bacon. It is, however, longer in the leg and less compact in symmetry than the tri-cross between the Suffolk, Berkshire, and Chinese. The improved Lincolnshire race is much valued in Suffolk, as is also the improved Essex breed, established by Lord Western, and esteemed throughout the kingdom. It is black, short-nosed, deep-jowled, short and thick in the neck, with small, sharp ears; the limbs are short and fine-boned, the barrel is rounded, the hams very full, the hair is spare and short, the skin fine; some have small wattles or appendages of skin depending from the neck. These animals fatten quickly, grow rapidly, and yield very superior meat; as porkers they are admirable, the meat being peculiarly delicate. The hogs, when fattened, will sometimes weigh 360 to 400 lbs., often 250 to 280.

This black breed is greatly crossed with the Neapolitan, and we believe the Sussex.

A modification of this breed is often seen in Essex; the pigs, like the Sussex, are generally black and white—the head and hinder parts being black, and the central portion of the body white. They are admirable in shape, with a deep round carcass, and fine skin, fine in the bone, and full in the hind quarters. The flesh is excellent. The sows produce large litters, but are said not to make the best nurses. We did not, however, hear this complaint from any of the Essex farmers, during our frequent visits to Rochford and the adjacent country. We suspect, however, that the Essex breed is delicate, and requires care, as indeed do all high-bred domestic quadrupeds.

Sussex possesses a breed very much like the last particolored race, of which it appears to be a variety. These pigs are well-made, of middle size, with a thin skin, and scanty bristles; the snout is tapering and fine, the ears upright and pointed, the jowl deep, the body compactly rounded. These pigs arrive early at maturity, and fatten quickly; the bacon hogs averaging a weight of 280 lbs. The flesh is excellent. Their bone, perhaps, is larger than in the Essex breed, but then the improved stocks of this latter race are remarkable for smallness of bone, and we doubt whether they are more bony than the improved stocks of the old Berkshire strain. The breed is undoubtedly valuable, and well adapted for crossing with the Essex, Neapolitan, or Chinese.

Sussex once boasted of a gigantic race of pigs, known by the name of the Rudgwick breed, (Rudgwick is a village in that county,) some of which were among the largest swine ever reared in our island. As is the case with all huge breeds, these animals were slow feeders and huge feeders; but yielded an enormous weight of excellent meat. Nevertheless, they became more and more influenced by the intercrossings of new breeds, till at length the old stock has become obsolete, its celebrity depending upon records and notices of the last century.

Bedfordshire has sent some admirable pigs to the great cattle-shows in London. Nevertheless, the animals could not be called truly Bedfordshire as to peculiarity of breed. They were crosses of various kinds, in which, as it appeared to us, the Suffolk strain was prevalent.

Crossings and intercrossings are everywhere taking place, and all the old stocks have become so altered, that the hog race of England is generally assuming an approach to universal uniformity. The modified New Leicesters and Yorkshires, the improved Berkshires, the Essex, and the New Suffolks, with various intermixtures of the Chinese and the Neapolitan races, are everywhere extending themselves. The gaunt, lanky, old breeds, flat in the sides and heavy in the bone, are now rare, and regarded as curiosities.

Among this diversity of intercrossings, certain strains are brought to high perfection by the breeder's skill and patience, and are deemed the highest even of the race to which they may belong. Thus, for example, in Berkshire we have the Coleshill strain, the pure Wadley strain, and the old Crutchfield strain; in Essex we have Lord Western's strain; and the same observations apply to other counties. But too often exorbitant overloading of fat is too much regarded—a point of less consequence than shape, fertility, and aptitude to fatten upon moderate rations; inasmuch as the wealthy have at their command the means of forcing animals unnaturally, and think little of the waste thereby incurred in order to accomplish their object. Pigs are shown not only incapable of standing, but also of seeing, from the enormous volumes of fat with which they are loaded. Such an accumulation of fat is in itself disease. Think what must be the state of the heart, the condition of the circulation, and the character of the muscular fibres. We have heard of mice burrowing in the fat of such animals, without appearing to occasion any pain or inconvenience. In cattle-shows there is, in many respects, sufficient evidence of the general and marked improvement which has taken place in this class of domestic animals; but we form our judgment rather from those which show their points, are really well fed, and not fattened up till they appear like bloated skins of lard—as destitute of definite shape, as of the power of moving about. What a waste of money must the forcing of such a monster occasion! The outlay would have sufficed to bring three pigs into fine and profitable condition. And what is the object? To show in how short a time a pig *can* be rendered a mass of fat, and upon what sort and quantity of food. The better aim would be, to show how many pigs could be well fattened in a given time upon a stipulated quantity of food—what breeds fattened the most kindly, and would be found the most profitable.

In Shropshire, Gloucestershire, Cheshire, Herefordshire, Oxfordshire, and other counties, the old races of pigs have passed away, and crosses with the Berkshire, and also with the Essex and the Chinese, have taken their place. In short, the change is universal; and even in the southern parts of Scotland, where formerly but few pigs were kept, and those of an inferior sort, excellent breeds prevail, and pigs are largely reared by the farmers.

5

In the Channel Islands—Jersey, Guernsey, Alderney, and Sark—the pig is an important animal, pork being the staple animal food of the Islanders during the winter. It is said to be very delicate, even more so than any in England. Almost every cottager keeps a pig, and is enabled to feed it the more easily, as his garden yields an abundant supply of produce.

The Channel Island breed, once gaunt and coarse, and of French extraction, is now greatly improved, and fattens rapidly. The pigs are kept in styes, and fed during the spring and summer months on buttermilk, bran, potatoes, cabbages, and all kinds of vegetables; in the autumn, almost exclusively upon parsnips. Bacon hogs are generally killed at about twenty months old, and average from 300 to 450 lbs. Sometimes, hogs attain to a much larger size; and instances have been known in which they have weighed 640 lbs., exclusive of the offal.

In the Isle of Man, the native breed closely approaches that of the Orkney and Shetland Isles. The animals resemble the wild boar in miniature, and roam about at liberty; yet they fatten readily, and yield excellent meat. Within the last few years, crosses from England have been introduced, and the plan of sty-feeding has been practised; but not with much success.

It is now time that we turn to Ireland, whence so much of the salted pork and bacon sold in England is exported.

The modern Irish pig has, within the last few years, become greatly improved. Formerly, it was a gaunt, flat-sided, large-boned, rough beast, long in the leg, sharp along the spine, long in the snout, and with huge flapping ears. It was a slow feeder, and yielded coarse meat. Latterly, the introduction of some of our best breeds, with which to cross the old Irish swine, has been attended with decided success, although there is still room for further improvement. The sides are sent, roughly salted, to certain houses in London, (and other large towns,) and are there finished off for the market.

Irish bacon is not to be despised, and, as we have said, the breed of pigs is generally much improved. Berkshire, Suffolk, Yorkshire, and even Chinese boars and sows, have been introduced, and by intercrossings, produced a considerable change—a change, however, neither quite so decided nor quite so general as is desirable. Besides, the plan of fattening upon potatoes is not calculated to do justice to the most improved stocks.

The Irish bacon is not of such good quality as that fed in England, as the animal is generally fattened on potatoes only, while the best practice here is, when half fat, to finish off with peas-meal, or barley-meal. The agricultural laborers, in counties where their condition is most comfortable, know that it is most profitable to buy the higher-priced English bacon, which swells in the boiling, and is at once more palatable and substantial than the potato-fed bacon of Ireland. In order to obtain the advantages of the English market, great improvements have taken place in the breed of pigs kept in Ireland.

As the Chinese pig is naturalized in our country, a few remarks upon it may not be out of place.

The Chinese pig is seldom kept in its pure state : its flesh indeed is exquisitely delicate, especially that of the sucking pig : and though it fattens rapidly and at little cost, yet, from the unctuous character of the fat, the sides are not calculated for making prime bacon. Besides, it is tender, susceptible of cold, and difficult to rear, the more so as the sows do not generally make good nurses. At the same time, as a source of improvement among our indigenous breeds, by judicious intercrossings, too much cannot be said in its praise ; indeed, it has been one of the most successful means of introducing reform among our old stocks ; it has corrected the faults of gauntness, of heavy bones, of slow feeding, of coarse flesh, and of a dense skin. True, it has caused a reduction in size, but not in hardiness, by its intercrossing; yet what advantages have not been gained by that very practice ?

Thus far have we endeavored to illustrate the various influential breeds of our own country, including Scotland, Ireland, and the smaller islands. To have rigidly analyzed, or rather attempted an analysis, of the varieties peculiar to each county or district, would have been folly—the thing is impossible. Mixtures and intermixtures are perpetually taking place, and individuals are from time to time establishing their own favorite crosses. In every county is this system of improvement in operation ; the whole is fluctuating, yet the broad strong current bears on towards improvement. Nevertheless, in this tideway impulse, the strong hand of a judicious steersman is the more necessary : the mark may be overshot. We mean that deficiency of profitable size, weakness of constitution, and infertility, may, unless judgment in crossing be exercised, detract from the merits of an otherwise most valuable stock.

It would be interesting, could we truly ascertain the amount of property invested in the United Kingdom, not only in the porcine race, but in other descriptions of live stock ; all the attempts of the kind are merely approximations, yet they are not therefore valueless—they give, at least, general ideas on the subject, and not unfrequently surprise us.

M'Queen, in his *Statistics of the British Empire*, has thus stated the enormous value of live stock in the United Kingdom, exclusive of domestic poultry (by-the-bye no trifle.) It appears that there are 2,250,000 horses, of the total value of £67,000,000, [the pound sterling is $4 86,6] of which more than 1,500,000 are used in agriculture, and valued at £45,000,000 ; the number of horned cattle in the kingdom is about 14,000,000, of the value of £216,000,000 ; the number of sheep 50,000,000, whose value is estimated at £67,000,000. The extent of the capital invested in swine is still more extraordinary, when we reflect how little it is thought upon or taken into account. The number of pigs of all ages, rearing, and breeding, is calculated to be upwards of 18,000,000, which, taking one third at £2 each, and the remainder at 10s. each, gives a value of £18,870,000, as the capital invested in pigs alone.

This is of course only an approximation to the truth, for the stock of all our domestic quadrupeds is liable, from various circumstances, both to increase and decrease; nevertheless, the statement, with every deduction, is calculated to excite some degree of surprise.—MARTIN.

ANATOMY AND DISEASES OF THE HOG.

CHAPTER VII.

A VERY slight acquaintance with that complicated and beautiful structure which we term the animal economy, will be sufficient to convince us that any rational method of investigating or treating disease must be founded upon an acquaintance with the general construction of the frame, the derangements and alterations to which it is liable, and a concise notion of the various systems or sets of organs of which the body is composed. Without this amount of knowledge it will be impossible correctly to interpret those signs of alteration of structure or function which constitute the symptoms of disease, and indicate its nature and seat.

If we would understand how to regulate the working of some complicated machine, we must not content ourselves with a mere cursory glance at its exterior, but closely inspect the different parts; make ourselves acquainted with their shape, situation, and arrangement; inquire into the principles upon which the whole is constructed, its mode of action, and the offices which each part was destined to perform. Proceeding thus, we shall arrive at a knowledge of the best means of preserving it from injury, repairing any accident that may happen to it, and maintaining it in a fit state for the efficient discharge of the duties it was intended to perform.

The animal economy consist of parts or organs, differing from each other in structure and function, yet all so intimately connected together, and so mutually dependent upon each other, that the coöperation of the whole is necessary to a state of perfect health; and if any one part suffer injury, the neighboring organs sympathize with it to a greater or less extent, and the working of the whole system is impaired. In order to arrive at a proper understanding of the functions of any one part of the body, we must study the whole; there is no other way of obtaining that insight into disease which will furnish us with a clear idea of the precise nature and seat of a malady, and the course of treatment most likely to be attended with success. The uninformed empiric who deals about his nos trums at random, is far more liable to put an end to the life of his patient than to arrest the progress of the disorder. Such men should never be allowed to tamper with the meanest animal. It is only to those who, from close study and long practice, have acquired an accurate knowledge of the anatomy, diseases, habits, and general management of domesticated animals, that their medical treatment can with safety be intrusted.

It is, however, by no means our intention in this work to give a formal treatise on the anatomy, physiology, and diseases of the pig, but simply to lay before our readers a tolerably comprehensive sketch of the general structure of the animal, and the alterations and evils to which certain parts are liable, and this divested as much as possible of all the technicalities of professional language. A description of the different parts, their form, situation, action, and functions, as well as their admirable adaptation to the ends for which they were designed, will lead us to a consideration of the diseases incidental to them—to the treatment proper to be adopted—and to some account of the various operations which it may occasionally be requisite to perform. In short, we would present them with a practical digest of all that is yet known relative to this too much neglected branch of veterinary science; one that shall serve as a book of reference in cases of doubt or emergency, and aid in introducing those great truths and leading doctrines, which form the groundwork upon which the practice of every branch of medical science ought to be based, into the last strongholds of ignorance and empiricism.

In entering upon the anatomy and diseases of swine, we may be said to take possession of a new and almost untrodden field, one as yet scarcely recognized as belonging to any earlier occupants; and here, in the onset, it will be as well to observe that, careful and lucid as we shall endeavor to make our descriptions, we should only mislead the agriculturist or grazier if we were to encourage him to believe that they will enable him wholly to dispense with a veterinary surgeon. Far from it; we would rather persuade him to seek at once the assistance of the well-educated and scientific practitioner, who, from close study, practical experience, and surgical skill, is qualified sucessfully to grapple with the most obscure and fatal diseases. We would enable him to assist the veterinary surgeon in his often arduous task, by giving him that information as to the previous symptoms, habits, &c., of the patient, which can alone enable him to proceed with certainty, and will tend to save the life of many a valuable animal; and, lastly, we would warn him against empirics.

Swine, from having been, until very lately, considered as a subordinate species of stock, have not yet, to any extent, become sharers in the benefits which an improved system of agriculture, and the present advancing state of veterinary science, has conferred upon other domesticated animals. When any thing goes wrong in the piggery, the farmer too often, instead of exercising that shrewd sense which he turns to so good an account in almost every other instance, either sends for the butcher, or consigns the sick tenants of the sty to the care of an ignorant " pig-doctor," whose whole pretensions to leech-craft rest on the possession of some antiquated recipe, which he uses indiscriminately as a grand panacea for " all the ills swine's flesh is heir to," or on the traditionary lore he inherits from some ancestor famous in his day for certain real or supposed wondrous cures. The treatment adopted in such a case is usually of a very summary nature : a drench is administered, the principal ingredients of which consist in whatever abominations happen to come to hand first when this learned practitioner is summoned. The unlucky patient's tail is next cut off, or he is bled " between the claws," and the " doctor," after some learned clinical remarks to the bystanders, swallows the customary mug of beer, and leaves his patient to contend with his disease and the remedy, one or the other of which in most cases speedily brings the matter to a conclusion, unless, with all the obstinacy inherent in a pig's nature, he lives on in spite of both.

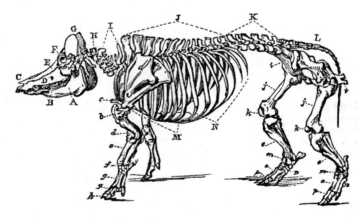

SKELETON OF THE PIG.

THE HEAD.

A. Maxilla inferior, vel posterior—lower jaw.
B. Dentes—the teeth.
C. Ossa nasi—the nasal bones

D. Maxilla superior, vel anterior—upper jaw.
E. Os frontis—the frontal bone.
F. Orbiculus—the orbit or socket of the eye.
G. Os occipitis—the occipital bone

THE TRUNK.

H. Atlas—the first vertel 'a of the neck.

I. Vertebræ colli, vel cervicales—the vertebræ of the neck.

J. Vertebræ dorsi, vel dorsales—the vertebræ
   of the back.

K. Vertebræ lumborum, vel lumbales—the ver
   tebræ of the loins.

L. Ossa coccygis—the bones of the tail.

FORE EXTREMITY.

a. Scapula—the shoulder blade.
b. Humerus—the round shoulder-bone.
c. Sternum—the breast bone.
d. Ulna—the elbow.
e. Radius—the bone of the fore-arm.

f. Os naviculare—the navicular bone.
g. g. Phalanges, vel ossa pedis—the first and
   second bones of the foot.
h. Phalanges, vel ossa pedis—the bones of the
   hoof.

HIND EXTREMITY.

i. i. Pelvis (ossa innominata) the haunch bones.
j. j. Os femoris—the thigh-bone.
k. k. Patella—the stifle bone.
l. l. Tibia—the upper bone of the leg.
m. m. Tarsus, (one of which is the (N) os
   calcis)—the hock bones.

n. n. Os naviculare—the navicular bone.
o. o. Digiti, vel phalanges (ossa pedis)—the
   first digits of the foot.
p. p. Digiti, vel phalanges (ossa pedis) the second digits of the foot.

THE SKULL AND SNOUT.

As the skull of the hog differs in many respects from that of the horse, ox, sheep, or dog, we shall now proceed to notice those points of difference.

From the point of the occiput to the tip of the nasal bone the profile presents an almost unbroken sloping line. The position of the orbit of the eye is lateral, giving to the animal a side, rather than a forward range of vision. The space occupied by the orbital processes of the frontal bone in the ox and horse, is in the hog supplied by a cartilage. The frontal bones unite together early, and the parietals appear to form but one piece. The frontal sinuses proceed to the occiput, and are only separated from each other by some longitudinal or somewhat oblique bony layers which do not entirely intercept communication : these and the sphenoidal sinuses render the cerebral cavity narrow, in fact the size of it is only half that of the cranium viewed from the exterior. The ethmoïd and turbinated bones are larger and more fully developed in the hog than in the ox or sheep, in fact they occupy an intermediate grade between those of the horse and dog, being larger than those of the former, and smaller than those of the latter ; they are spiral, complicated, cellular, and offer an extensive surface for the expansion of the olfactory nerve ; the ethmoïdal fosset is very much sunk, of moderate size, divided by a very salient crest, and riddled with numerous holes.

The nasal bones of the hog are situated low down in the face, flattened, and well adapted to the situation and wants of the animal. They are attached to the frontals in a slightly curved direction across the face, by a strong denticulated suture. All communication be tween them and the lachrymal bones is cut off by the interposition of a projection of the frontals on either side; the suture between them and the superior maxillary is mortised; the anterior maxillary sends up a broad deep process more than half the length of the nasal bones, and the suture here is exceedingly strong. The bony nasal opening is but small, not one-sixth of the size of that of the sheep, and the apices of the bone form one sharp but rapidly widening point, which is carried forward to the anterior extremity of the maxillary. The suture between the nasals themselves is often so intricate, that before the animal is two years old, the upper part of it is perfectly obliterated, and the nasal cavity appears as if only covered by one bone. A very slight comparison of the face of this animal with that of any other will prove that strength is the object here in view; strength towards the inferior part of the bone. In point of fact the snout of the hog is his spade, with which, in his natural state, he digs and grubs in the ground for roots, earth-nuts, worms, &c. And to render his implement more perfect, an extra bone is added to the nasal bone. This one is short and trificial and placed directly before the nasal bones, with which, and with the edges of the anterior maxillary, it is connected by strong ligaments, cartilages, and muscles. This bone has been termed the *spade-bone*, snout-bone, and by some writers, the *vomer*, from its supposed resemblance to a ploughshare. By it and its cartilaginous attachment is the snout rendered strong as well as flexible, and far more efficient than it could otherwise be; and the hog often contrives to give both farmers and gardeners very unpleasant proofs of its efficiency, by ploughing up deep furrows in newly-sown fields, and grubbing up the soil in all directions in search of his living and dead food.

The palatine bones constitute the crescentic and posterior border of the palate and nasal cavity; they do not advance further than just before the last molar tooth, instead of occupying a considerable portion of the palate. The palatine processes consist merely of bony laminæ.

As roots and fruits buried in the earth form the natural food of the hog, his face terminates in a strong muscular snout, insensible at the extremity, and perfectly adapted for turning up the soil. There is a large plexus of nerves proceeding down each side of the nose, and ramifying over the nostril, and in these doubtless reside that peculiar power which enables the hog to detect his food though buried some inches below the surface of the ground. The olfactory nerve, too, is large, and occupies a middle rank between that of the herbivorous and carnivorous animals; it is comparatively larger than that of the ox: indeed few animals, with the exception of the dog, are gifted with a more acute sense of smell than the hog. We have already spoken of the sow which was taught to hunt partridges, and proved as sure a finder and as stanch a backer as any pointer

5*

ever bred. To the acute sense of the hog are epicures indebted for the truffles which form such a delicious sauce, for they are the actual finders. A pig is turned into a field and suffered to pursue his own course and watched. He stops and begins to grub up the earth, the man hurries up, drives him away, and secures the truffle, which is invariably growing under that spot, and the poor pig goes off to sniff out another, and another, only now and then being allowed by way of encouragement to reap the fruits of his research. And how many a school-boy has by watching a hog along the hedge sides, and driven him away just as he began to dig, secured a fine juicy earth-nut!

The muscles, too, of the snout of the hog require some notice. According to Cuvier, there are four principal muscles proceeding to it; the superior of these proceeds from the lachrymal bone, which occupies a rather large rhomboidal space upon the cheek, and its tendon bears upon the snout, but does not approach sufficiently near it to unite with it. The next two are situated immediately beneath, and proceed from the maxillary bone; these are partially united, but their tendons pass on separately, one on the one side, and one on the other of the extremity of the snout; and the fourth and smallest passes obliquely beneath the tendons of the others, from the nasal bone towards the insertion of the second and third muscles. These longitudinal muscles are enveloped in annular fibres, which appear to be a continuation of the *orbicularis* of the lips, and give to the snout its extreme flexibility.

THE TEETH.

The hog has fourteen *molar* teeth in each jaw; six *incisors* and two *canines*; these latter are curved upwards, and commonly denominated *tushes*. The molar teeth are all slightly different in structure, and increase in size from first to last; they bear no slight resemblance to those of the human being. The incisors are so fantastic in form as to baffle description, and their destined functions are by no means clear. Those in the lower jaw are long, round, and nearly straight; of those in the upper jaw four closely resemble the corresponding teeth in the horse, while the two corner incisors bear something of the *fleur de lis* shape of those of the dog. These latter are placed so near to the tushes as often to obstruct their growth, and it is sometimes necessary to draw them, in order to relieve the animal and enable him to feed.

It is seldom that it becomes necessary to ascertain the age of the hog by inspecting his teeth, nor is it by any means an easy task to do so, but still it may occasionally be interesting. and, with reference to those intended for breeding, important to be able to do so when necessary.

The calculation of the age of the hog by means of reference to the mouth, has not yet been carried beyond three years; no writer seems to have gone much beyond the protrusion of the adult middle teeth of the lower jaw.

The hog is born with two molars on each side of the jaw; by the time he is three or four months old, he is provided with his incisive milk teeth and the tushes; the supernumerary molars protrude between the fifth and seventh month, as does the first back molar; the second back molar is cut at the age of about ten months, and the third generally not until the animal is three years old. The upper corner teeth are shed at about six or eight months, and the lower ones at about seven, nine, or ten months old, and replaced by the permanent ones. The milk tushes are also shed and replaced between six and ten months old. The age of twenty months, and from that to two years, is denoted by the shedding and replacement of the middle incisors, or *pincers*, in both jaws, and the formation of a black circle at the base of each of the tushes. At about two years and a half or three years of age, the adult middle teeth in both jaws protrude, and the pincers are becoming black and rounded at the ends.

After three years, the age may be computed by the growth of the tushes; at about four years, or rather before, the upper tushes begin to raise the lip; at five they protrude through the lips; at six years of age, the tushes of the lower jaw begin to show themselves out of the mouth, and assume a spiral form. These acquire a prodigious length in old animals, and particularly in uncastrated boars; and as they increase in size they become curved backwards and outwards, and at length are so crooked as to interfere with the motion of the jaws to such a degree that it is necessary to cut off these projecting teeth, which is done with the file or with nippers. (*Traité de l'Age du Cheval, du Bœuf, du Mouton, du Chien, et du Cochon,* par N. F. et J. Girard.)

THE BRAIN.

This important organ is not so large as from an external view of the cranium we should be led to suppose, the frontal and sphenoidal sinuses contracting the limits of the cranial cavity and rendering it narrow; it is, however, considerably larger in proportion to the size of the animal than that of the ox or sheep, being about 1-500th part of the weight of the animal, while that of the ox is only 1-800th part, and that of the sheep only 1-750th part. The irregularities of the surface, or those prominences and depressions which define the organs in phrenology, are more marked in the pig than in the horse, taking the size of the animal into consideration, but not so much marked as in the dog.

The brain of the hog, like that of our other domesticated animals, is composed of two substances differing materially in appearance and structure; the one is of a pale gray or ashy hue, and termed the *cortical* or *cineritious substance,* and the other, from its pulpy nature and from being found deeper in the brain, the *medullary substance.*

These two distinct component parts of the brain are allowed by all scientific men to be intended for the discharge of two distinct functions. The mind or reasoning power is supposed to reside in the cineritious portion; and hence the preponderance of that substance in the human brain; while the medullary portion is merely the recipient of outward impressions upon the senses. There is very little difference between the proportions of these two substances in the brain of the hog and that of the sheep; if any thing, the hog has more of the cineritious portion than the ox; a proof, physiologists would say, that his reasoning powers or moral faculties are greater. We have already endeavored, we know not how successfully, to vindicate him from the charge of utter stupidity and unteachableness so generally brought against him, and pleaded the slight intercourse, compared with that enjoyed by other animals, which he has with man as the cause of it. There are anecdotes enough to prove them possessed of memory, attachment, and social qualities; but at present the system of treatment affords no scope for the development of any but mere brute and gluttonous instincts.

APOPLEXY.

As this is a disease which is chiefly induced by plethora, laziness, want of exercise, high feeding, and such like causes, it is not to be wondered at that it is frequent among swine; and in by far the majority of cases it is fatal; for either the animal dies suddenly without any precursory symptoms, or the progress of the attack is so rapid that before help can be obtained or remedies administered all is over. Where, however, the apoplexy does not destroy its victim in a short space of time, it may be subdued and the animal temporarily cured; but only for awhile; it invariably dies soon afterwards of inflammation of the brain. Sometimes apoplexy will run, like an epidemic, through a whole piggery, and where this is the case the causes of it must be diligently sought out and carefully removed.

The precursory symptoms which prognosticate apoplexy are dullness, disinclination to move, heaviness of the head, an uncertain and staggering gait, wildness and inflammation of the eyes, with apparent loss of sight, no appetite, and general numbness. The treatment must be prompt and energetic: bleeding from the palate; Epsom salts and sulphur as purgatives; or emetic tartar dissolved in water to induce vomiting. Strict attention to diet will be requisite for some time afterwards. No stimulating food should be given; the water should be slightly nitrated, and the animal bled at least every three months.

INFLAMMATION OF THE BRAIN.

Inflammation both of the substance and of the membranes of the brain is by no means of unfrequent occurrence, and almost invariably follows an attack of apoplexy. It is also induced by heating or exciting or indigestible food, as an over-feed of grains, or new corn, &c. The precursory symptoms are dullness, redness of the eyes, and disinclination to move; but as the inflammation becomes more intense the animal runs wildly to and fro, seems blind and unconscious where he is going, runs against every thing; the pulse is small and rapid; and the breathing slightly accelerated. The first thing to be done is to bleed, from the palate if possible; if not, or if sufficient blood cannot be obtained from there, let incisions be made in the ears, and these repeatedly washed with warm water, which materially increases the bleeding. *Magn. sulph.* with ginger should be given internally as a purgative. Enemas (clysters) have also a beneficial effect, and then the animal should have repeated cooling doses of sulphur. Castor oil and jalap have been given as purgatives; and the system stimulated by the application of a blister to the throat.

PHRENITIS.

This is a disease very much resembling the last mentioned, and is often called brain-fever or frenzy; it arises pretty much from the same cause; all excitants of the system, all things which tend to drive the blood to the head, will induce it. The symptoms are prostration of strength, blindness, frenzy, and often convulsions. The treatment must consist in copious bleedings and strong purgatives, which should be followed up by doses of sulphur to keep the bowels open. Croton oil with tincture of ginger has been given in extreme cases, and with beneficial effects. The dose for a moderate-sized animal is about two minims of croton oil and one dram of tincture of ginger.

SPINAL CORD.

Next to the diseases of the brain follows a consideration of those arising from the spinal cord. This proceeds from the brain to the tail, and is divided by a central line on the upper and under surface throughout its whole extent, forming it into two separate columns, each of which has been proved to possess a distinct and separate function, the inferior surfaces being connected with voluntary motion, and the central ones on the upper surface with sensation.

EPILEPSY.

The pig occasionally exhibits all the symptoms of epilepsy in their most frightful intensity, and whoever has carefully marked the habits of swine when not confined to the sty will easily be able to account for this; for, obtuse and stupid as it is the custom to denominate them, there is more excitability and nervousness in these animals than in many that have the credit of being more delicately organized. Note the manner in which they are affected by the approach of wind or storms—how they run about in a state of highly nervous excitement with straw in their mouths; note the sympathy and terror a whole herd will exhibit while one of them is undergoing the operation of spaying or ringing, how they squeak in concert with his cries; see them at a fair under the irritation of strange scenes and noises, and we shall find sufficient indications of a susceptibility of impression to account for swine being peculiarly subject to epilepsy.

The prognostics are constant grunting, restlessness, acceleration of breathing, pallor of the skin, and a staggering gait. Then the animal suddenly falls as if struck by lightning, and for a few moments lies perfectly motionless; after which convulsions come on gradually, increasing in intensity until they are fearful to behold; the countenance is distorted, the neck curved in every direction, and the legs alternately drawn up to the body, and extended with momentarily increasing rapidity. The eyes protrude, the pupils are distended, and the balls roll about. The tongue is protruded and fixed between the clenched jaws; the teeth grind together, foam and saliva flow from the mouth. The pulse is wiry and small at first, then hard and bounding, and, as the intensity of the fit decreases, irregular and intermittent. Throughout the whole of the fit the animal remains perfectly unconscious, and as he recovers gets up, tries to hide himself in the litter or in a corner of the sty, and looks terrified and wild; then gradually the impression passes away, and he creeps out and begins to eat again. The seizure of one pig is often but a prelude to that of the greater number of those contained in the sty. The fits often succeed each other rapidly, two or three occurring in one day; and the cries uttered by the animals while in them are distressing in the extreme.

Medical treatment can only be resorted to in the intervals between the fits, and is seldom successful. It consists of cold affusions applied to the head, bleeding, and energetic purgatives, followed up by low diet, perfect quiet, and cooling medicines. The best way of keeping the head cool is to tie a piece of cloth about it, and then keep this constantly wet. A very efficient cold lotion for this purpose may be composed of a pint of vinegar to two quarts of water, and one ounce of *sal ammoniac*. Salts and calomel may be given as purgatives.

It is often difficult to determine what are the precise causes of epilepsy; the immediate one is generally some excitant or stimulant acting on a system predisposed by cerebral inflammation, or by intestinal irritation arising from worms, or other sources, to take on disease.

We quote a case communicated by Mr. Cartwright, of Whitchurch, to whom we are indebted for much useful information relative to the diseases of swine:—

"In 1825, I saw a pig that was taken ill in the following manner: He was a little stupid and dull, and now wandered about the sty unconsciously for a few minutes, and then appeared to be quite well; but in a few days after he became worse: he would move forwards until he came to one wall, and then retreat backwards until he came to the other wall; and made a grunting and squealing noise all the time the fit was on him, which was usually a few minutes, and sometimes longer; and he had them every quarter of an hour, and even oftener. His fits continued to increase; when he had been thus for about five days he began, after so backing himself, to fall down at full length, stretch out his legs and tumble about, and appear as if dying, and make a shrieking noise as if in great pain, and seem to be blind. His pulse was very quick and full during the fits, but subsided a great deal when they were over. He ate at intervals between the fits when food was *put* to him. He continued in this latter bad state for three or four days, and got well in a few days after. I gave him salts and calomel during his illness, bled him in the tail and ears, and between his claws; but little blood, I fancy, was obtained from all the places; and I kept his head wet with cold water.

"About the same time a miller in this neighborhood lost five or six in a similar way, but I had not an opportunity of opening any of them."

PALSY OR PARALYSIS.

This is by no means a disease of frequent occurrence in our own country. It is treated of by French writers, who attribute it to low, marshy situations, bad or damaged food, or the avarice of the pig-owner, who, in order to fatten the animals more rapidly, gives them highly stimulating food, which irritates the intestinal canal, and through it the spinal cord. Eric Viborg, an authority quoted by Hurtrel D'Arboval, recommends wholesome food, clean straw, a dose of common salt as a purgative, and drenches of common salt and gentian.

But there is a kind of partial palsy which is caused by the presence of *cysticercus cellulosa*, a hydatid peculiar to the pig. M. Dupuy gives the following case which came under his observation:—

"Palsy of the hind limbs, with loss both of motion and feeling

was observed in a pig eighteen months old. On carefully examin
ing him after death, the muscles were discolored and softened.
There were in the psoas muscles numerous cysts inclosing hydatids.
Other cysts with their parietes, more thickened and fibrous, inhabited
the muscles surrounding the trochanter, containing likewise hydatids.
These parasites are also found in the lungs, the liver, and the cortical substance of the kidneys.

"Between the internal surface of the cyst and the hydatid was a
fine white powder, resembling pulverized bones. The spinal marrow
was softened about the lumbar and sacral regions, and the membranes were slightly reddened, particularly about the roots of the
lumbar nerves."

It is generally the hinder parts of the pig which are paralyzed,
either wholly or partially; in the former case the animal is totally
unable to rise, in the latter he totters in his gait and falls when
attempting to walk. Paralysis frequently accompanies chronic disease of the digestive organs, and is attended with loss of appetite,
acceleration of the pulse, and swelling of the tongue. This disease
is seldom obstinate; a removal of the predisposing cause, good
nourishing food, a clean and well-ventilated sty, moderate exercise,
and gentle purgative or cooling medicine, will generally restore the
animal to perfect health in a short space of time.

TETANUS, OR LOCK-JAW.

This disease, which is commonly denominated *Locked-jaw*, is by no
means an unfrequent malady among pigs. The symptoms are at
first spasmodic motion of the head and of one or more of the extremities, grinding the teeth and rigidity of the jaws. This is soon followed by stiffness of the neck and greater part of the frame, and an
unnatural upraised position of the head. The castration of young
pigs will frequently produce this disease, especially if the animal is
too well fed for a few days after the operation. It also often appears
among pigs that are driven far to market, especially if when heated
by travelling or exposure to the sun, they are suffered to roll themselves in ditches or streams, as they will endeavor to do. Bleeding,
warm baths, lotions, &c., friction with stimulating oils, purgatives if
they can be got into the mouth, if not, enemas and anodynes are the
most efficient remedies. But the disease is too often fatal, and runs
its course very speedily; if the animal survives the first twelve or
eighteen hours, some hopes of his eventual recovery may be entertained.

RABIES.

Swine are by no means exempt from this frightful disease; there
are numerous cases on record in which they have been inoculated by

the bite of rabid dogs, and Hübner relates a case of inoculation from the bite of a rabid fox. The symptoms of rabies in the hog are peculiarly interesting at times from the resemblance many of them bear to those of the human being. At first there is dullness and indisposition, and the pig is continually licking the bitten part. Subsequently some are exceedingly ferocious, snapping at every body, gnawing every thing which comes in their way, dashing themselves against walls, or leaping over all obstacles. Others, again, are dull, stupid, refuse their food, stagger when they attempt to rise, and are paralyzed in the hinder parts. There is no absolute dread of water, but evident inability to drink. An animal that we saw went to the trough, smelt at the food, and brought his nose nearly in contact with it, then started back, trembled violently, and elevated his snout high in the air. Once or twice he attempted to take portions of meat or vegetable from the wash, but the attempt was always accompanied or followed by universal rigor and shuddering, during which the food was dropped from the mouth, evidently proving that the organs of deglutition were powerfully affected.

The animal is in a highly nervous state, and the sensibility of the skin is so excessive, that even if his mother licks him he screams with agony, and buries himself in the litter, uttering shrill squeaks on the approach of any one, or springs up into the air if he hears a loud noise, and falls down again in convulsions. There is in general no great secretion of saliva in these animals, and the delirium which characterizes rabies in the dog is rarely seen, or when met with is less evident and distinctive.

And yet this disease has been but little studied in pigs. Mr. Pritchard, V. S., of Wolverhampton, gives the following interesting account of some cases he met with :—

"A rabid dog entered the farm-yard of Mr. George Strongitharm of Calderfield, near Walsall, on the 27th of December, 1835, and attacked some pigs, which making a considerable noise, aroused Mr. S. and his servants from their beds, and they proceeded with their guns already loaded, discovered him, and succeeded in destroying him. Two of the pigs had evidently received wounds in their noses from the dog, which soon got well, no curative or preventive measures being had recourse to, and without much irritation or swelling taking place. After a fortnight had elapsed, nothing outward being observable in them, they were again turned into the yard to their old companions.

"A day or two after, on the entrails of a sheep being thrown to the pigs, all came and partook of it except the two that had been bitten. One of these was found dead in the litter, with a quantity of froth and slaver about his mouth; the other, in coming out of his bed into the air, immediately jumped up on all four legs like the bound of a deer, a yard at least from the ground, and threw from his mouth a portion of thick slaver and froth. Upon being again placed in the sty he was much convulsed, and made a shrill squeaking noise; his mouth was filled with saliva, and held continually open, nearly half an inch, except when champing his under jaw, which he frequently did with considerable twitching of the superficial muscles. He refused to eat or drink, gradually got worse, and died on the third day.

"Three weeks after, another of the pigs was taken ill. The symptoms were much the same. The effect of water was tried, and upon being thrown upon him caused him considerable distress, so that he leaped into the air and dashed his head against the wall, appearing quite delirious. He died on the second day. Not long afterwards another pig was attacked, the symptoms being similar to those in the former cases, only more violent; he died twenty-four hours afterwards, nothing having been done to disturb him. None of the pigs ate or drank any thing after they were first taken ill."

And the case we are now about to quote was communicated by Mr. Heaton, a human surgeon :

"About May, 1829, while visiting a patient, I was told that in a sty at the bottom of the yard there was a mad pig. Thither I repaired, when I was informed by its owner that the animal had been bitten about three weeks before by a strange dog, which had passed through the yard, and who was at the time, by those who saw it, declared to be mad ; the dog appeared to be greatly alarmed and proceeded with swiftness ; it was afterwards seen for the last time in some fields at the outskirts of the town. From the statement of the man it would appear that, on the morning of the day previous to that on which I saw the pig, the animal began to exhibit symptoms of great oppression at the præcordia ; to this succeeded gradual inability to stand, fearful cries, and general uneasiness when disturbed, foaming at the mouth, and a disposition to eat whatever came in the way, &c. At six o'clock in the afternoon of the second day I first saw it, covered with straw and apparently quiet, until the rattling of the sneck of its door seemed to awaken the most painful apprehension, and its mental agony seemed almost insufferable. The sense of sight seemed no less acute than that of hearing, which was manifested by the animal's convulsive efforts to hide even its head beneath the straw ; this accomplished, it became somewhat tranquil, and was constantly devouring its own litter, excrement, &c., &c. Its eyes had the suspicious glance of those of a phrenetic patient, its breathing was preternaturally quick, and its efforts to stand wholly abortive. In this state it continued two hours, when half a pint of train oil was attempted to be poured into its mouth, the greater part being wasted, and the animal instantly expired. I regret that the approaching night, and the man's desire to bury the carcass, restricted the post-mortem examination, which merely went to show that upon the division of the costal cartilages the lungs protruded, as if too large for the cavity of the thorax, and, being cut into, poured forth a frothy mucus, resembling in color and consistence soap lather ; the stomach and duodenum were filled with the matters above described to have been eaten, not however impacted, probably owing to the premature death. I have little doubt from the symptoms that, had the examination gone so far, the vessels of the brain and spinal cord would have been found injected. The splash of water certainly caused disquietude ; but, inasmuch as noise of any sort produced similar effects, it is doubtful whether aversion to fluids existed ; and yet the circumstance of death instantly following the oil-draught, would warrant the belief that spasms of the muscles of deglutition, with the temporary closure of the glottis, occasioned suffocation and death."

Among all the numerous cases of rabies which we have met with in the course of our practice, we have never had the opportunity of examining the post-mortem appearances of a rabid pig ; but it seems to be generally admitted by those who have done so that there is invariably inflammation about the glottis, and very considerable inflammation of the villous coat of the stomach, especially about the pylorus, towards the cardia, and on the surface of the two rugæ ; in some parts the inflammation had almost merged in mortification. The stomach is generally filled with every kind of filth and rubbish, and the bladder distended with urine.

The disease generally appears in the third or fourth week after the animal has been inoculated, but it has been known to lie dormant for two months.

Incision of the part and the application of the cautery as soon as possible after the animal has been bitten, are the only preventive means : cure there is none when once this disease has made its appearance, and those who rely on the infallible nostrums of some learned "pig-doctor," will find themselves disappointed ; the symptoms may be alleviated by certain drugs, but rabies is incurable.

We are not aware that rabies has ever been known to be communicated by the bite of a pig, but Julian Palmarius states that he has seen horses, cattle, and sheep, become rabid from eating the straw in which rabid pigs had lain ; and Dr. Shackmann corroborates the fact.

It has been a much disputed point whether or not the flesh of animals which have died rabid can be eaten with safety. Two eminent scientific men in Paris ate of such flesh without experiencing any bad effects. The carcass of an ox that had been bitten by a rabid dog, and had exhibited all the symptoms of rabies, was cut up and sold, but it did not appear that any of those who ate of it experienced the slightest inconvenience. Again, at the Royal Veterinary School at Alford, the tongue of a rabid horse was given to a dog ; the animal devoured it, and lived on in perfect health.

But the opposite party bring forward as many authenticated facts in support of the contrary opinion, and the one with which we now chiefly have to do is narrated by Schenkius: "A tavern-keeper in the duchy of Wurtemberg, served up the flesh of a pig that had died rabid to some customers who were dining at his inn. All those who partook of it were shortly afterwards attacked with rabies." Pierre Borel records a very similar case.

We should most strongly urge the prudence of abstaining from the flesh of all rabid animals, and not only of abstaining from it ourselves, but putting it out of the reach of other animals; and the best way to do this is to bury the carcass six or eight feet under ground, and cover it carefully and closely up.

NASAL CATARRH.

We have already spoken of the formation of the nose or snout of the pig, and will now proceed to describe a disease vulgarly called the *snuffles*, or *sniffles*. It is characterized by defluxion from the nose in the first place, and its advance is so gradual as to be almost imperceptible. But it gains ground daily—attacks the respiratory passages—cough and sneezing come on—there is evident difficulty of swallowing, and the respiration is impeded by the mucus formed. After some time the membrane of the nose becomes thickened, the nostril swelled and deformed, and the snout drawn on one side. Blood is often discharged from the nostril, and when this has been the case all the symptoms are abated and the animal seems relieved for awhile. But it too frequently happens that this discharge or hemorrhage returns again and again, each time in increasing quantities, until the strength of the animal becomes so undermined that notwithstanding the utmost care and the most nourishing diet, he dies of exhaustion, or perhaps, as it may be more properly termed, consumption.

This disease, which strongly resembles glanders and distemper, is like them hereditary, and may be communicated from either the male or female parent. It also results from exposure to damp or cold.

Emetics and tonics are the best means of combating it. A solution of sulphate of copper in doses of from three to five grains morning and night will sometimes eventually effect a cure, assisted by strict attention to diet and regimen. But in by far the majority of cases the disease runs its course and terminates fatally, for it has generally gained the upper hand before much notice is taken of it.

THE LARYNX.

This instrument of voice consists of five cartilages united to one another by a ligamentous substance, by distinct articulations, and by a seemingly compl.cated but really simple muscular apparatus. In form it is an irregular oblong tube, exceedingly flexible, and capable of adapting itself to all the natural or morbid changes of the respiratory process, and to the production of all the various intonations of sound or voice by which the animal expresses his emotions. It is placed at the top of the windpipe, guards the exit from the lungs, and prevents the passage of food into the respiratory canals.

The *Ericoid cartilage* constitutes the base and support of this organ, and serves in great measure as a bond of union to the rest.

Placed above and resting upon this are the *Arytenoid cartilages*, prolongations of which rest upon the *Chordæ vocales*, and influence their action. The vocal ligaments take an oblique direction across the larynx in the pig instead of a straight one, so that the angle is at a considerable distance from the thyroid cartilage. They have also a curious slanting direction, the anterior angle being depressed and the arytenoid portion elevated. About the middle of the chordæ vocales, and immediately above them, are two sacculi, which are generally supposed to be concerned in the act of grunting. From the anterior parts of the larynx springs the *epiglottis*, a heart-shaped cartilage placed at the extremity of the opening into the windpipe, with its back opposed to the pharynx; its use is this: food passing from the pharynx in its way to the œsophagus presses down the epiglottis, which, closing the aperture of the larynx, prevents any portion of the food from entering it. As soon as the food has passed, the elasticity of the epiglottis, assisted by that of the membrane at its base, and still more by the power of the *hyo-epiglottideus* muscle, enables that cartilage to rise up and resume its natural position.

The *thyroid cartilage* envelops and protects all the rest, and shields the lining membrane of the larynx, which vibrates under the impulse communicated by the passage of the air, and gives the tone or voice.

In the larynx of the hog we find that beautiful adaptation of means to the end. The space between the arytenoid cartilages is less, comparatively speaking, than in the horse or dog, speed not being required in swine. The epiglottis, too, is larger than in the ox, sheep, or horse, and differently constructed; it is more flexible, from the cellular ligamentous substance at the base of it being looser; and from its increased size, and the curved direction of its edges, it not only covers the opening into the windpipe, but in a manner embraces the arytenoid cartilages when pressed down by the passage of food, a formation admirably suited to an animal who is constantly plunging his nose and muzzle into the mud or dirt, and who, by blowing into his food in the peculiar way pigs are apt to do in order to stir up the sediment, would otherwise be constantly getting some irritating and noxious matters into his windpipe. The inferior cornu of the thyroid bone is comparatively more developed in the hog than in other domesticated animals.

The pharynx, to which we just now alluded, is a membranous, muscular, funnel-shaped bag, extending from the root of the tongue to the larynx and œsophagus, wide in front and becoming gradually narrower until it terminates in the œsophagus. Its office is to convey the food from the mouth to the upper part of the gullet, and this it performs by means of its lining muscles. Properly speaking, we ought perhaps to have noticed it when speaking of the digestive system, but as we are proceeding from the head to the neck we have included it in this division of our subject.

This is a body which embraces the thyroid cartilage of the larynx, and gives support and protection to it, and also affords attachments to the *hyo-glossus longus* muscle, or that which draws the tongue into the mouth; the *brevis*, which fulfils a similar office; the *hyo-pharyngeus*, which dilates the pharynx; the *anterior constrictor pharyngeus*, which contracts the pharynx, and several others.

This bone in the human being is supposed to resemble the Greek letter upsilon; in the horse it may be compared to a spur, but in the swine it is different. This animal requires a freer use of the tongue. The shorter cornua are stronger than in the horse, or even the ox and dog; the central one is less developed, and the longer cornua is thin and insignificant. There is also considerably less ligament interposed between this bone and the thyroid cartilage, which it almost closely embraces. We will now proceed to a consideration of the diseases of the throat and neck.

These diseases are of very frequent occurrence, and as they are rapid in their progress, generally exceedingly fatal. They chiefly attack fattening hogs.

The glands under the throat begin to swell, and thus affect not only the respiratory organs but the act of swallowing · impeded respiration, hoarseness, and debility then supervene; the pulse becomes quick and unequal, the head to a certain extent palsied, the neck swells, tumefies, and rapidly goes on to gangrene; the tongue hangs from the mouth, and is covered with slaver, and the animal gradually sinks. In the commencement of the disease very simple treatment, as cooling medicines, attention to diet, and care and warmth, will often suffice to check it; but when the swelling, impeded respiration, and difficulty of swallowing has come on, recourse must be had to more energetic treatment. Bleeding and purgatives are first indicated ; setons and puncture of the swollen glands have also been recommended, and in extreme cases there is no reason why we should not have recourse to blisters and external stimulants as counter-irritants.

A diseased animal should never be allowed to remain aomng healthy ones, as this malady is so infectious that it may almost be regarded as an epizoõtic.

Mr. Cartwright, veterinary surgeon, of Whitchurch, who has paid much attention to the diseases of swine, gives the following account of some fatal cases of inflammation of the glands of the throat in the "*Veterinarian:*"—He says that he had six pigs attacked at nearly the same period. Their respiration was very quick ; they husked and foamed at the mouth. They could not bear to be pressed on the throat, and swallowed liquids with difficulty. To some of them jalap was given, and to others castor and goose oil. One was blistered under the throat, and all bled by cutting off their tails. They died in the course of eight-and-forty hours from the commencement of the disease.

On examination he found much inflammation under the jaws and throat, and also much of swelling with effused serum. In some of their windpipes, and the branches of the bronchia, there was a great quantity of mucus, but no apparent inflammation. In one the heart appeared to be inflamed, but most probably sympathetically.

Columella thus speaks of these diseases :—"Such swine as have swellings of the glands under the throat must be let blood under the tongue ; and when it has flowed abundantly, it will be proper that their whole mouth be rubbed over with bruised salt and wheat-meal. Some think it a more present and effectual remedy when they pour into each of them, through a horn, three cupfuls of *garum*, or salt-fish pickle ; then they bind cloven tallies, or cuttings of fennel-giant with a flaxen cord, and hang them about the necks, so that the swellings shall be touched with the fennel-giant cuttings."

If we may judge by the writings of the ancients, the most prevalent diseases among pigs were those of the glands of the throat. Didymus gives a long and accurate description of them.

Hurtrel D'Arboval also gives an account of a disease of the glands of the throat, which he denominates *Poil piqué, maladie piquante,* or *soie,* and states it to be peculiar to swine : he thus describes it :—

It is situated on one or both sides of the neck, between the jugular vein and the tracheal artery. On the part affected is seen a raised tuft of hairs, differing from any of the others, being hard, rough, dull, and discolored, and exceedingly painful to the touch ; and if one be pulled out the skin comes away with it. At first there is only a slight depression or concavity of the part ; but the skin soon becomes red, then violet-colored, the hairs conglomerate, the parts become softened, tumefied, and even proceed to mortification. Meanwhile the animal betrays symptoms of thirst, there is dulness, loss of appetite, and grinding of the teeth. As the malady progresses the patient becomes inert, deaf, insensible to blows, lies down constantly, and totters and falls if compelled to rise; the flanks heave, the mouth is hot and full of slaver, the tongue red and inflamed, the lower jaw convulsed, and the conjunctiva injected; the animal utters plaintive moans, and if not speedily relieved dies of suffocation, from the effects of the pressure of the tumor upon the air-passages.

D'Arboval attributes this disease to the irritation caused in some of the cutical tissues by the abnormal growth of the tuft of hair, which, uniting with some internal sympathetic irritation induced by heating food, damp litter, hot ill-ventilated styes, or such like prejudicial influences, acts locally and determines this disease of the glands. Other French writers believe it to be epizoötic and to arise from certain miasmatic influences.

Tonics, acidulated drinks, warmth, cleanliness, strict attention to diet, and the application of actual cautery to the root of the evil— the tuft of hair—is the treatment prescribed.

THE CHEST OR THORAX.

In the human being this constitutes the superior, and in quadrupeds the anterior portion of the body; it is separated from the abdomen by the *diaphragm*. This latter is of a musculo-membranous nature, and is the main agent in respiration; in its quiescent state it presents its convex surface towards the thorax, and its concavity towards the abdomen. The anterior convexity abuts upon the lungs, the posterior concavity is occupied by a portion of the abdominal viscera. The diaphragm of the pig resembles that of the ox and sheep.

The chest is divided into two cavities by a membrane termed the *mediastinum*, which evidently consists of a duplicate of the *pleura* or lining membrane of the thorax. The pleura is a serous membrane possessed of little or no sensibility, and acted upon by but few nerves. It it smooth and polished; covers the bony wall of the thorax from the spine to the sternum, and from the first rib to the diaphragm, and dilating and forming a kind of bag which spreads over and contains the whole of the lung.

The lungs form two distinct bodies, the right being somewhat larger than the left one; they are separated from each other by that folding over of the pleura termed the mediastinum, and hence may be said to be inclosed in separate bags, or to have distinct pleuras. Each lung is subdivided. The right one consists of three unequal lobes, the smallest of which is again subdivided into numerous lobules, differing in number in different swine. The left lung consists of two lobes, and the scissure between these is not very deep.

Beneath the left lung the heart is situated and partially inclosed in another membranous bag termed the *pericardium*, which closely invests, supports, and protects it. The heart has two sides, the one devoted to the circulation of the blood through the lungs, and the other to its circulation through the frame generally. Each side is divided into two compartments, the one above, the other below, which are termed the *auricles* and *ventricles*. The right auricle as well as the ventricle is larger than the left, and its parietes are thinner. The longitudinal tendinous cords of the ventricle are more firm and distinct in the pig than in the ox or sheep, and the fleshy prominences shorter. The tendinous cords of the left ventricle are few in number, large, and ill defined. The aorta of the pig separates almost immediately after its commencement into two trunks, the smaller of which leads forwards and gives forth those arteries which in other animals arise from the cross of this artery; and the other, which is longer in diameter, inclines backwards: these are usually termed the anterior and posterior aorta.

The beating of the heart may be felt on the left side, whence also the pulse may be taken, or from the femoral artery which crosses the inside of the thigh in an oblique direction. In swine in a state of health the pulsations are from seventy to eighty in a minute.

DISEASED VALVES OF THE HEART.

This appears to be a more common malady than is generally suspected, for in repeated cases of sudden death, where a post-mortem examination has been made, there have been found fleshy excrescences or tumors on the tricuspid valves. We believe Mr. Cartwright, whose name we have already mentioned, was one of the first persons who drew attention to this disease. The only marked precursory symptoms appear to be inappetency and very shortly before death difficulty of breathing and evident distress. In one pig that died thus suddenly, Mr. Cartwright found several uneven watery excrescences, some as large as marbles, growing from the edge of the auricula-ventricular valves of the left side; also several small papillary growths, all of which served three parts to close up the ventricular opening.

In another case he found a loose, jagged, watery excrescence growing from the whole surface of the tricuspid valves, closing up, in a great measure, the ventricular opening, and projecting at least half an inch into the left auricle. In a third, the valves of the left auricle were thickened, schirrous, and presented a ragged uneven surface. The orifice of the ventricle was almost closed up by this diseased substance, and a portion had forced its way into the aorta. This disease was always found in the left side of the heart, and in

6

no case did it extend beyond the circumference of the valves; the lining membrane of the heart always remained intact.

BRONCHIAL TUBES.

Swine are very susceptible of *bronchitis*, and also liable to worms in the *bronchia*, both of which affections manifest themselves under the form of cough, inappetency, and loss of flesh. The former may be subdued by bleeding and cooling medicines, as sulphur, cream of tartar, or pulv. antimonialis : the latter almost invariably cause the death of the animal from the irritation they create and the inflammation which is thus set up.

m-n

INFLAMMATION OF THE LUNGS.

This disease is perhaps more generally known under the term of *rising of the lights ;* it is one of the most prevalent and too often the most fatal of all the maladies that infest the sty. It has been supposed by some persons to be contagious, by others to be hereditary, but there does not appear to be any actual foundation for either of these opinions. By far the most probable supposition is, that it arises from some atmospheric influences or agencies which create a tendency to pulmonary affections, and these, acting upon a system heated and predisposed to disease by the mode of feeding adopted in most piggeries, give a serious and inflammatory character to that which would otherwise be merely a simple attack of catarrh; or it may arise from some irritating influence in the food itself, or from damp, ill-ventilated styes: whatever be its cause, it generally runs through the whole piggery when it does make its appearance. The prominent indications of disease are loss of appetite, incessant and distressing cough, and heaving at the flanks.

As soon as the first symptoms are perceived, the animal should be bled; the palate perhaps will be the best place in this case to take blood from ; purgatives must then be given, but cautiously; Epsom salts and sulphur will be the best, administered in a dose of from two to four drachms of each, according to the size of the animal. To these may succeed sedative medicines: digitalis, two grains, pulv. antimonialis, six grains, nitre, half a drachm, forms a very efficient and soothing medicament for moderate-sized pigs, and will often produce very satisfactory effects ; cleanliness, warmth, and wholesome, cooling, nutritious food, are likewise valuable aids in combating this disease. But whatever measures are taken, they must be prompt; for inflammation of the lungs runs its course with rapidity and intensity, and, while we pause to consider what is best to be done, saps the vital energies of the patient.

PLEURO-PNEUMONIA.

This disease often breaks out among pigs as well as horses, cattle, and sheep, and commits great devastation. We shall quote some accounts of its progress, treatment, and post-mortem appearances given by English and foreign veterinarians, by whom it is classed under the head of

EPIDEMICS.

M. Saussol narrates that during the summer of 1821 nearly all the swine in the neighborhood of Mazamet were attacked by a violent and mortal disease that spared neither age nor sex, fat nor lean. He rates its ravages at about one-fifth of every four hundred patients.

The first symptoms were inappetency, thirst, dullness, groaning, and seeking of moist places; then followed hardness of the belly, heat of the skin, constipation, diminution of the urine, difficulty of respiration, heaving of the flanks, and short cough; the eyes were full of tears, and the mucous membranes inflamed. All these symptoms came on in the course of twelve hours. If the disease continued, the succeeding symptoms were still more alarming; the animals began to stagger about, the limbs were stretched out in an unnatural position, rattling in the throat came on, they supported themselves against the wall, and only fell to die a few minutes afterwards. Death usually came about the third day, and was in some cases preceded by convulsions of the face and extremities.

Treatment.—Copious bleedings from the *sacro-coccygean* arteries and veins, or, if these did not yield blood enough, amputation of the tail, hot baths, a seton covered with blistering ointment inserted in the chest, camphorated and laxative drenches, and a decoction of borage, mallows, and lettuces, slightly acidulated, to drink.

Causes.—Exposure to the heat of the sun, want of water, feeding on dry plants; returning home in the evening exhausted, receiving a hearty feed, and being then shut up in ill-ventilated styes without drink until morning.

Preventive treatment.—Troughs of acidulated nitrated water placed in the styes and frequently renewed; non-exposure to the heat of the day, means of bathing, bleeding, cleanliness, and ventilation; moderate feeding, and gentle exercise after the sun had set. These precautionary measures, M. Saussol says, arrested the progress of the disease.

Post-mortem appearances.—The thoracic cavity was filled with bloody limpid fluid; the lungs much inflamed; the pleura thickened, inflamed, and injected; the diaphragm covered with black patches of the size of a shilling; the mucous coat of the intestines slightly inflamed; the windpipe and bronchial tubes full of reddish froth; the brain covered with reddish serosity.

The next account we come to gives a description of a somewhat different epidemic which occurred in Aveyron and its environs, attacking both the respiratory and digestive organs, and running its course with astonishing vigor and rapidity, frequently sweeping off all the inhabitants of a piggery in from twelve to fourteen hours, and in the more virulent cases in less than half this time.

Symptoms.—In the worst cases these are sudden loss of appetite, small and frequent pulse, haggard eyes, the conjunctiva inflamed, the mouth open, red, and filled with foam, the respiration laborious, plaintive cries, convulsions, palsy of the hind limbs, and involuntary discharge of highly fetid fæces. Death here is the inevitable termination, and that in a short time. But where the progress of the disease is less rapid, the symptoms assume a milder form, and medical aid is available and often beneficial. Pregnant sows escape the attack of this malady, but as soon as they have farrowed they lose this immunity and they and their young take it. It also seems to spare leprous swine. It appears at all seasons of the year, but is most malignant in the summer and at the commencement of autumn. There can be no doubt as to its contagion, and from some experiments made, it can be reproduced in other animals by inoculation, particularly in sheep. The flesh of pigs that have died of this disease has been given to dogs and eaten by them without producing any bad effects.

Causes.—Unwholesome food, ill-ventilated styes, want of attention to cleanliness, exposure to heat, wet, or cold, are the predisposing causes; and probably some miasmatic influence develops the disease.

Treatment.—In the most virulent cases almost all modes of treatment are unsuccessful; or if they do succeed in rescuing the animal from death, he generally falls into a state of marasmus, or becomes paralytic. In the milder cases the following means have often proved efficient:—Seton in the chest; a decoction of sorel, with camphor, nitre, and calomel, as a drench; emollient injections, slightly acidulated; stimulating frictions of the dorsal and lumbar regions, or bathing these parts with hot vinegar; and water thickened with oat or barley-meal as the sole diet and drink. Venesection is here dangerous, tending only to undermine the strength of the patient, this disease being evidently one which alters, decomposes, and vitiates the blood. Acetate of ammonia, administered in doses proportionate to the size of the patient, has been of service. Purgatives should be avoided, as they are of very uncertain benefit. Directly an animal is attacked he should be removed from the others, and placed in some comfortable place.

Prevention.—Strict attention to diet, cleanliness, ventilation, and comfort; and a plentiful supply of clean water, both for the animals to drink and to bathe themselves in. In cold and rainy weather they should be kept in their styes; and during the heat of summer their drink should be slightly nitrated, acidulated, or salted. Whey is an excellent thing for those that are weakly. Small doses of camphor and nitre, with the addition of a few grains of calomel, administered in some cooling vegetable decoction, is a useful preventive. If one pig is attacked he should be removed, and the others taken out while the sty is well fumigated.

In 1838 we have accounts of an inflammatory epizoötic among pigs, rapid and fatal in its course, and attacking by preference store pigs rather than those put up to fatten.

Symptoms.—Prostration of strength, difficulty of breathing, discharge from the mouth and nostrils, constant cough, and reddish hue of the skin. These went on increasing in intensity until death put a period to them, which usually occurred in from three days to three days and a-half after the commencement of the attack.

Treatment.—Bleeding and laxative medicines, stimulating frictions of the trachea and parietes of the thorax, seemed to be the most efficient remedies. Doses of tartarized antimony and Hydrarg. Sub. Mur. in three grains of each, administered every twelfth hour, produced vomiting, and appeared to give ease. Sulphate of magnesia relieved those cases in which there was constipation.

The causes seemed obscure. The epidemic prevailed in the summer; but whether it arose from the warmth of the weather, from want of a sufficient supply of water, or from dry and heating food, was not at all evident.

Paulet has described a very similar epidemic among swine, which frequently prevails in one or the other of the *arrondissements* of the south of France. He describes it as highly inflammatory, rapidly going on to gangrene, and exceedingly contagious, but is at a loss to what cause to attribute it.

The precursory symptoms are, according to him, restlessness, cough, loss of appetite, dullness, and a weak tottering gait. These gradually go on increasing in intensity until the seventh or eighth day, when they have become very marked. Then alternations of heat and coldness of the body come on; the ears droop and are cold, the head is heavy, and the tongue becomes discolored; the breath is fetid, and there is a copious discharge of mucus from the nostrils. The skin is tinged with red, but the hue is not very evident except-ing under the belly: the animal appears to be in great suffering, and cries out pitifully. This general inflammation of the integuments rapidly goes on to gangrene, which alteration is evidenced by the livid violet hue of the diseased surfaces. Death then rapidly follows.

He, too, prescribes bleeding, and from the ears and veins of the belly, while many authors condemn it as debilitating. The only thing he recommends besides, is thin oatmeal gruel, acidulated with white-wine vinegar; for he appears to consider the malady to be so fatal that medical treatment avails nothing against it. Here, however, we cannot but deem him wrong; many of the most virulent, and, if neglected, fatal of the diseases to which our domesticated animals are subject, will yield to the influence of a judicious course of treatment, and many a valuable animal has been saved by the skill and attention of a veterinary surgeon. We should recommend laxative drenches, stimulating frictions, warmth, and cleanliness, and a seton in the chest.

In the epidemic which prevailed in 1841, throughout the greater part of England, swine were affected, as well as horses, cattle, and sheep, and often took it before any of the rest of the stock, but in general had it more mildly. This malady was of a highly contagious, inflammatory character, and affected chiefly the mucous and secretory tissues. When once it entered a farm-yard, it spread rapidly, until every ox, sheep, or pig was infected, and in some instances it passed to the human being. Damp, wet weather appeared most favorable to its development; and, from all accounts, it seems to have arisen from some atmospheric agency.

Symptoms.—Lameness of one or more of the feet, accompanied with heat around the hoof and lower part of the leg; discharge of saliva from the mouth and nostrils; champing or grinding of the lower jaw; ulceration of the mouth and tongue, extending even to the snout; dullness, inappetency, constipation, rapid emaciation, and cough.

Treatment.—The ulcerated portions of the feet and the detached pieces of horn should be carefully pared, and the parts daily washed with a solution of blue vitriol, or smeared with warm tar; the mouths also dressed with a strong solution of alum; and from an ounce and a half to two ounces of Glauber salts, dissolved in water, and given in their food. Where the malady was attacked in its onset, these simple remedies sufficed to produce convalescence in from fourteen to one-and-twenty days.

Post-mortem appearances.—There were patches of inflammation throughout the whole of the intestines, both externally and internally; the liver was sound; the heart flabby and soft; the lungs shrivelled, flattened, and diminished to one half their natural size, and in some cases hepatized; the diaphragm, pleura, and bronchial tubes of a greenish hue, and evidently gangrenous.

The flesh of pigs that had died of this epidemic was eaten by some persons without their suffering any ill effects; nevertheless the experiment was hazardous.

CHAPTER VIII.

Anatomy of the Stomach — Gullet—Intestines — Duodenum—Jejunum—Ileum—Cœcum and Colon : Diseases to which these parts are liable—Enteritis—Colic—Diarrhœa—Garget of the Maw—Anatomy of the Liver and Spleen : Splenitis—Rupture of the Spleen—Absorption of the Spleen—Peritoneum—Worms—The Bladder and its diseases—Protrusion of the Rectum.

THE GULLET.

THE gullet, or *œsophagus,* is a musculo-membranous tube, commencing at the pharynx, passing down the throat on the left side of the windpipe, entering the chest in company with that tube, penetrating through the folds of the diaphragm, and terminating in the stomach through an orifice termed the *cardia.*

THE STOMACH.

The stomach of the hog is a much more simple apparatus than that of the ox and sheep ; it is a truly omnivorous one, and beautifully adapted by its pyramidal appendage and glandular structure, as well as by the villous mucous membrane with which it is lined, for the digestion of the heterogeneous food which it is destined to receive, being, perhaps, more analogous to that of the horse than to any other animal. In form it is globulous. Its large blind cavity is very voluminous, and is surmounted in front by a hood-like appendage. The narrow long portion which abuts on the pylorus, greatly resembles this hood-shaped appendage. On each side of the cardia are two transversal folds, and the cardia itself is half way between the pylorus and the large cavity.

The stomach has three coats,—the outermost, or *peritoneum,* which constitutes the common covering of all the intestines ; the muscular or fibrous coat, which acts upon, and mingles the food, and prepares it for digestion ; and the mucous or villous coat, which is peculiarly developed in the pig, and into which open the mouths of numerous little vessels, conveying the gastric juice to the semi-digested food, and by its action conveying it into a pultaceous fluid, commonly called *chyme.*

THE INTESTINES.

The intestines of the hog bear a stronger resemblance to those of the human being than we find in any other animal. They are sixteen times the length of the body of the animal, and the proportions of the small intestines to the large, are as three to one. They are composed of four coats or layers. The outer or peritoneal one is formed of that membrane which invests and retains in its proper position every portion of the contents of the belly. The second layer is muscular, and by its action propels the contents of the stomach gradually onwards. The office of the third is to lubricate the innermost coat, and for this purpose, it is supplied with numerous glands surrounded by cellular tissue. The fourth or lining coat is soft, villous, and, in a healthy state, always covered with mucus. The food, having been sufficiently converted into chyme by the action of the stomachs, is gradually propelled through the pyloric orifice by

THE DUODENUM,

or first intestine, where it is submitted to the influence of two fluids, the one secreted by the pancreas, the other by the liver, and the combined action of which separates the nutritious from the worthless portion, causing the former to assume the appearance of a thick whitish fluid, and the latter that of a yellow pulpy substance. It next passes into

THE JEJUNUM AND ILEUM,

where it undergoes still further alteration, and whence a considerable portion of it is taken up by the lacteal vessels which open into these two small intestines, and conveyed away to nourish the frame, and become mingled with the blood and supply the waste in it. These intestines are of equal diameter in the pig throughout their whole extent, and the termination of the jejunum and commencement of the ileum is by no means distinctly defined; the latter is, however, longer than the former, and opens into

THE CŒCUM,

with a valvular opening close to the aperture into the colon. The cœcum is a kind of bag supplied with numerous secretory glands, which furnish it with a fluid which once more acts upon those portions of the digested food which reach it, extracting from them any nutritive portions which may chance still to remain. The matter having reached the base of this intestine, is returned by the muscular action of its coat, and being prevented by the valve from re-entering the ileum, passes into

THE COLON,

the largest of the large intestines, some of the convolutions of which equal the stomach in size, while others are as small as the small intestines. Here the watery parts of the mass are extracted, and the residuum or hard fæcal portion is retained for awhile, and finally **expelled** through the *rectum*. It will be readily imagined that this complicated and beautiful process must occasionally become deranged by various causes, and that hence will arise different diseases of a more or less serious nature. This is, however, less the case in swine than in most of our other domesticated animals, from the circumstance of their stomachs and intestines being prepared by the softening power of their highly mucous villous lining for the reception and digestion of a heterogeneous mass of food, which to other animals would be actually poisonous; rendering it evident that, although the hog in a state of nature is a herbivorous animal, he was also destined to become omnivorous for the service of man.

ENTERITIS.

This disease consists in inflammation of one or more of the coats of the intestines, and is capable of being produced by various irritating causes, as the foul air of badly ventilated styes, unwholesome food, &c.

The symptoms are dullness, loss of appetitite, constipation, spasms, or convulsions, continued restless motion, either to and fro, or round and round, staggering gait, evident symptoms of suffering.

The most successful treatment is warm baths, dry litter, and general warmth and comfort; and internally, purgatives and enemas. Castor oil, calomel, or rhubarb, are the best purgatives for cases of this nature, and the enemas should be of an emollient oleaginous nature. The diet should be restricted to the simplest and lightest food; oatmeal, porridge, skim-milk, or whey, are the best things.

COLIC.

The hog is frequently attacked by this malady, which generally arises from unwholesome food, cold, or wet filthy styes; and is evidenced by restlessness, cries of pain, rolling on the ground, &c. A dose of castor oil proportionate to the size of the patient, with perhaps a little of ginger in it, and administered in warm milk, will generally give speedy relief; or if the first should not, the dose must be repeated. Some practitioners recommend Glauber's or Epsom salts, but we consider oleaginous purgatives to be best adapted for attacks of colic.

DIARRHŒA.

This is a disease very common among all our young domesticated animals, and one that is also repeatedly met with in older ones; a scanty allowance, or unwholesome food will produce it, as will also over feeding, or too nutritious diet It consists in a frequent dis-

6*

charge of the fæcal matter in a thin or slimy state, but not actually altered, and arises from inflammation or congestion of the mucous lining of the intestines. What we conceive to be an attack of diarrhœa, is often only an effort of nature to throw off some offensive matters, and will cease of itself in the course of twenty-four hours; but where it goes on for any length of time, it must be taken seriously in hand, as it will otherwise weaken the animal and impair its value. The best remedy for it is the compound commonly called calves' cordial, viz: Prepared chalk, one ounce, powdered catechu, half an ounce, powdered ginger, two drachms, powdered opium, half a drachm, mixed and dissolved in half a pint of peppermint water. From half an ounce to an ounce of this mixture, according to the size of the animal, should be given twice in the day; and strict attention paid to the diet, which should consist as much as possible of dry, farinaceous food.

GARGET OF THE MAW.

This is a disorder arising from repletion, and is found alike in older animals and in sucking pigs. Its symptoms strongly resemble those of colic. The remedies, too, are purgatives. Epsom salts is here, perhaps, as good a thing as can be given, in doses of from a quarter of an ounce to an ounce. It might as well be termed *indigestion*, for such it actually is, the stomach being overloaded with food. In sucking pigs it usually arises from the coagulation of milk in the stomach.

THE LIVER.

This organ in swine does not appear to be so subject to disease as it is in most of our other domesticated animals; we have only, therefore, to glance at its use and anatomy as we pass. It is smaller in swine than in sheep, and larger than we find it in the dog, in accordance with that anatomical law, which seems to be in force in all animals; namely, that the size of the liver shall be in inverse proportion to that of the lungs. It is situated in the anterior part of the abdomen, and its upper surface rests against the concavity of the diaphragm. Its office is to receive the blood that is returned from the intestines, separate from it and secrete the fluid termed *bile*, and then forward the residue of the blood onwards to the lungs, where it undergoes the usual aërating process, and becomes transmuted into arterial blood.

The fluid or *bile* thus secreted, when in a healthy state, and not in undue proportion, stimulates the mucous membrane, and increases the peristaltic motion of the intestines, excites the secretion of that mucus requisite to preserve these parts in a healthy state, hastens the process of separating the nutritious from the innutritious parts of the food, and facilitates the escape of the fæcal matters. It also acts chemically upon the various substances which are devoured by the animal, and is the chief agent in neutralizing the acidity which some of these would otherwise create. The liver of the pig has four distinct lobes.

THE SPLEEN.

In the hog the spleen is very long, and nearly of a uniform breadth and thickness throughout its whole extent. It lies on the left side of the abdomen, and is attached to the stomach by the folds of the epiploön. Its texture is almost like that of a sponge in appearance, consisting of innumerable cells of every size and form, yet it is firm to the touch. In color it is a dark, deep reddish brown.

There has been much dispute as to the functions and use of this organ. Some persons, arguing from its situation, contend that it is a powerful agent in the process of digestion; but this is strongly negatived by the fact, that it has been removed from some animals which have existed for a considerable time afterwards, without apparent injury to that function. Others again, and with more probability, assume that it has to do with the coloring and conversion of the chyle into blood as it passes through the mesentery, where it becomes mixed with the red coagulable fluid furnished by the spleen. But with these physiological questions we have at present nothing to do: our purpose is simply to consider it with a view to understanding and treating those diseases of which it is not unfrequently the seat. Little attention has hitherto been paid to them, probably from their symptoms being somewhat obscure; but nevertheless, different morbid affections of the spleen are by no means uncommon among the lower domesticated animals. This viscus is often ruptured, distended with blood, inflamed, or softened, from the effects of different causes, but chiefly of damp, heat, or foul air.

SPLENITIS.

Swine suffering under this malady are restless and debilitated, shun their companions, and bury themselves in the litter. There is loss of appetite and excessive thirst, so excessive that they will drink up any thing that comes in their way, no matter how filthy. The respiration is short; they cough, vomit, grind the teeth, and foam at the mouth; the groin is wrinkled, and of a pale brownish hue, and the skin of the throat, chest, and belly, (which latter is hard and tucked up,) is tinged with black.

The remedies are copious blood-letting, gentle purgatives, as Epsom or Glauber's salts, followed up by cooling medicines. Cold lotions of vinegar and water, to bathe the parts in the neighborhood of the spleen, or a cold shower-bath applied by means of a watering-pot, are also efficacious in these cases.

Columella, in his quiet style, thus treats of this disease :—

"Also the pain of a distempered spleen uses to plague them ; the which chiefly happens when there chances to be great droughts, and, as the Bucolic poem speaks—

> When on all sides the apples scattered lie,
> Each under its own tree ;

for it is an insatiable cattle the swine, which beyond all measure eagerly seek after that which is sweet. They labor and are affected in the summer and early autumn with a swelling or growth of the spleen, from the which they are relieved if troughs be made of *tamarisks* and *butcher's broom*, and filled with water, and set before them when they are thirsty ; for the medicinal juice of the wood being swallowed with the drink, puts a stop to their intestinal swelling."

The great difficulty here is, how troughs can be made of the *museus* (butcher's broom.) In all probability the true meaning is, that the trough should be lined with the branches of this plant ; and the *tamarisks* signifies doubtless the *tamaricus e trunco* mentioned by Pliny, lib. xxiv. 9, where he speaks of canals and troughs being made of the *tamarix*. Translators are given occasionally to make a similar mistakes or alterations of text.

RUPTURE OF THE SPLEEN.

We quote this case from the "*Veterinarian*" for 1841 :—

"A pig belonging to Mr. Roberts of Whitchurch, died after having only been ill for a day or so, and that unattended by any definite symptoms. On post-mortem examination the spleen was found to be of about three or four times its natural size, and completely congested. In one place there was a small rupture surrounded with coagulated blood. All the other viscera were perfectly sound."

ABSORPTION OF THE SPLEEN.

This case is also derived from the same source, and we present it to our readers as a testimony of the different forms of disease which occur in the spleen of the swine.

"A fat pig, weighing fifteen score, was killed, and upon cutting it up, the spleen was found to be almost entirely absorbed. It was of the usual length, but not above half an inch in width or the eighth of an inch in thickness in any part, and weighed but seven drachms. What there was of it, however, appeared to be perfectly sound, and was surrounded by a considerable portion of adepts."

PERITONEUM.

This portion of the contents of the abdomen is composed of cellular tissue, and amply supplied with absorbent vessels; its office is to separate the different viscera from each other, to envelop them, and to attach them to, and support them in their proper position. It is subject to attacks of inflammation, technically termed

PERITONITIS,

the symptoms of which closely resemble those of splenitis; and the causes too are very similar, being chiefly improper food, repletion, or exposure to extremes of temperature. Oleaginous purgatives are here the only ones which are admissible, and emollient clysters; great attention must also be paid to the diet, and nothing of an acrid or indigestible nature given to the animal. This disease is too often fatal, gradually wasting away its victim. The post-mortem appearances are as follows: the intestines have become so adherent to each other that it is scarcely possible to believe that any false membranes were ever interposed; the peritoneal surfaces present evidences of inflammation, and are often covered with confluent ulcerations resembling those seen in glanders of the horse; there is considerable inflammation of the muscular coat of the intestines, and the whole of these parts are thickened and corrugated.

WORMS IN THE INTESTINES.

These entozoaria are very troublesome in swine, and often exceedingly fatal. The *spiroptera strongylina* is of the kinds most common to the hog, but the *ascarides tænia* and *echinorhinc* are likewise often found in considerable numbers.

The presence of worms may be inferred when the animal eats voraciously and yet continues lean and out of condition; coughs, runs restlessly about, uttering squeaks of pain, becomes savage, snapping at his companions, and destroying all rabbits and poultry that come in his way. The excrements are generally hard and highly-colored, the eyes sunken, the animal becomes daily more debilitated, and frequent attacks resembling colic tend still further to weaken him. Too often he dies; for before these symptoms have been noticed the evil has generally attained to such a height as to be beyond the power of medicine; for these parasites, and the *echinorhinc* especially, multiply with incredible rapidity.

Drastic purgatives constitute the most efficient means of combating worms; but they must be cautiously administered, as they are but too apt to dissolve and force away with them the lining mucus of the intestinal canals. Turpentine is exceedingly destructive to worms, and although to many of our domesticated animals a dangerous medicine, it may be administered with perfect safety to the hog. Common salt may be also given with advantage, and should be mingled with the food. Nor must it be supposed that because no worms are seen to come away from the animal the treatment may be discontinued, or that there are none; hundreds of them die in the intestines, and there become digested and decomposed, and go through the same processes as the food.

THE BLADDER.

This organ seems to be but little subject to disease in swine. Its position beneath the rectum and genital organs contained in the pelvic cavity protects it in all animals from external injuries; and the pig not being exposed to those causes which render the horse and dog peculiarly liable to disease of the bladder, namely, speed, long and fatiguing exercises, &c., seems to be comparatively exempt from it.

There is, however, a case narrated in the " Veterinarian," by Mr. Reid, V. S., which we shall quote.

VESICAL CALCULI.

"A barrow-pig that to the seventh month had manifested perfect health, from that period fell rapidly away (although its appetite remained unimpaired,) so much so in fact that in two months more it was a mere bag of bones, and the owner had it destroyed. He attributed this decline to a difficulty in passing its urine, which distressed the animal to such a degree that every time it wanted to stall it quite moaned with pain, rolling upon its back, arising, and again posturing itself for stalling, arching its spine, and making violent efforts, which too often were ineffectual. At other times, and indeed oftenest, he after much straining succeeded in passing a little urine, but this was speedily followed by fresh efforts. Occasionally, after having rolled about and laid on its back, it obtained relief by a flow of urine in a full stream. The urine was at all times perfectly clear."

This account was sufficient to draw Mr. Reid's attention to the presence of vesical calculi. He regretted that he had not been called in during the life of the animal, that he might have made it the subject of operation, and requested permission to examine the carcass.

The bladder was half full of limpid urine, in which floated the stone. The internal coat of the bladder about the inferior part exhibited slight blushes of inflammation. All around the neck it was deeply inflamed, and thence the reddening spread about an inch into the urethra. The peritoneum also exhibited a light tint.

INVERSION OF THE BLADDER.

A sow littered in the morning and brought forth ten pigs without any apparent difficulty, and immediately afterwards something resembling the bladder, and which appeared to be about half full, came out. The owner seeing that it did not come away, became alarmed and sent for the pig-butcher, who said it was the womb, and that it must be put back, which he accordingly endeavored to do, and having passed two or three stitches of small twine across the labia to retain the parts, left the animal. Mr. Neale, V. S., of Burbage, happening to hear of the occurrence, called to see the sow. He found the vagina considerably protruded, or at least that there was a protrusion of the size of a man's fist, and in a sloughing state there. She appeared, however, in good condition, got up without apparent pain or difficulty, and was suckling her young well. The urine was flowing drop by drop. As the owner declined having any thing done to her, Mr. Neale ordered the parts to be bathed with a decoction of bark. Four months afterwards she was killed for bacon, and weighed 160 lbs. Upon opening her the uterus was found to be perfectly healthy, the vagina as clean as possible, and the tumor reduced by sloughing to the size of a lemon; the bladder was completely gone. The kidneys were full of white purulent matter of about the consistence of cream. The uterus led directly from the kidneys to the protruded part, at the inside of which, and just below the anus, was a formation of matter about the size of a hen's egg. There was not the slightest trace of inflammation in any of the surrounding parts.

PROTRUSION OF THE RECTUM.

This is an evil of not unfrequent occurrence in swine, arising chiefly from obstruction of the intestines. Where the cause is simply obstruction, an operation will remedy it; but as the obstruction is too frequently attended with rupture of some of the intestines, it will perhaps be as well to have the animal slaughtered at once, especially if it is in tolerably good condition.

HERNIA.

There is little doubt but that umbilical and congenital hernia are of frequent occurrence among swine; but as yet the attention devoted to the diseases of these animals has been so slight that we dare not venture positively to assert the fact.

CHAPTER IX.

THE SKIN.

THE skin of the hog, like that of most other animals, is composed
of three separate parts or layers.   The first or exterior of these is
the *cuticle* or scarf skin, which covers the whole surface of the body
and protects the more sensitive parts from the injuries which might
result to them from immediate contact with external agents.   It is
a thin, tough, callous texture, perforated with innumerable holes or
pores, through which pass the hairs and bristles, and whence exude
those transpirations by means of which the body throws off all
vapors injurious to the system.   Chemical analysis has proved it
to be chiefly composed of gelatine, and consequently insoluble in
water of common temperature.   This layer is considerably tougher
and denser in the hog and other of the pachydermata than it is in
the horse, ox, and most of our domesticated animals.

Beneath this is the *rete mucosum*, a soft expansion of tissue which
overspreads, and can with difficulty be separated from the layer below
it.   Its purpose appears to be to protect the terminations of the
blood-vessels and nerves of the skin, which it in a manner envelops
or covers.   This layer determines the color of the body and of the
hair.

The third and undermost part is the *cutis vera* or true skin, an
elastic texture composed of innumerable minute fibres crossing each
other in all directions, fitting closely to every part of the frame,
yielding by its elasticity to all the motions of the body, and interpos-
ing its dense, firm structure between the more vital parts of the
system and external injuries.   Innumerable blood-vessels and nerves
pass through it, and appear upon its surface in the form of papillæ;
it is in fact far more sensitive than the muscles or flesh.

The skin varies in density in different breeds of swine.   In some
of the large, old breeds it is thick, coarse, tough, and almost as im-
penetrable, in comparison, as the hide of a rhinoceros; while in
many of our smaller breeds, and particularly in those which have a
considerable admixture of Asiatic blood, and in the Chinese pigs
themselves, it is soft, fine, and delicate, and bears no slight degree
of resemblance to the skin of the human being.   It is not to be
wondered at, that a structure so delicately organised as the one we
have been describing should be subject to disease.   In the hog it is
peculiarly so; many of the most serious maladies to which he is

subject, have their seat in the skin : it were a point well worthy of study to inquire into the reason of this fact, but as the present work is devoted to practice rather than theory, we must leave it to abler hands, and pass onwards to a consideration of some of the most prevalent diseases of the skin in swine.

GANGRENOUS ERYSIPELAS.

This disease, which is frequently spoken of by the ancient writers, as prevailing to a greater or less extent, and often almost as an epidemic among sheep and swine, is now of rare occurrence. Poulet thus describes the symptoms :—

"The first of these, which last some five or six days, are uneasiness, inquietude, depression, loss of appetite, and inertness. About the seventh or eighth day these gradually increase in intensity ; the limbs totter, the body is alternately hot and cold, the ears droop and are cold, the head appears heavy, the tongue is discolored, the breath fetid, a thick mucus flows from the nostrils, and the whole of the skin becomes tinged with an erysipelatous redness, which is most evident under the belly; the animal utters almost incessant screams of pain. This inflammatory state of the integuments rapidly merges into decided gangrene, and the whole of the diseased surface becomes of a livid blue or violet hue. The skin is first covered with blisters containing a thin reddish watery fluid ; and as these break, the gangrenous, dark colored scabs are formed. The disease is, however, by no means of so fatal a character in swine, as it is in sheep, probably from the former being the stronger animals. A little blood should be taken from the ears, once at any rate, and the bleeding should be repeated if it appears at all necessary. A dose or two of Epsom salts, cooling drinks slightly acidulated, and strict attention to diet and cleanliness, are generally all that will be requisite. Should the skin appear to be very irritable, a little sweet oil may be rubbed over it, or some sulphur made into a kind of ointment with sweet oil or palm oil; but local applications are not generally requisite."

Exposure to great heat or cold, or any sudden transition from one extreme of temperature to another, are supposed by some authors to be the causes of this disease ; while others, and we think with justice, attribute it to unwholesome or putrid food, and to general inattention and neglect.

LICE.

Pigs, when allowed to wallow in the mire, and to dwell in filthy styes, are very apt to engender these disgusting vermin, which eat into the skin and render it scabby and ulcerated, and by the irritation they keep up, worry and fatigue the animals, and effectually prevent them from thriving. Eric Viborg states that these vermin sometimes burrow their way into the flesh and come out through the eyes, nostrils, or mouth, or have even been known to be voided in the urine.

The first step to be taken towards effecting a cure is thoroughly to cleanse the skin from every particle of dirt, and to clean out and whitewash the styes and put in fresh dry litter.

Mercurial ointment, turpentine, or tobacco-water, are the most efficient agents in the destruction of these unwelcome parasites. A little sulphur or Ethiop's mineral and bay-salt may be given internally.

The preventive means are strict attention to cleanliness both in the styes and in the animals themselves. Whenever a pig is observed to be lousy, which will quickly be perceived by his rubbing himself against the gates, trees, and walls, he must be immediately separated from his companions, or they too will become infested with lice, if they are not already so.

Parkinson is of opinion that "the cause of vermin infesting animals clearly arises, in a general way, from bad feeding, which occasions weakness of the blood; for," says he, "if an animal be ever so lousy, by giving him strong food for a few days the vermin will disappear, probably because the rich blood is poison to them." He considers that a free access to water for bathing, and also occasional exposure to heavy rain, is not only necessary to the general health of swine, but a most excellent preservative against vermin.

LEPROSY.

This disease has apparently existed in swine from the remotest periods, and Tacitus gives it as his opinion that it was because the hog was subject to leprosy that the Jews were forbidden to eat of its flesh. It consists in the development of certain vesicles, or whitish granulations, in all parts and portions of the cellular tissue; which vesicles have been proved to be neither more nor less than a species of worms termed the *cysticercus cellulosa*, supposed by some French authors to be of the same species as that found in the brain of sheep. There are however considerable differences between these two. The cysticercus is found in all the cellular tissues and soft parts throughout the whole of the body; in the fat, in the adipose matter, in the interstices between the muscles, in the viscera, and, in short, in every crevice into which they can insert themselves. The thigh or ham has been mentioned by some authors as the principal seat of these vesicles, but they are also found on the shoulders, around the jaws, along the neck and belly, and even underneath and around the root of the tongue, where alone can any outward lesions indicative of leprosy be in general discovered; and even here they are not constant, but are chiefly evident in those animals in which the disease has attained to a great height. The progress of leprosy is very insidious, and the early symptoms so little marked that a practised eye only can detect them.

In the onset all that is observable is a certain marked stupidity or obstinacy in the animal; a state of languor and apparent general debility; an evident thickening of the skin; a slight adhesion of the bristles; a tendency in the hair to fall off, caused by the development of a greater or less quantity of those vesicles of which we have spoken, as being scattered in different parts of the fatty tissue, either on its surface or in the interstices of the muscles; under the coats of the viscera, or on the sides of the tongue.

In its successive progress this disease attacks the animal economy more or less profoundly without the functions appearing otherwise troubled. There is ulceration of the cellular tissue, and even of the organs that surround or penetrate it: the animal does not however appear to be generally and seriously ill. Far from losing his appetite, he is occasionally extremely voracious. He does not appear to suffer in the lungs; his breath is not embarrassed, nor is his voice hoarser than usual.

Such is at least what may be observed to take place when the leprous vesicles are not numerous. It is when they increase in quantity and the disease increases that they begin to affect the health of the patient. He then becomes indifferent to every thing; moves about slowly; totters as he walks; his eyes are dull; the buccal membrane is pale, and sometimes strewed with violet spots. The expired air is fetid, the breathing slow; the pulse small and irregular, the bristles easily plucked, and sometimes a little blood accompanies them. Strength begins to abandon the patient; he can no longer sustain himself on his hind legs; the posterior part of the trunk becomes paralyzed, the body exhales an unpleasant smell; the skin is thicker, and the cellular tissue is raised in different parts, especially about the kernals of the neck. There is swelling about the roots of the hair, which often proceeds to ulceration; the skin comes off in patches; large tumors are developed; the teeth are ground convulsively together; the tongue is dark colored, hot, thickened, and covered with slime; the body swells; the animal utters feeble cries of pain, and seldom survives many hours.

This is a very obstinate disease, probably from its having usually taken so great a hold of the system before it is suspected, and numerous have been the medicaments recommended for it. Antimony, sulphur, small and repeated doses of Epsom salts, and general bleedings, seem to be the course of treatment most likely to be attended with success; and these must be aided by strict attention to diet and cleanliness; cooling wholesome food alone should be given, and water, in which barley-meal has been dissolved. Nothing of a rich or heating nature should be allowed to come within reach of the animal. As external applications, mercurial ointment may be moderately applied to the ulcerated parts, or the common mange ointment composed of sulphur and antimony.

In all probability the reason why this and many other diseases of swine have hitherto been regarded as incurable, is that men of science, educated veterinarians, have as yet given but little of their attention to these useful animals, and deemed the study of their diseases and of the means of treating them beneath their notice. Nor is the owner without his share of blame, for he too often either abandons the poor brute to its fate, or calls in the aid of the pig-butcher or some ignorant empiric.

There have been numerous opinions advanced relative to the predisposing causes of leprosy; some authors attribute it to exposure to the inclemency of the weather, insufficient food, and damp marshy localities; and urge in support of their opinion that the disease was much more prevalent and fatal when swine were turned into the woods and forests during certain periods of the year to seek their own food than it is now when they are comfortably lodged and more care devoted to their feeding. Others have attributed it to some pernicious qualities in the water which the animals drink, or in the food which is given to them; and with both these parties we are inclined to agree, and to attribute this disease in a great measure to vitiation of the blood.

The wild boar appears to be exempt from it; nor is leprosy known in America, Russia, or Spain, if we may believe the testimony of various authors and travellers.

Some have asserted it to be hereditary; but there are numerous facts on record in which some of the progeny of a perfectly healthy boar and sow have proved leprous, while a diseased sow has produced sound and healthy young.

Another question has likewise been much discussed, namely, the propriety or safety of eating the flesh of pigs that have died of this disease. These animals, however good condition they may appear to be in, are rather bloated than fat; the flesh is soft and flabby, and tasteless, and will not keep; the bacon pale in color and wanting consistency. Soup made with such flesh is white, greasy, and insipid, and has been known to produce vomiting and diarrhœa. We are not aware that there are any records of disease or other evil resulting from the eating of the flesh of leprous pigs; nevertheless it stands to reason that it cannot be wholesome, and should not be made use of, for although no immediate ill effects may follow the eating of it, we cannot tell what insidious evils such vitiated and diseased food may engender in the human frame.

MANGE.

This cutaneous affection, which was formerly attributed to want of cleanliness, or to some peculiar state of the blood, is now generally admitted to arise from the presence of certain minute insects termed *acari*. It is identical with the *scab* in sheep, and the *itch* in the human being, which also were supposed to arise from corruption of the blood, or acrid humor subsisting in it, or from filthiness, but which arise from this scabious insect. As far back as the twelfth century these *acari scabiei* were described by an Arabian physician; subsequently they were noticed and described by several German and Italian writers, and in 1812 and 1814 Herr Walz, a German veterinarian, and M. Gohier, an eminent French veterinary surgeon, found these insects in, and gave drawings of, and described those peculiar to, almost all our domesticated animals.

There is a very interesting translation from a pamphlet by Dr. Hertwig, given in the *Veterinarian* for 1838, in which a detailed account of the habits and history of these insects will be found.

The hog does not appear to suffer so much from mange or scab as the horse, sheep, and dog; in swine, the pustules are usually chiefly developed under the arm-pits, and on the interior of the thighs. They at first consist simply of red spots, vesicles, or pimples; but these gradually become connected together by minute burrows, or furrows existing beneath the skin, and eventually unite in the form of large scabs, which the animal, irritated by the itching, rubs into large blotchy sores.

Where the mange is recent, a tolerably strong decoction of tobacco or digitalis will often prove an efficacious wash for the diseased parts, or a solution of corrosive sublimate; but if the eruption is of long standing, and has degenerated into scabs, a solution of arsenic in the proportion of one ounce to a gallon of water, or, what is still better, sulphur and mercurial ointment in the proportion of an ounce of the former to a drachm of the latter, carefully and thoroughly rubbed into the skin, must be resorted to. A decoction of soot has also been recently discovered by an eminent French physician to be exceedingly efficacious in cases of cutaneous disorders. Two handfuls of soot are boiled during half an hour in a pint of water, the fluid is then strained off, and the lotion when cold used two or three times in the day. Creosote has also been used with success in the treatment of cutaneous eruptions. If the animal is in high condition, blood should be taken, and two or three doses of cooling physic given, or sulphur mingled with the food. Strict attention must be paid to cleanliness, and the animal kept apart from the rest of the herd. Mange is both hereditary and infectious. There are numerous instances of its having been communicated from one animal to another of a different species, and even to the human being.

In Austria, if mange appears in the hog within eight days after the sale, it is presumed to have existed at the time of the said sale, and the animal is returnable to the vendor; and when it can be proved that he was aware of the unsoundness, he not only has to return the purchase-money, but also to indemnify the purchaser for any loss or inconvenience he may have sustained, besides paying a fine equal to one-tenth of the value of the animal.

That the actual disease, namely, the scab and the irritation, arises from the presence and proceedings of the *acari*, there can be no shadow of doubt; but the question is, whence do these acari arise? Are they the product of some morbid state of the skin, arising from constitutional derangement, or created by miasma or effluvia? We find mange in animals that are fed on too stimulating food, we also find it in others that are neglected and badly fed. How can these contradictions be reconciled? Here is a vast field for scientific research and experiment. As every grain of earth, and every drop of water, and every particle of air, is peopled with living beings, developed by certain causes, it is by no means an improbable theory to suppose that the germs of the *acari* may exist in a dormant state in the skin, and only be called into actual life by some of the vitiating influences which neglect or mismanagement produces, and once existing, they follow the law of every created being, and propagate and multiply, and pass from one animal to another either by actual contact, or by the intermediation of some other substance which both had touched. We admit, however, that this is mere theory, and call upon our professional brethren to aid us by their researches in our endeavors to discover the actual truth.

MEASLES.

This is rather a sub-cutaneous than an actual disease of the skin, consisting in a multitude of small watery pustules developed between the fat and the skin, and indeed scattered throughout the cellular tissue and adipose matter. It has, by many, been regarded as a milder form of leprosy; and so far as our present limited knowledge will allow us to judge, this supposition appears by no means an erroneous one.

The external appearances attending it are the development of reddish patches, somewhat raised above the surface of the skin, on the groin, the arm-pits, and the inside of the thighs at first, and subsequently on other parts of the body. The attendant symptoms are acceleration of the pulse, heat of the skin, cough, discharge from the nostrils, loss of appetite, nausea, swelling of the eyelids, feebleness of the hinder extremities, and the formation of blackish pustules under the tongue : eventually the skin usually comes off in patches.

The measles in swine is seldom fatal, and will gradually yield to the simplest cooling treatment, or even to mere attention to diet, temperature, and ventilation. Didymus tells us that Democrates prescribed bruised asphodile roots to be mingled with the food given to hogs, as an excellent remedy for this disease. It sadly injures the quality of the meat, rendering it insipid, flabby, pale, and indisposed to take the salt. We should say that the flesh of measly pigs is positively unwholesome, although, perhaps, there are no cases on record in which it is proved that bad effects have resulted from the use of it.

The following was a remedy for this disorder used by the ancients : "A hog having measles must be put in a sty and kept there three days and nights without food. Then take five or six apples, pick out the cores and fill up the holes thus made with flour of brimstone; stop up the holes and cast in the apples to the measly hog. Give him first one or two, then one or two more, and then, as being hungry he will eat them, give him all. Let him have nothing more to eat until the next day, and then serve him so again. Thus use him for five or six days, and he will become as well and as wholesome as ever." In our opinion it is one very likely to be beneficial.

It yet remains to be discovered whether measles in swine is an epidemic, like that disorder in the human being, or whether it is hereditary, or whether, as many suppose, it arises from the development and presence of a variety of the *cysticercus*.

DESQUAMATION OF THE SKIN.

The following singular case, communicated to *The Veterinarian*, by Mr. J. Sherwood, of Sittingbourn, appears to us not unworthy of record here.

"A few weeks ago the skin became hard on either side about nine or ten inches from the spine, and afterwards kept gradually separating towards the centre of the spine from the shoulder to the insertion of the tail. The bailiff cut off portions from time to time of the weight of nearly 10 lbs. in order to make the load with which the animal was encumbered the lighter, until the last week, when the hog lay down, and after taking his rest with his brethren (for he fed and looked as well as the rest, with the exception of the load on his back) he got up and left the substance behind him. It consisted of the entire skin so far as it had sloughed, with about two inches of adeps adhering to it in the middle, getting gradually thinner towards the sides, and weighing 20 lbs., which, added to the portions before removed, made a total of 30 lbs. The hog is now computed to weigh 400 lbs. He had not any medicine administered, as he did well the whole of the time."

CHAPTER X.

BLEEDING.

THIS is a most useful and necessary operation, and one which in many diseases is of vital importance. The common and vulgar mode of getting blood from the pig is by cutting off portions of the ears or tail; but these modes of proceeding should only be had recourse to when local and instant blood-letting is requisite. The jugular veins of swine lie too deep and are too much imbedded in fat to admit of their being raised by any ligature about the neck; it is therefore useless to attempt to puncture them—we should only be striking at random. Those veins, however, which run over the interior surface of the ear, and especially towards its outer edge, may be opened without much difficulty: if the ear is turned back on to the poll, one or more of them may easily be made sufficiently prominent to admit of its being punctured by pressing the fingers on the base of the ear near to the conch; when the necessary quantity of blood has been obtained, the finger may be raised and it will cease to flow.

The palate veins which run on either side of the roof of the mouth are also easily opened by making two incisions, one on each side of the palate, about half way between the centre of the roof of the mouth and the teeth. The flow of blood may be readily stopped by means of a pledget of tow and a string, as in the horse.

M. Gohier, who had considerable practice in bleeding swine, was of opinion that the cephalic and sephena veins might be opened without any great exertion of skill by any one who possessed a little knowledge of anatomy. The lancet should be used somewhat obliquely, and a sufficient quantity of blood having been obtained, the flow arrested in the usual manner.

Mr. Cupiss recommends the brachial vein of the fore-leg (commonly called by farriers the *plate*-vein) as a favorable place for bleeding. This vein runs along the inner side of the fore-leg under the skin, and the best place for puncturing it is about an inch above the knee, and scarcely half an inch backwards from the *radius*. No danger need be apprehended from cutting two or three times if sufficient blood cannot be obtained at once. The vein will become easily discernible if a ligature is tied firmly round the leg just below the shoulder.

Columella tells us "to let blood from the ear," or "strike a vein beneath the tail at the distance of two inches from the buttocks, where it attains sufficient size for the purpose, and it must first be beaten with the sprig of a vine ; then, when swelled up by the stroke of this rod, opened with a lancet, and, after enough blood has been drawn, the vein must be bound up with the rind of the willow or elm-tree."

This operation should always be performed with the lancet if possible : in cases of urgent haste, when no lancet is at hand, a small penknife may be used; but the fleam is a dangerous and objectionable instrument.

CASTRATION OR SPAYING.

This operation is performed on many of our domesticated animals, with a view of increasing their docility and usefulness, and on others to dispose them to fatten and attain to early maturity; it consists in removing the testicles of the male, and the ovaries, and sometimes a more or less considerable portion of the uterus, of the female.

Pigs are chiefly castrated with a view to fattening them; and doubtless castration has the required effect, and therefore is less objectionable when performed on the pig, than when the horse or dog is subjected to it; for at the same time that it increases the quiescent qualities of the animal, it diminishes his courage, spirits, and nobler attributes, and even affects his form. The tusks of a castrated boar never grow like those of the natural animal, but always have a dwarfed, stunted appearance.

If possible, this operation should be performed in the spring or autumn, as the temperature is then more equable, and care should be taken that the animal is in perfect health. Those which are fat and plethoric should be prepared by bleeding, cooling diet, and quiet. Pigs are castrated at all ages, from a fortnight to three, six, and eight weeks, and even four months old. There are various modes of performing the operation: we will begin by quoting those described by Professor Vatel :—Vatel's Eléments de Pathologie Vétérinaire.

"*Castration by simple division of the spermatic cord.*—If the pig is not more than six weeks old, an incision is made at the bottom of the scrotum, the testicle pushed out, and the cord cut without any precautionary means whatever. But when the animal is older, there is reason to fear that hemorrhage to a greater or less extent will supervene; consequently it will be advisable to pass a ligature round the cord a little above the spot where the division is intended to take place.

"*Castration by tearing the cord.*—Swine are thus operated on by some cutters :—An assistant holds the pig, pressing the back of the animal against his chest and belly, keeping the head elevated, and grasping all the four legs together ; or, which is the preferable way,

7

one assistant holds the animal against his chest, while another kneels down and secures the four legs. The operator then grasps the scrotum with his left hand, makes one horizontal incision across the base of it, opening both divisions of the bag at the same time. Then laying down his knife, he presses the testicles out with his finger and thumb, grasps them between his teeth and tears them out. He then closes the wound by pressing the edges gently together with his fingers; the tearing prevents all hemorrhage, and the wound speedily heals. This mode of operation is sometimes performed on animals two and three years old. Some break the spermatic cord without tearing it: they twist it, and then pull it gently and firmly until it gives way.

"*Castration by sawing or scraping.*—Here a portion of the base of the scrotum is cut off, the testicles forced out, and the cord sawn through by a somewhat serrated but blunt instrument. The hemorrhage, if any there be, is arrested by introducing ashes into the wound. The animal is then dismissed, and nothing further done with him. Fromage de Feagre has castrated many pigs of three or four months old by dividing the spermatic cord in this way. This mode of operating, however, should only be practised on very young animals.

"*Castration by ligature.*—Here a waxed cord is passed as tightly as possible round the scrotum above the epididymes, which completely stops the circulation, and in a few days the scrotum and testicles will drop off. This mode of operating should never be performed on pigs more than six weeks old, and the spermatic cord should always be first of all uncovered."

We cannot approve of the tearing or gnawing the testicle with the teeth; it is a disgusting practice, and inflicts unnecessary pain on the patient: the use of a blunt knife is far preferable, as this lacerates the part equally as much without so bruising it and rendering it painful; and it is the laceration only we require, in order to prevent the subsequent hemorrhage which would occur if the cord were simply severed with a sharp instrument.

The castration by ligature requires great nicety and skill, otherwise accidents will occur, and considerable pain and inflammation be caused. Too thick a cord, a knot not tied sufficiently tight, or a portion of the testicle included in the ligature, will prevent the success of the operation.

The most fatal consequence of castration is tetanus, induced by the shock communicated to the nervous system by the torture of the operation.

In spaying the sow the animal is laid upon its left side and firmly held by one or two assistants; an incision is then made into the flank, the fore-finger of the right hand introduced into it, and gently turned about until it encounters and hooks hold of the right ovary, which it draws through the opening; a ligature is then passed round this one, and the left ovary felt for in like manner. The operator then severs off these two ovaries, either by cutting or tearing, and returns the womb and its appurtenances to their proper position. This being done, he closes up the womb with two or three stitches, sometimes rubs a little oil over it, and releases his patient, and all generally goes on well; for the healing power of the pig is very great, as the following fact will testify.

Mr. Thomson, veterinary surgeon at Beith, N. B., was castrating a pig, and while cutting through the peritoneum, one of the assistants lost his hold, and the animal sprang up. The scalpel was plunged deep into the belly, entered one of the convolutions of the ileum, and divided one of the guts almost through, besides making a wound in the mesentery. Mr. Thomson sewed up the mesentery with a fine needle and thread, and restored it to its place, and secured the side with firm stitches—not, however, with much hope of seeing his patient recover. But, to his surprise, two days afterwards little appeared to be the matter, and in a short time the animal was well.

The after treatment is very simple. The animals should be well littered with clean litter, in styes weather-tight and thoroughly ventilated; their diet should be attended to; sour milk or whey, with barley-meal, is an excellent thing to give at these times; it is well to confine them for a few days, as they should be prevented from getting into cold water or mud until the wound is perfectly healed, and also from creeping through hedges or fences.

The best age for spaying a sow is about six weeks; indeed, as a general axiom, the younger the animal is castrated the better it gets over the operation, which is seldom attended by fatal results. Some persons, however, have two or three litters from their sows before they operate upon them; where this is the case, the consequences are more to be feared, as the parts have become more susceptible, and are consequently more liable to take on inflammation. Lisle says:—" Where this is done, it is best to spay a sow two or three days before her litter of pigs are weaned, because then, if harm follows the operation, the young ones will draw off the venom."

CATCHING AND HOLDING THE PIG.

Swine are very difficult animals to obtain any mastery over, or to operate on or examine. Seldom tame or easily handled, they are at such periods most unmanageable, kicking, screaming, and even biting fiercely. Hurtrel d'Arboval recommends the following means of getting hold of them:—" Fasten a double cord to the end of a stick, and beneath the stick let there be a running noose in this

cord ; tie a piece of bread to the cord and present it to the anima.,
and when he opens his mouth to seize the bait, catch the upper jaw
in the noose, run it tight, and the animal is fast."

Another means is to catch one foot in a running noose suspended
from some place, so as to draw the imprisoned foot off the ground ;
or to envelop the head of the animal in a cloth or sack.

But, so far as it can be, all coercion should be avoided, for the
pig is naturally so averse to being handled, that in his struggles he
will often do himself far more mischief than the disease we seek to
investigate or remedy would effect.

DRENCHING.

Here again the observations with which we closed the preceding
paragraph are applicable, for there are more instances than one on
record in which the pig has, in his struggles, ruptured some vessel
and died on the spot, or so injured himself as to bring on inflammation and subsequent death. Whenever it is possible, the medicine
should be mingled with a portion of food, and the animal thus cheated
or coaxed into taking it. Where this cannot be done, the following
is the best method :—

Let a man get the head of the animal firmly between his knees,
without, however, pinching it, while another secures the hinder parts.
Then let the first take hold of the pig's head from below, raise it a
little, and incline it slightly towards the right, at the same time
separating the lips on the left side so as to form a hole into which
the fluid may be gradually poured, not more being introduced into
the mouth at a time than can be swallowed at once. Should the
beast snort or choke, the head must be released for a few moments,
or he will be in danger of being strangled.

RINGING.

The operation of ringing is performed in order to counteract the
propensity swine have to dig and furrow up the earth. The ring is
passed through what appears to be a prolongation of the septum,
between the supplemental, or snout-bone, and the proper nasal. The
animal is thus unable to obtain sufficient purchase to use his snout
with any effect without causing the ring to press so painfully upon
the part that he is speedily compelled to desist. But the ring is
apt to break, or it wears out in process of time and has to be replaced. The operation is most painful, and the shrill squeaks of the
animal undergoing it cause it to be a perfect nuisance to the neigh
borhood.

John Lawrence gives the following directions concerning this operation: "The snouts of pigs should be perforated at weaning-time, after they shall have recovered from castration; and it will be necessary to renew the operation as they become of large growth. It is too generally neglected at first; but no pigs, young or old, should be suffered to roam at large unrung. It should be ascertained that the sow's rings are sufficiently strong previously to her taking the hog, on account of the risk of abortion from the operation being renewed while she is in pig. Care must be taken by the operator that he go not too close to the bone, and that the ring turns easily."

The far better mode of proceeding is, when the pig is young, to cut through the cartilaginous and ligamentous prolongations by which the supplementary bone is united to the proper nasals. The divided edges of the cartilage will never unite again, and the snout always remains powerless.

CHAPTER XI.

WE now approach one of the most difficult and important divisions of our subject—breeding.

The object of the farmer or breeder is to produce and retain such an animal as will be best adapted to the purpose he has in view, be that the consumption of certain matters which could not be otherwise so well disposed of; the converting into hams, bacon and pork; or the raising of sucking-pigs and porkers for the market. Almost all farmers, nay, we might almost say, every cottager who has a bit of ground, keep one or more pigs to devour the offal and refuse which would otherwise be wasted; and the farmer finds a sufficiency for their keep, while the cottager begs wash and other matters, or turns the beast out into the lanes to forage for himself. But this is a matter totally distinct from "breeding swine." In the former case the animal or animals are purchased young, for a small price (each person buying as many as he considers he shall have food enough for,) and then sold to the butcher when in proper condition to be killed; and thus a certain degree of profit is realised. In the latter many contingencies must be taken into calculation, viz., the available means of feeding them; whether or not that food might be more profitably disposed of; the facilities afforded by railways, by the vicinity of towns, or large markets, &c. for disposing of them. And the rapid growth of railways is now affording these facilities to all parts of the United Kingdom. Formerly the inhabitants of remote localities had no means of conveying their swine to a favorable market except the tedious one of driving them, or the expensive one of conveying them in carts.

Agricultural writers seem to be very much divided in their opinions as to the relative advantages of breeding or buying, but all allow that the keeping of swine is one of the most profitable parts of the business of a farm. Whoever determines upon breeding must make up his mind in the first place what is the shape and what the qualities he wishes to obtain, and then steadily bear this in mind as he pursues his object; not with wavering caprice, now selecting a cross of one sort, now one of another, but adhering to a system well laid down, and then he will find his efforts attended with success. The great *desideratum* in almost all establishments is an animal that will grow rapidly, and attain to the earliest maturity and greatest weight in the shortest period, and on the smallest and most economical amount of food.

It is a generally admitted fact in the principles of breeding, that the offspring usually inherit the bodily and constitutional qualities of one or both parents; and in swine it is the boar whose qualities chiefly predominate in the offspring; hence it will be necessary most carefully to select the male animal. Thäer, in his admirable work, says:—

CHOICE OF THE BOAR AND SOW.

"In the breeding of swine, as much as in that of any other live stock, it is important to pay great attention not only to the breed, but also to the choice of individuals. The sow should produce a great number of young ones, and she must be well fed to enable her to support them. Some sows bring forth ten, twelve or even fifteen pigs at a birth, but eight or nine is the usual number, and sows which produce fewer than this must be rejected. It is, however, probable that fecundity depends also on the boar; he should therefore be chosen from a race which multiplies quickly.

"Good one-year bacon-hogs being much in request, we must do all we can to obtain a breed well adapted for producing them. Swine of such a breed may be known by their long bodies, low bellies, and short legs. Long pendulous ears are usually coupled with these qualities, and attract purchasers. If, however, as is often advisable in large dairies and cheese factories, hogs are to be sold at all seasons to the butchers, great attention must be paid to quickness of growth and facility of gaining flesh, so that the animals may attain their full growth and be ready for killing before they are a year old. This quality is particularly prominent in the Chinese and African breeds; but among our ordinary varieties, hogs are often met with which are better adapted for this purpose than for producing large quantities of bacon and lard.

" The boar should be selected from a breed well suited to these several purposes; he must be sound and free from hereditary blemishes; and should be kept separate from the sows till he is about a year old, and has finished his growth, or he will begin to leap too early. He is usually castrated before completing his third year, otherwise his flesh becomes uneatable. If, however, he is of a peculiarly excellent breed, one which cannot be easily replaced, his flesh may be sacrificed for the sake of preserving him for breeding from a few years longer.

"A boar left on the pasture at liberty, with the sows, might suffice for thirty or forty of them; but as he is usually shut up, and allowed to leap at stated times only, so that the young ones may be born nearly at the same time, it is usual to keep one boar for ten or twelve sows. Full-grown boars being often savage, and diffi cult to tame, and attacking men and animals, must be deprived of their tusks.

" The sow must be chosen from a breed of proper size and shape, sound and free from blemishes and defects. She should have at least twelve teats; for it is observed that each pig selects a teat for himself and keeps to it, so that a pig not having one belonging to him would be starved. A good sow should produce a great number of pigs, all of equal vigor. She must be very careful of them, and not crush them by her weight; above all, she must not be addicted to eating the after-birth, and what may often follow, her own young ones. If a sow is tainted with these bad habits, or if she has diffi cult labors, or brings forth dead pigs, she must be castrated forth with. It is therefore proper to bring up several young sows at once, so as to keep those only which are free from defects. Breeding sows and boars should never be raised from defective animals."

According to Varro and Columella, the ancients considered the distinguishing marks of a good boar to be—a small head, short legs, a long body, large thighs and neck, and this latter part thickly covered with strong erect bristles.

Our most experienced breeders prefer an animal with a long cylindrical body, small bones, well-developed muscles, a wide chest— which denotes strength of constitution, a broad straight back, short head and fine snout, brilliant eyes, a short thick neck, broad well-developed shoulders, a loose mellow skin, fine bright long hair, and few bristles, and small legs and hoofs. Some give the preference to long flapping ears; this is the case especially in several of our western counties, but experience seems to demonstrate that those animals are best which have short, fine, erect ears. The boar should always be vigorous and masculine in appearance.

That quaint old writer Lisle in his " Husbandrie," gives the following advice on this subject—advice more suited to swine " as they were," than to the improved breeds which are now so generally replacing the heavy old races, but still worthy of some degree of attention :—

·" In all kinds of four-footed beasts, the shape and form of the male is chosen with great care, because the progeny is frequently more like the father than the mother ; wherefore, in swine-cattle also, certain of them must be approved, which are choice and singular for the largeness of their whole body, and such as are rather square (than those that are long and round), with a hanging-down belly, vast buttocks, but not so long legs and hoofs, of a large and glandulous neck, with short snouts, and turned upwards; and especially, which is more to the purpose, the males must be exceedingly salacious, and such as are proper for gendering from the age of one year till they come to their fourth year ; nevertheless, they can also impregnate the female when they are six months old. Sows of the longest size and make are approved, provided they be, in the rest of their members, like the boars which have been already described.

" If the country is cold, and liable to hoar-frost, the herd must be chosen of an exceeding hard, thick, and black bristle. If it be temperate, and lie exposed to the sun, the cattle that is smooth and has no bristles, or even that which is white, and proper for the mill and the bakehouse, may be fed."

But although the chief care must be bestowed on the selection of the male animal, we must not be led to imagine that the female may be chosen at random. One of good form and breed, free from constitutional defects, and from disease of any kind; not addicted to vice, and especially not to feeding on flesh or carrion, or destroying rabbits, or poultry, should be chosen. Also those which produce the finest and most numerous progeny should be kept for breeding, especially if at the same time they are good nurses ; and the comparatively barren animals spayed and fattened. Sows that have very low bellies almost touching the ground, seldom produce large or fine litters. A good-sized sow is generally considered more likely to prove a good breeder and nurse, and to farrow more easily and safely, than a small delicate animal. Few of our domesticated animals suffer so much from being bred in-and-in as swine. Where this system is pursued, the number of young ones is decreased at every litter, until the sows become, in a manner, barren. As soon as the slightest tendency to this degeneracy is observed, the breed should be crossed from time to time, keeping sight, however, while so doing, of the aim in view. The Chinese and Siamese pigs will generally be found to be the best which can be used for this purpose, as a single, and even two crosses, with one of these animals, will seldom do harm, but often effect considerable improvement. The best formed of the progeny resulting from this cross must be selected as breeders, and with them the old original stock crossed back again.

"Selection, with judicious and cautious admixture, is the true secret of forming and improving the breed," says an old and well-established axiom; and so it is. Repeated and indiscriminate crosses are as injurious as an obstinate adherence to one particular breed, and as much to be avoided; and of this most persons seem to be fully aware, for a systematic alteration is extending itself throughout all our English breeds of swine; the large, heavy, coarse breeds are almost extinct, and a smaller race of animals—more apt to fatten, less expensive to keep, attaining earlier to maturity, and furnishing a far more delicious and delicate meat—have taken their place.

It would be useless to point out certain breeds as being the most profitable or advantageous, so much depends upon the object for which the animals are raised; and besides, each breeder of any experience has in general his own pet stock breed, frequently one that has been "made," if we may be allowed the expression, by himself or his progenitors. This will be found to be the case in all great pig-breeding localities, and it frequently happens that the actual stock from which some of the present choicest races of swine sprang cannot be traced farther back than some ancestor or ancestress celebrated for the number of prizes he or she, or their immediate descendants, have won. At least we have found this to be the case in almost every instance in which we have endeavored to arrive at a knowledge of the actual parent stock of some of the most perfect and valuable animals we have met with or heard of. The Berkshire, the Improved Essex, and the New Suffolk and Bedfordshire breeds may, however, with the Chinese and Neapolitan, be instanced as the best stocks from which to raise a small-boned, thriving, profitable race, adapted for almost every purpose.

A sow is capable of conceiving at the age of from seven to ten months, but it is always better not to let her commence breeding too early, as it tends to weaken her when she does. From ten to twelve months old will be about the best age. Thäer says, "Sows are almost always in heat until they have received the boar; this state commences even as early as at the age of four or five months, but they are usually a year old before they are allowed to be put to the boar."

The boar should be at least a twelvemonth old before he is employed for the purpose of propagating his species, and during that time should have been well and regularly fed and exercised. On

7*

boar may be allowed to serve from six to ten sows, but on no account more. The best plan is to shut up the boar and sow in a sty together; for when turned in among several females, he is apt to "ride" them so often, that he exhausts himself without effect.

The period of gestation averages from seventeen to twenty weeks, according to the age, constitution, &c., of the mother; young or weakly sows farrow earlier than those of more mature age or stronger constitutions. It is commonly asserted that three months, three weeks, and three days, is the period of gestation; but, from M. Tessier's observations on twenty-five sows, it appears that it varies from 109 to 123 days.

A good breeding sow will produce two if not three litters in a year, but two should be the outside number; for where she is suffered to have more, the pigs are not so fine or so many in number, nor can she suckle them so well. How many years they would continue to breed is scarcely known, as it is generally considered to be most advantageous to spay them in their second, or at any rate early in their third year, and then fatten them for the butcher, especially where there is always a stock of young sows to replace them; for after the just-mentioned period the litters are seldom so fine, and the animal herself deteriorates in value. Some breeders, indeed, only suffer a young sow to have one litter, and then immediately spay and fatten her, as the bacon is then supposed to be equally as good as that of an animal spayed in the very onset. This is mainly a question of choice or economy. An agricultural author of some repute states that "a sow is fit for pigging up to her seventh year, and many will continue to be so even longer. The more prolific, however, the animal is, the sooner does she grow old and her fruitfulness decay."

But they doubtless would go on farrowing for many years, for there are instances on record of sows that have produced as many as eight or ten pigs at a litter when in their eighth and tenth years. Selbourne, in his "Natural History," gives an account of a half-bred bantam sow, kept by a friend of his, more from curiosity than with any view to profit, "who was as thick as she was long, and whose belly swept on the ground, till she was advanced to her seventeenth year; at which period she showed some tokens of age by the decay of her teeth and the decline of her fertility.

"For about ten years this prolific mother produced two litters in the year, of about ten at a time, and once above twenty at a litter; but, as there were near double the number of pigs to that of teats, many died. From long experience in the world, this female was grown very sagacious and artful. When she found occasion to converse with a boar, she used to open all the intervening gates, and march, by herself, up to a distant farm where one was kept, and, when her purpose was served, would return by the same means

At the age of about fifteen, her litters began to be reduced to four or five; and such a litter she exhibited when in her fatting-pen. She proved, when fat, good bacon, juicy and tender; the rind or sward was remarkably thin. At a moderate computation she was allowed to have been the fruitful parent of three hundred pigs—a prodigious instance of fecundity in so large a quadruped. She was killed in the spring of 1775."

Although we should by no means advise the keeping of an animal to such an age, still, notwithstanding that it is the fashion or custom to do otherwise, we would advise every breeder never to part with a sow while she continues to bring forth a numerous and fine progeny, which many will do for years, and to be a good nurse; and in general these animals become better nurses the oftener they farrow: her value he knows; the value of the young animal that he intends should succeed her, has yet to be tested; and if one of the two must be fattened for the butcher, we should decidedly recommend that it were the untried one. Varro states that we may judge of the fruitfulness of a sow from her first litter, the subsequent ones being generally all of about the same number.

A sow that brings forth less than eight pigs at a birth the third or fourth time she farrows is worth little as a breeder, the sooner she is fattened the better; but a young sow that produces a great number at her first farrowing cannot be too highly valued.

Whenever it is practicable, it should always be so arranged that the animals shall farrow early in the spring, and at the latter end of the summer or quite the beginning of the autumn. In the former case the young pigs will have the run of the early pastures, which will be a benefit to them and a saving to their owners; and there will also be more whey, milk, and other dairy produce which can be spared for them by the time they are ready to be weaned. And in the second case there will be sufficient time for the young to have grown and acquired strength before the cold weather comes on, which is always very injurious to sucking pigs.

Martin says: "None of the *pachydermata* are, as a general rule, remarkable for fertility. The elephant, the rhinoceros, the hippopotamus, &c., appear to produce only a single offspring at a birth, and that after a long period of gestation; for example, the gestation of the elephant is said to extend to twenty months and eighteen days. It is then not until after a considerable lapse of time that she again becomes pregnant, and she produces only a single young one. The hog-like peccaries produce, according to Azara, only two at a birth. To this rule the swine is an exception; it may be that the wild species are less prolific than the ordinary domestic variety of the genus *sus*, yet they are fertile, but in the ordinary hog this fertility is at a maximum. Ordinarily, a healthy sow produces eight, ten, or twelve young ones twice a year. The period of gestation is some-

what variable: Cuvier says, " quatre mois;" others give it as three
months. three weeks, and three days; that is, 108 days.   According
to Mr. Tessier, out of fifteen sows, one littered in 109 days, and one in
123 days, the latitude being fourteen days; according to others, the
range of gestation extends from seventeen weeks, or 119 days, to
twenty weeks, or 140 days.   According to Desmarest, the wild
sow goes with young four months and a few days, and produces from
three to nine at a birth, suckling them from three to four months.
It would appear, then, from these observations, that the period of
gestation in the domestic sow varies according to age, constitution,
food, and the peculiarities or idiosyncrasies of the peculiar breed.
Young and weakly sows not only produce fewer pigs, but farrow ear
lier than those of more mature age and sounder constitution; and
moreover, as might be expected, their offspring are deficient in vigor,
often indeed puny and feeble.   Here, having trenched upon the subject, we may advert to the principles upon which the breeding of
swine should be conducted.   Two great objects are in view, fertility
and early fattening.   With respect to fertility, we rather advocate
moderation than excess, both on account of the strength and
health of the mother, and the improvement of her progeny from
a full supply of nutriment.   How long a sow should be kept for
breeding depends on circumstances; generally speaking, however,
after three or four years the most fruitful sows, exhausted in their
reproductive energies, evince a great falling off both in the number
and vigor of their young.   There are, however, exceptions.   .   .   .
.   .   .   . Generally speaking, it is most advantageous to allow the
sow to breed only two or three years, and her successors being ready,
to fatten her off for the knife.

"A leading principle in breeding this animal,—and it applies equally
to the horse, the sheep, the ox, the dog,—is to make a cautious selection of the male by whom the female is destined to conceive her
first progeny, for that male stamps a character upon every subsequent produce (whether for good or bad) by other males; 'the subsequent progeny of the mother will always partake more or less of
the character of the father of the first offspring.'   This law is mysterious, but it has been abundantly proved (See Giles, in *Philoso-
phical Transactions* for 1821,) and need not be here further insisted
on; the fact is established.   The selection of the male, then, is of
primary importance; of whatever breed he may be, he should be
as perfect as possible in the good qualities of his race; he should be
free from all blemishes, and be, moreover, the offspring of parents
in all points unexceptionable.   A young boar intended for breeding
from, should be kept separate from the sows until about a year old,
when his physical energies will be fairly developed.   Form is of
more importance than size; in this latter respect the breeds differ,
as they do also in the size of the ears, which in some breeds are

flapping, especially in those which incline to the old stock. Good pigs, it is true, may show such ears, but small sharp erect ears accompany what may be called *blood*. In a well-formed boar the barrels should be rather long and cylindrical, the limbs should be small in the bone, the hoofs neat and compact, the skin should be rather loose and mellow, with the bristles fine but scanty ; the snout should be short and sharp, the forehead rise boldly between the ears and merge into an arched neck ; the back should be straight and broad ; the hams rounded and ample ; the chest should be wide, indicative of the amplitude and vigor of the vital organs. The tail should be slender, the eyes should be lively, the temper or disposition cheerful, without moroseness. As to color, some breeds are black, others are white ; but we think black pigs are thinner in the skin, and are moreover less subject to cutaneous affections.

" Equal care should be taken in the selection of a breeding sow as of a boar ; she should be of good stature and form, sound, healthy, and free from defects ; she should have twelve teats at least ; for, as may be observed, each little pig selects its own teat, and keeps to it, so that a pig not having one belonging to it would in all probability be starved. A sow not pregnant, whose belly hangs low, almost touching the ground, seldom produces large litters or fine pigs ; the pendulous condition of the abdomen is the result of weakness and relaxation from ill-feeding and ill-breeding, neglect, with other causes, and is generally accompanied with flat sides, a long snout, and a raw-boned, unthrifty carcass, yielding coarse meat, which will not repay the outlay of feeding.

" Early breeding not only weakens the sow, but, as her physical powers are not yet fully developed, results in the production of undersized weakly pigs, and perhaps incomplete as to number ; and these, perhaps, she will scarcely be able to nourish. A young sow of good stock, who produces a large litter at her first parturition of pigs, all of equal size, and proves a good nurse, is valuable ; she promises well, for her first litter may be taken as an example of those to succeed. As long as such a sow continues to return to the breeder such litters twice a year, he will do well to keep her, more' especially, if he finds upon trial that her progeny fatten kindly, whether as porkers or bacon hogs. Some persons, after obtaining one or two litters from a sow, have her spayed, and then fattened off as quickly as possible for bacon. Some keep to their second or even third year of breeding ; but if the last litter was good, and the sow continues vigorous, it becomes a question how far it may not be more advantageous to keep her still longer, even until the diminished number of pigs produced indicates a decline in fruitfulness.

"Cold sleety weather, with keen winds, is very detrimental to young pigs, and not favorable to their mother ; hence, early in the spring, and late in the summer or early in the autumn, are the best periods of the year for the production of the litter. In the spring, the fields and paddocks offer fresh grass and various vegetables, and a run upon the pastures will be not only a saving to the farmer, but of benefit to the young pigs; besides which, at this season of the year, whey and buttermilk are abundant, and so continue to be during the greater part of summer. An autumnal litter, again, will have sufficient time to grow and acquire strength before the severities of mid-winter; besides, the refuse of the potato crop, and the carrot beds, of the garden generally, and of the mill, is now at hand in abundance.

"A breeding sow should never be overfed; not that she should be starved—on the contrary, she should be kept by a judicious allowance of food, in good condition and perfect health, but not fat. A sow when fat is not likely to be fertile, and, moreover, her parturition is sure to be more difficult and dangerous, and her milk in insufficient quantity, perhaps even of inferior quality, while her unwieldiness renders her more liable to overlay her young. When with pig she should have a commodious and clean sty to herself, and be supplied with sufficient straw to render her comfortable. She should be sufficiently fed, and all her wants supplied. All sources of irritation or annoyance should be avoided, and especially as the time of parturition approaches. From these causes—sometimes, perhaps, from craving hunger—a sow will devour her young; it is said also, that if she be allowed to devour the after-birth, a morbid appetite, leading her to fall upon her litter, will be engendered. For these reasons the sow should be carefully watched and fed, especially if the parturition be her first; and not for these reasons only, but lest her parturition should prove dangerous or in any way difficult.

"On no account should two pregnant sows be placed in one sty, however commodious. They will assault each other, and at last, perhaps, destroy each other's young.

"'Selection, with judicious and cautious admixture, is the true secret of forming a breed.' It is thus that all our improved breeds of domestic animals have been produced, those of the hog not excepted. Hence the old, coarse, large-boned swine have now almost disappeared, and given place to small-boned breeds, apt to fatten, mature at an earlier age, affording more delicate meat, less expensive to keep, and, therefore, altogether more profitable breeds. Such are rapidly extending themselves, and improvements are going on. Many landed proprietors pride themselves on the possession of a particular breed of their own establishment, and remarkable for good qualities of every kind. In the establishment of such a stock, indiscriminate selection, and a repetition of crosses, with no definite object, must be avoided; while, at the same time, a pertinacious adherence to the plan of breeding in and in from the same stock, however excellent, will ultimately result in its degeneracy. Com paratively speaking, it is only within a few years that the improved breeds of pigs have risen up to reward the skill of the breeder. The Chinese or Siamese, the Neapolitan, and the African varieties have greatly contributed to their creation, and continue to modify those in which a farther cross is desirable. After one or two crosses, the best progeny is generally selected to inter-breed again with the original stock, and thus is its improvement effected. Among the numerous admirable breeds which now exist, it would be difficult to say which has the superiority, or which it is most profitable and advantageous to rear. As in the case of cattle and sheep, much depends on contingent circumstances, on locality, and the kind of food most readily obtainable. No doubt each breeder prefers his own strain. Berkshire and Essex boast of their respective races; Yorkshire, Suffolk, Sussex, and Bedfordshire put in their claims for praise."

"The following rules for the selection of the best stock of hogs will apply to all breeds:—

"*Fertility.*—The strain from which the farmer or breeder selects ought to be noted for fertility. In a breeding sow this quality is essential, and it is one which is inherited. The same observation applies to other domestic animals. But besides this, she should be a careful mother, and with a sufficient number of dugs for a family of twelve at a single litter. A young untried sow will generally display in her tendencies those which have predominated in the race from which she has descended, and the number of teats can be counted. Both boar and sow should be sound, healthy, and in fair but not over fat condition, and the former should be from a stock in which fertility is a characteristic.

"*Form.*—It may be that the farmer has a breed which he wishes to perpetuate; it is highly improved, and he sees no reason for immediate crossing. But, on the other hand, he may have an excellent breed, with certain defects, as too long in the limb, or too heavy in the bone. Here, we should say, the sire to be chosen, whether of a pure or cross breed, should exhibit the opposite qualities, even to an extreme, and be, withal, one of a strain noted for early and rapid fattening.

"But what is meant by *form*, as applied to a pig? A development of those points connected with the profit of the owner. In these points high or low blood is demonstrated. The head should be small, high at the forehead, short and sharp in the snout, with eyes animated and lively, and thin, sharp, upright ears; the jowl, or cheek, should be deep and full; the neck should be thick and deep, arch gracefully from the back of the head, and merge gradually into a broad breast; the shoulders should be set well apart at the clavicular joint; the body should be deep, round, well-barrelled, with an ample chest, broad loins, and a straight, flat, broad back; the tail should be slender; the hams should be round, full and well deve. loped; the limbs, fine-boned, with clean small joints; and with small compact hoofs, set closely together, with a straight bearing upon the ground. If in perfect health, young store hogs, or young stock selected for breeding, will be lively, animated, hold up the head, and move freely and nimbly.

"*Bristles.*—These should be fine and scanty, so as to show the skin smooth and glossy; coarse, wiry, rough bristles usually accompany heavy bones, large spreading hoofs, and flapping ears, and thus become one of the indications of a thick skinned and low breed.

" *Color.*—Different breeds of high excellence have their own colors: white, black, parti-coloured, black and white, sandy, mottled with large marks of black, are the most prevalent. A black skin, with short scanty bristles, and small stature, demonstrate the prevalence of the Neapolitan strain, or the black Chinese, or perhaps an admixture of both. Many prefer white; and in sucking pigs destined for the table, and for porkers, this color has its advantages, and the skin looks more attractive; nevertheless, we think that the skin of black hogs is in general thinner than that of white hogs, and less subject to eruptive diseases."—MARTIN.

TREATMENT OF SOWS DURING PREGNANCY.

Sows with pig should be well and judiciously fed; that is to say, they should have a sufficiency of wholesome nutritious food to maintain their strength and keep them in good condition, but should by no means be allowed to get fat, as when they are in high condition the dangers of parturition are enhanced, the animal is more awkward and liable to smother or crush her young, and besides, never has as much or as good milk as a leaner sow. She should also have a separate sty: for swine are prone to lie so close together, that if she were amongst others her young would be in great danger; and this sty should be perfectly clean and comfortably littered, but not so thickly as to admit of the young being able to bury themselves in the straw.

As the time of her farrowing approaches she should be well supplied with food, especially if she be a young sow, and this is her first litter, and also carefully watched in order to prevent her from devouring the after-birth, and thus engendering a morbid appetite which will next lead her to fall upon her own young. A sow that has once done this is never afterwards to be depended upon. Hunger, thirst, or irritation of any kind. will often induce this unnatural conduct; and this is another reason why a sow about to farrow should have a sty to herself, and be carefully attended to, and have all her wants supplied.

ABORTION.

This accident is by no means of so common occurrence in the sow as in many of our other domesticated animals. There are various causes which will tend to produce it; insufficiency of food, eating too much succulent vegetable food, or unwholesome unsubstantial diet; blows and falls will also induce it; and one very prevalent cause arises from this animal's habit of rubbing itself against hard bodies in order to allay the irritation produced by the vermin or cutaneous eruptions to which swine are subject.

Reiterated copulation does not appear to produce abortion in the sow, at least to the extent it does in other animals.

The symptoms indicative of approaching abortion are similar to those of parturition, only more intense. There is generally restlessness, irritation, and shiverings: and the cries of the animal testify the presence of severe labor-pains. Sometimes the rectum, vagina, or uterus becomes relaxed, and one or the other protrudes, and often becomes inverted at the moment of the expulsion of the fœtus, preceded by the placenta, which presents itself foremost.

Nothing can be done to prevent abortion at the last hour; all that we can do is, from the first to remove every predisposing cause. The treatment will depend upon circumstances. Where the animal is young, vigorous, and in high condition, bleeding will be beneficial, not a copious blood-letting, but small quantities taken at different times; purgatives may also be administered. If, when abortion has taken place, the whole of the litter are not born, emollient injections may be resorted to with considerable benefit; otherwise the after treatment should be much the same as in parturition, and the animal should be kept warm, and quiet, and clean, and allowed a certain degree of liberty.

Whenever one sow has aborted, the breeder should immediately look about for the causes likely to have induced this accident, and endeavor, by removing them, to secure the rest of the inhabitants of his piggery from a similar fate.

In cases of abortion, the fœtus is seldom born alive, and often has been dead for some days; where this is the case—and whether it is so or not will be easily detected by a peculiarly unpleasant putrid exhalation, and the discharge of a fetid liquid from the vagina—the parts should be washed with a diluted solution of chloride of lime, in the proportions of one part chloride to three parts water, and a portion of this lotion may be gently injected into the uterus if the animal will submit to the doing so. Mild doses of Epsom salts, tincture of gentian, and ginger will also act beneficially in such cases, and with attention to diet, soon restore the animal.

PARTURITION.

The approach of the period of farrowing is marked by the immense size of the belly, by a depression of the back, and by the distension of the teats. The animal gives evident symptoms of acute suffering, and wanders restlessly about, collecting straw, and carrying it to her sty, grunting piteously the while.

As soon as this is observed, she should be enticed into a separate sty and carefully watched. On no account should several sows be permitted to farrow in the same place, as they will inevitably irritate each other, and devour their own or one another's young.

The young ones should be taken away as soon as they are born, and deposited in a warm spot, for the sow being a clumsy animal, is not unlikely, in her struggles, to overlay them; nor should they be returned to her until all is over, and the afterbirth has been removed, which should always be done the moment it passes from her; for young sows, especially, will invariably devour the afterbirth if permitted, and then, the young being wet with a similar fluid and smelling the same, will eat them one after another. Some persons advise washing the backs of the young pigs with a decoction of aloes, colocynth, or some other nauseous substance, as a remedy for this; but the simplest and easiest one is to remove the little ones until all is over and the mother begins to recover herself and seeks about for them, on which they should be put near her.

It has been frequently observed that each little pig has its own peculiar teat, and will not willingly suck from any other; therefore, as the front teats yield most milk, the smallest pigs should be placed to them. If more young are farrowed than the mother has teats, the most weakly-looking must be destroyed, unless it should so happen that there is another sow at hand which has fewer pigs than teats, in which case they may be put to her, if this can be done without her knowledge; though some writers affirm that a sow will give her teats indifferently to her own offspring or to that of a stranger.

It does not, however, always happen that the parturition is effected with such ease. Cases of false presentation, of enlarged fœtus, of debility in the mother, often render it difficult and dangerous. The womb will occasionally become protruded and inverted in consequence of the forcing pains of difficult parturition, and even the bladder has been known to come away. These parts must be returned as soon as may be; and if the womb has come in contact with the dung or litter and acquired any dirt, it must be first washed in luke-warm water, and then returned and confined in its place by means of a suture passed through the lips of the orifice. Some foreign veterinarians place a pessary high up the vagina, and secure it in its situation by means of an iron ring or wire; but this is a complicated operation, and could not be performed without great difficulty on so obstinate an animal. The easiest and perhaps the best way is not to return the protruded parts at all, but merely tie a ligature around them and leave them to slough off, which they will do in the course of a few days, without effusion of blood or further injury to the animal. No sow that has once suffered from protrusion of the womb should be allowed to breed again.

Mr. Ramsden, of Ripon, gives the following account of a case of difficult parturition :—

"About the middle of August, 1840, I was called in and requested to assist a sow that was in labor, could not rise, and seemed to be in great suffering. I relieved her of one, gave her some gruel, and hoped that she would be able to effect the parturition of the remaining ones without aid.

" On my return she was perfectly senseless. The young pig was endeavoring to suck. The parturition had not in the least degree advanced. I pressed with my left hand over the diaphragm, which recalled in a slight degree the pains, and empounded my right hand gradually. I then drew out a second pig; it lay about four inches anterior to the pelvis. The stupor of the mother was a little removed, and at length I got the whole litter of ten pigs, and also the placental membrane. This was the first case of the kind that ever came under my notice."—*The Veterinarian,* vol. xiv.

Another and still more interesting case is given by Mr. Cartwright, veterinary surgeon :—

" On the 11th of July, 1839, I was requested to attend a sow, the property of a farmer near this town. The poor animal had been in labor six days. During the last three days she was not able to stand, nor had she taken any food, and her death was expected every hour. She was a very fat animal, and the owner informed me that she was about ten days past her time of pigging, and that he was confident the pigs were dead. I was of the same opinion; and, after a minute examination, felt confident that nothing short of the Cæsarean operation could save her; at the same time informing the owner that she might die in consequence of, or during, the operation.

" The operation was consented to; and I proceeded first to secure her legs, and to have them firmly extended their full length, and retained there by assistants. I next placed a bundle of straw underneath her, which gave the belly a round and prominent position, rendering it more tense and firm, and at the same time giving me considerable advantage in operating.

" My first proceeding was to clear away the hair in the direction of my intended incision, in which I, at the onset, had made up my mind to follow the theory taught in operative surgery, viz. always to make the incisions in the same direction as the muscular fibres, and, above all, never to sever a muscle if it could be avoided. The hair being removed, I was about to make the incisions lengthways, in the course of the linea alba, when it suddenly occurred to me that I should not, in this case, be able to keep the lips of the wound approximated by sutures or bandages, on account of the depending state of the abdomen and its contents.   I therefore determined to make the incisions more on the side, and across the oblique externus abdominis.   I accordingly cut freely through the integuments for about eight inches in length, which I accomplished with a common scalpel.   Next I penetrated through the adipose or fatty matter underneath, of which there was no lack ; and then cut down on the muscle, at the superior part of the incision, quite through, and exposing the peritoneum.   I now introduced my forefingers as directors, and with the curved bistoury laid the abdomen freely open.

" The lips of the incision or wound of course receded from each other to a great distance, and a slight arterial hemorrhage ensued, which I thought proceeded from the circumflex artery of the ileum. If the incision had been made longitudinally, this might have been prevented, but as the hemorrhage soon ceased, it was of little consequence.   The intestines were much inflated with gas, and protruded as far as the wound of the peritoneum extended.

" I now introduced my right hand, and distinctly felt the situation of the uterus, when the animal made a desperate struggle, and some of the small intestines escaped.   I found it necessary for an assistant to introduce his hand, to prevent a repetition of this.   The bladder was distended with urine, which proved somewhat troublesome, and I had no catheter at hand.   I was now about to make a second attempt to open the uterus, when I accidently felt the pulsation of a large artery.   Had I divided the uterus in the same direction as the incision in the abdomen I should have cut the artery. Was it the uterine or vaginal artery ?   I placed my hand inferior to the vessel, and felt a young one.   Next, with a scalpel in my right hand, guarded at the point with my forefinger, fearing that the sow might struggle and the instrument wound some of the intestines, I cut through the uterus, introduced my finger guarding the scalpel, and effected an opening into it about six inches in length.   I then introduced my hand, laid hold of one of the fœtal pigs, and drew it out.   In this way I proceeded until I removed the whole number, which amounted to seven.

"The operation being thus far completed, her legs were drawn towards each other, which brought the lips of the wound into approximation, and I retained them there by strong adhesive plasters, over which I placed a roller passing three times round her body.   I now proceeded to examine my patient : she was, as might be expected, in a very weak state ; and when her head was raised, it fell again upon my hand as if she was dead.   As she lay in this exhausted state, not a muscle except the involuntary ones moving, I gave her a little brandy and water, and then closed the door and left her. The general opinion of the by-standers was, that in a few minutes she would be dead: this was about 4 p. m. Indispensable business prevented me from seeing her until 10 o'clock, when I was glad to find my patient somewhat revived. I gave more brandy and beef-tea, and left her for the night.

"At 6 a. m. there was a decided improvement; the extremities were warm, the respiration tranquil, with an occasional grunt and pricking or moving of the ears; some fæces had passed during the night. I doubted whether the bladder had been emptied, and therefore introduced a small catheter which I use for sheep, &c., and took away a great quantity of water. I ordered more weak brandy and water and broth.

"At 6 p. m. the symptoms were improving, excepting that the side surrounding the incision was a little swelled; I therefore ordered fomentations to be applied, using hot cloths, with but little water.

" 18th.—Doing well; the secretions regular; and she for the first time voluntarily took a little milk, with a drachm of brandy, of which she appeared fond. From this time she continued to improve daily; and on the fifth day from the operation she was able to stand, and fed well. The roller round her body was not removed for a month, and the plaster remained for nearly three months. When it came away the wound was beautifully healed. This animal has attracted considerable attention in the neighborhood, and she is now as fat as she can be, and a fine specimen of the short-eared breed."

MONSTROSITIES.

Monstrosities are often farrowed by swine. It would be difficult to assign any cause for this, did we admit, with most persons, that these are peculiarly stupid and unimaginative animals; but as in Chapter III. we have already declared our opinion to be a contrary one, the inexplicability of the matter is done away with.

Mr. Ellis, V. S., of Liverpool, gives an account of six sows belonging to one person which all produced blind young ones, the greater part of which were without the least semblance of an eye, the orbit being quite empty. Some of them had four ears each. Only four out of the whole lot lived; they were either brought forth dead or died immediately after birth.

One of the sows could not farrow any of her young ones, they being three times the proper size, and in a state of decomposition. The Cæsarean operation was therefore performed, as the only means of saving her; but it had been delayed too long; she only lived three hours after it.

These pigs were all got by one boar, but the sows were of different breeds.

More depends upon this than many persons seem to have the least
idea of, both as regards the mother and the young; and many a fine
sow and promising litter have been ruined for want of proper and
judicious care at this period.

Immediately after farrowing, many sows are apt to be feverish;
where this is the case, a light and sparing diet only should be given
them for the first day or two, as gruel, oatmeal-porridge, whey, and
such-like. Others, again, are very much debilitated, and require
strengthening; for them strong soup, bread steeped in wine or in a
mixture of brandy and sweet spirits of nitre, administered in small
quantities, will often prove highly beneficial.

Gradually the rations must be increased and given more frequently; and they must be composed of wholesome, nutritious, and
succulent matters. All kinds of roots—carrots, turnips, potatoes,
and beet-root—well steamed or boiled, may be given, but never raw;
bran, barley and oatmeal, bean-flower, Indian corn, whey, sour, skim,
and butter-milk, all are perfectly well adapted for this period; and,
should the animal appear to require it, grain well bruised and macerated may also be added. Bean-flour is considered by many persons
to create an abundance of milk; and there are many who deem
barleymeal too stimulating, and advise that it should never be used
alone, but always one-third oatmeal to two-thirds of the barleymeal.
Whenever it is possible, the sow should be turned out for an hour
each day, to graze in a meadow or clover-field, as the fresh air and
exercise and herbage, will do her an infinity of good. The young
pigs must be shut up for the first ten days or a fortnight, after which
they will be old enough to follow her and take their share of the
benefit.

The rations should be given regularly at certain hours; small and
often-repeated meals are far preferable to large ones, for indigestion or any disarrangement of the functions of the stomach vitiates
the milk, and produces diarrhœa and other similar affections in the
young.

The mother should always be well, but not over-fed; the better
and more carefully she is fed, the more abundant and nutritious will
her milk be, the better will the sucking-pigs thrive, and the less will
she be pulled down by suckling them.

When a sow is weakly, and has not a sufficiency of milk, the
young pigs must be taught to feed as early as possible. A kind of
gruel, made with skim-milk and bran, or oatmeal, will be the best
thing for this purpose; or a soup composed of potatoes, boiled, and

then mashed in milk or whey, with or without the addition of a little bran or oatmeal.

Towards the period when the pigs are to be weaned the sow must be less plentifully fed, otherwise the secretion of milk will be as great as ever; and it will accumulate, and there will be hardness, and perhaps inflammation of the teats. Should it appear requisite, a dose of physic may be given to assist in carrying off the milk; but in general a little judicious management in the feeding and weaning will be all that is requisite.

Martin says: "From some ill-understood cause, several domestic animals, as the rabbit, and sometimes the cat, seem to forget all instinctive ties, and turning upon their offspring, ravenously and unnaturally devour them. This is not unfrequently the case with the sow; and it is remarkable, that when this revolting act has been once committed, its re-occurrence may be expected. This disposition is not always or necessarily connected with general ferocity, nor even with the fierce anxiety which the sow, with other animals, displays in the protection of her young; it may be that the animal is ordinarily mild and gentle, and yet at this juncture becomes madly ferocious. We are not aware whether or not such tragic scenes take place among animals in a state of natural independence; most probably they never do, or but very rarely. Yet in early ages the sow was evidently subject to this morbid propensity; for among the regulations respecting swine, laid down by Hoel Dha, one of the good qualities of a sow expressly noticed is, that she do not devour her young ones. The less the sow, after bringing forth her young, is meddled with, the more comfortable her bedding, the more regularly and gently she has been previously managed and treated, the less likely is she to violate one of the great laws of nature.

"The wild boar, as we have said, is a dangerous animal; and so indeed, to a certain extent, is the domestic boar of some of the larger breeds. Instances are not unfrequent of boars turning furiously upon their keepers, especially if interfered with when in company with the female, or if constrained to quit her society.

"It is not, however, only at certain times and under certain circumstances that the boar is dangerous: a boar, especially one of the large old breeds, is by no means a safe animal to venture near at any time, and we have more than once seen sows almost equally savage; this, however, is not generally the case."

TREATMENT OF THE YOUNG WHILE SUCKING.

For the first ten days or a fortnight, the mother will generally be able to support her litter without assistance, unless, as has been already observed, she is weakly, or they are too many in number;

in either of which cases they must be fed from the first. When the young pigs are about a fortnight old, warm milk should be given to them. In another week, this may be thickened with some species of farina; and afterwards, as they gain strength and increase in size, boiled roots and vegetables may be added. As soon as they begin to eat, an open frame or railing should be placed in the sty, under which the little pigs can run, and on the other side of this should be the small troughs containing their food; for it never answers to let them eat out of the same trough with the mother, both because the food set before her is generally too strong and stimulating for them, and besides, the chances are they would not get a mouthful. Those intended to be killed for "sucking-pigs" should not be above four weeks old; most persons kill them for this purpose on the twenty-first or twenty-second day. The others, excepting those which are kept for the purpose of breeding, should be castrated at the same time.

WEANING.

The age at which pigs may be weaned with the greatest advantage is when they are about eight or ten weeks old; many persons, however, wean them as early as six weeks, but then they seldom turn out so well. They should not be taken from the sow at once, but gradually weaned. At first they should be removed from her for a certain number of hours each day, and accustomed to be driven by hunger to eat from the trough; then they may be turned out for an hour without her, and afterwards shut up while she is turned out also by herself. Subsequently they must only be allowed to suck so often in twenty-four hours; perhaps six times at first, then four, then twice, and at last only once; and meanwhile they must be proportionally better and more plentifully fed, and the mother's diet in a like manner diminished; thus will the weaning be accomplished without danger or evil consequences to either. Some persons have advised that the whole litter should not be weaned at once; we do not, however, agree with them, unless it should happen that one or two of the young ones are much weaker and smaller than the others; in such case, if the sow remains in tolerable condition, they might be suffered to suck for a week longer; but such a mode of proceeding should be an exception, not a general rule.

Pigs are more easily weaned than almost any other animals, because they learn to feed sooner; but nevertheless this is always a somewhat critical period, and great attention must be paid to them if we would have them grow up strong, healthy animals. Their styes must be warm, dry, clean, well ventilated, and weather-tight. They should have the run of a grass meadow or paddock for an hour or two every fine day, in the spring and summer, or be turned into the farm-yard among the cattle in the winter, as fresh air and exercise tend to prevent them from becoming rickety or crooked in the legs.

Butter-milk, whey, and the refuse of the dairy, with boiled or steamed potatoes, pollard, and oat or barleymeal, may be given as food; also boiled cabbage and lettuce, macerated and bruised oats, barley, and even wheat; in short, the most nutritious and succulent food that circumstances will permit of, and a daily run at grass wherever it is possible. At first their food should all be given to them warm, and be tolerably soft, in order better to assimilate with the state of the digestive functions; gradually and soon they must be accustomed to take it cold, it being far better for them so when once they are used to it; and they must also learn to masticate their food.

Newly-weaned pigs require five or six meals in the twenty-four hours. In about ten days one may be omitted; in another week, a second; and then they must do with three regular meals each day.

But let it be understood that, while we would enforce the necessity of good and ample feeding, we highly deprecate all excess, and all stimulating, heating diet, such tending to vitiate the animal powers, often to lay the foundation of disease, and never to produce good, sound, well-flavored flesh.

A little sulphur mingled with the food, or a small quantity of Epsom or Glauber's salts disolved in the water, will frequently prove beneficial.

A plentiful supply of clear cold water should always be within their reach; the food left in the trough after the animals have done eating, should be removed, and the trough thoroughly rinsed out before any more is put into it. Strict attention should be paid to cleanliness; indeed, many persons assert that there is no comparison in point of thriving between an animal well cleaned and repeatedly brushed and another that is left to itself; although both shall be in feeding and all other respects treated exactly the same, the latter will not weigh so much as the former by many pounds.

This treatment will bring them on to the time when the owner must separate those he intends for breeders from those which are to be fattened for the market. The boars and sows should be kept apart from the period of weaning.

The question of which is most profitable—to breed swine, or to buy young pigs and fatten them—will best be determined by the individuals who have to study it, for they know best what resources they can command, and what chance of profits each of these separate branches offers.

There was an interesting paper published some little time since in the *Farmer's Magazine*, calculating the number of pigs which, in the course of ten years, may be raised from two one year old sows.

We give it verbatim, as many of our readers have probably never
entered into such a calculation, or formed the least idea of the amazing quantity of animal food which may be derived from this kind of
stock :

"I am indebted to a worthy and sensible friend, and a friend also
of the poor, for the following estimate of what I shall term 'pig
population,' and set it in array against the increasing demands of the
home population, which goes on at the rate of not quite 1½ per cent.
per annum—nay, little more than 1¼ by the last ten years' census.
I think, with the assistance of my above-mentioned friend, I can feed
the supernumeraries well, and in this way, at all events, save their
bacon. Would you credit the assertion that in ten years—ten short
years—and from two breeding sows, many millions can be produced ? Would you suppose (for I certainly had no conception of
the fact) that more than the present or even anticipated population
of the country for ten years to come is not equal to the number of
pigs to be thus born and bred in the same period, if we choose ?
But I shall proceed to proof and give the figures, which are un-
answerable arguments when well founded. His calculation, then, is
as follows, viz.: that in one year two sows (one year old) will
breed ten each, of which we shall assume that one-half are females,
and so proceed on that assumed equality.

"The first year there will be males and females.................... 20
From which take the males.................................... 10

And we have the result as breeders...................... 10
At the second year, then, we may fairly take the same ratio of ten to
each, viz.:.. 10
                                                            2)100
And it gives us a hundred males and females, leaving, con-
    sequently, for the third year, breeders................. 50
I shall now drop the text, and merely give the figures, the same prin-
    ciple applying throughout 10

Third year.. 2)500
                                                            250
                                                             10
Fourth year.......................   .... 2)2,500
                                                          1,250
                                                             10
Fifth year...............   .... 2)12,500
                                                          6,250
                                                             10
                                                          62.500

Sixth year .. .. 2)62,500

                                                            31,250
                                                               10

Seventh year...2)312,500

                                                           156,250
                                                               10

Eighth year...2)1,562,500

                                                           781,250
                                                               10

Ninth year..2)7,812,500

                                                         3,906,250
                                                               10

Tenth year, males and females.........................39,062,500

"I hope my friend has brought his pigs to a good market; but to equalize the supply, I shall, for the present purpose, take only the male half of the pig population for food, leaving the breeders to go on. In this way we can kill and eat ten the first year—no bad increase from two sows, recollect; the second year, 50; the third, 250; the fourth, 1250; the fifth, 6250; the sixth, 31,250 (pork in abundance now); the seventh, 156,250 (still more abundant); the eighth, 781,250; the ninth, 3,906,250; and the tenth, when divided in like manner, the enormous number of 19,531,250 for food, without interfering with the breeders, who, I presume, by this time will probably require killing also. Now, I am not aware that much commentary is required on this prolific subject; every man who reads this short paper will at once draw his own conclusions from the facts. They are, however, of a very cheering description, and drawn from the breeding of one domestic animal only, and amply prove what abundant stores nature and the God of nature have provided for human subsistence. I shall close this paper with the sensible practical observation of my friend in reference to this subject, as, after all, it is in practice only that the benefits open to all are to be received by any. In the county of Kent, he informs me, there are 31,000 agricultural families or farmers. It is a very easy matter for each to keep two breeding-sows, which in three years would produce in round numbers 15,000,000 of pigs.

"In the fifty-two counties of England, he also adds, the number of agricultural families is 760,000; so that, by the same mode of calculation as for Kent, every farmer keeping two sows, the produce would be, in the like period, 380,000,000 pigs. One good breeding sow to each would consequently produce 15,000,000. As I have

said, and say again, is this all true ? for if so, what prevents the immediate use of the same beneficial proceeding to every one, not even
omitting the allotment tenant ?   What more easy and practicable
than to breed on a small scale, or to join two or three families together, and thus diminish expense and increase profits ?   I throw out
the hint, and hope that good may arise from a due consideration of
the prominent facts already stated."

With the following valuable remarks by that well-known practical
agriculturist and grazier, Arthur Young, we will conclude this chapter :—

"The breeding of swine being one of the most profitable articles
in the whole business of a farm, the husbandman cannot pay too
much attention to it.   I shall, in as few words as the subject will
admit, give an account of the best system to be pursued in this
branch of his business.   The farmer who would make a considerable
profit by hogs must determine to keep a proper number of sows in
order to breed many pigs ; but this resolution ought to be preceded
by the most careful determination to prepare crops proper for supporting this stock.   The proper ones for that purpose are barley,
buck, beans, peas, clover, potatoes or carrots.   In the common management, a farmer keeps only a sow or two because his dairy will
do no more ; but in the system of planting crops purposely for swine,
a different conduct must necessarily be pursued.   Potatoes, carrots,
Swedish turnips, and cabbages, must be provided for the sows and
stores from October till the end of May, by which time clover, chicory, or lucerne should be ready to receive them, which will carry
them till the stubbles are cleared ; so that the whole year is filled
up with these plants, and the common offal of the barn-door and the
corn-fields.   When the sows pig, meal must be provided to make
wash by mixing it with water.   This in summer will be good enough
for their support, and in winter it must be mixed with boiled roots,
oats, and pea-soup, for the young pigs.   If cows are kept, then the
dairy-wash is to be used in the above mixtures.

"Upon this system, a farmer may proportion his swine to his
crops, or his crops to his swine ; and he will find that for the whole
year he should have about an equal quantity of roots and grass, and
half as much corn as potatoes.   For carrying the profit to the highest
advantage, the sows should pig but twice a-year, that is, in April and
August, by which means there will never be a long and expensive
season for rearing pigs before they are put to the staple food of clover
or potatoes, &c. ; but this circumstance is much removed by the
provision of crops raised expressly for the swine.

"Upon this plan the annual sale of lean hogs should be in October,
the litters of April sold then as stores, and those of August kept till
October twelvemonth to sell for baconers, if the farmer feeds none
himself. The stock upon hand this month will therefore be the sows,

and the pigs littered in the preceding August, all which should have roots from the store, and run at the same time in the farm-yard, for shacking the straw of the barn-doors. In proportion to what they find in this, you must supply them with roots, giving enough to keep them in growth."

CHAPTER XII.

On Feeding Swine—Fat Pigs—Cattle Shows—Whey, Milk, and Dairy Refuse—Refuse and Grains of Distilleries and Breweries—Residue of Starch Manufactories—Vegetables and Roots—Fruits—Grain—Soiling and Pasturing Swine—Animal Substances as Food for them— General Directions for Feeding and Fattening.

MARTIN says:

"That great attention should be paid to the hog, especially in a country like England, and when we consider its importance as a flesh-giving animal, is not surprising. There is, in fact, no part of the hog, its bristles excepted, which is not consumed; the very intestines are cleansed, and knotted into chitterlings, by many persons exceedingly relished; the blood, mixed with fat and rice, is made into black puddings; the skin of pork roasted, is a *bonne bouche;* a roast sucking pig is hailed with satisfaction; salt pork and bacon are in incessant demand, and are important articles of commerce. Great quantities are prepared in Ireland for exportation, and great quantities are also prepared in England. It is stated by Dr. Mavor, in his 'Survey of Berkshire,' that at Farringdon fully four thousand are annually killed and cured.

"One great value of the hog arises from the peculiarity of its fat, which, in contradistinction to that of the ox or that of the sheep, is termed lard, and differs from them in the proportion of its constituent principles, which are essentially *olein,* or *elain,* and *stearin.* All fats agree in being insoluble in water. It may not be uninteresting to the reader to know the distinguishing characters of the fat of our three most important flesh-giving domestic animals.

"*Ox Fat.*—When this has been fused, it begins to solidify at 98°, and the temperature then rises (on account of the evolution of latent heat) to 102°. Forty parts of boiling alchol of sp. gr. 0·821 dissolve one part of it, and it contains about three-fourths its weight of stearin, which is solid, hard, colorless, not greasy, and of a granular texture. It fuses at about 112°, and may then be cooled to 102°, when, on congealing, it rises to 112°. It burns like white wax. Of this stearin, about 15·5 parts are dissolved by 100 parts of anhydrous alcohol.

" The olein of ox fat is colorless, nearly inodorous, and its specific gravity 0·913 ; boiling alcohol dissolves nearly one-fourth more than its weight.

"*Sheep's Fat*, or *Mutton Suet*, greatly resembles that of the ox. It is, however, whiter, and, by exposure to the air, acquires a peculiar odor. After fusion, it congeals at a temperature varying between 98° and 102°. It dissolves in 44 parts of alcohol of sp. gr. 0·821. The stearin is white, translucent, and, after fusion, but imperfectly crystalline. About 16 parts are dissolved by 100 parts of boiling anhydrous alcohol. The olein of mutton suet is colorless. Its specific gravity is 0·913, and 80 parts of it are dissolved by 100 parts of anhydrous alcohol at 168°.

"*Hog's Fat*, or *Hog's Lard*, is a soft, colorless solid, which fuses between 78° and 86°. Is specific gravity at 60° is 0·938. By powerful and long-continued pressure between folds of blotting paper, it is stated to yield 62-100ths of its weight of colorless olein, of specific gravity 0·915. Of this, 100 parts of boiling alcohol dissolve 123 parts. The stearin of hog's lard is inodorous, solid, and granular, which, after fusion, remains liquid down to 100°, and then, on congealing, the temperature rises to 109°. It becomes acid by exposure to the air.

" Different as are the qualities of stearin and olein, analysis shows that their composition is less remote than might be expected. The subjoined analysis of mutton may be taken as a general example :—

					Stearin.			Olein.
Hydrogen	.	.	.	.	11·770	.	.	11·090
Carbon	.	.	.	.	78·776	.	.	79·354
Oxygen	.	.	.	.	9·454	.	.	9·556
					100·			100·

" One great value of the hog, arises from the peculiarity of its fat. The great mass of this fat is laid on under the skin, and between the superficial muscles.

" Vancouver, in his 'Survey of Essex,' makes the following judicious observations relative to the management and value of hogs :— ' There is no animal in the whole economy of good husbandry that requires more attention as to breed, number, and supply of food, or will better requite the care and trouble of the farmer, than a well-managed and proper stock of hogs. These things, however, are too much overlooked, or rather disregarded, by farmers in general, though all are ready to agree that an overstock in other respects must ever prove fatal to the interests of the farmer. Hogs are too frequently conceived to be a trifling and unimportant part of the stock of a farm; whereas, if their first cost and the value of their food were duly considered, with their improving value, it would certainly bear them out against some of the more costly animals, and challenge more care and attention than are usually bestowed upon them. A due regard to the breed which the peculiar circumstances of the farm may call for is particularly necessary, as some breeds are much better suited to pasture, and feed upon grass and nerbs, than others. The most hardy and best qualified to prog for themselves are the Chinese, a cross with which breed upon almost any other may, under most circumstances, be prudently recommended. Let the breed be what it may, a well-proportioned stock to every farm will most abundantly requite the care and repay the expense of the necessary food provided for them. A few acres of clover would be well applied to the use of the hogs in summer; but in the sty it would be well to restrain them to a certain quantity of water, and to lodge them clean and dry, notwithstanding the wilful neglect and too prevailing opinion to the contrary; for cleanliness is as essential to the preservation of their health and well-doing as to that of any other animal.'

"These views are very different from those of a writer in the *Quarterly Journal of Agriculture*, who says, ' It is greatly doubted by many competent judges, whether swine form a profitable stock, at least when fed on food which requires to be raised for the purpose. The results deduced from calculations entered into, to show the probable return for a given quantity of grain, roots, or other vegetable produce, are, however, so discordant as to avail but little in the formation of a settled and conclusive opinion. In connexion with distilleries, dairies, breweries, and other large establishments, they are of much higher and assured importance, and return, in proportion to the offal they consume, a great quantity of meat. Their chief advantage as live stock probably consists in their being nourished by what would otherwise either prove nearly useless, or be entirely lost. When potatoes are raised as a fallow crop, exceeding the demands of human consumption, the rearing of swine for bacon and pickled pork becomes an advisable branch of rural economy.'

"No one, we presume, would keep pigs without having the means of feeding them at his command, all necessary conveniences, and a proper system of management. Under such circumstances they will return ample profit, a fact well known in America, where the hog is important to a degree elsewhere unknown, Ireland not excepted.

"If this animal is profitable to proprietors of large establishments, to great distillers, to millers, to farmers and dairymen, so it is to the laboring peasant who cultivates a little garden, and collects the refuse of the kitchens of his wealthier neighbors; he will have two or three litters in the course of the year, saleable as ' sucking pigs' at the age of three or four weeks, and at Christmas he will kill two, three, or four fat pigs, and find a ready sale for the meat, besides turning part into bacon for his own family. This is no theory;

we ourselves know those who act upon the plan, and find it a source
of profit and comfort. It would not, however, do for the idle or the
improvident ; it demands industry, order, and fore-thought, ard that
assistance, which, while the man is going on with his regular work,
his wife or some part of his family can render.

"Exclusive of bacon, hams, &c., great is the demand for fresh
pork throughout our island—much greater, indeed, than formerly,
and this is in some measure owing to the improvement of our breeds;
our porkers are small-sized, with fine-grained delicate flesh, and firm
fat, sufficiently but not superabundantly laid on, and the skin is thin
and clear ; the limbs are round and fine-boned. Such is the country-
fed pork to be seen in London and in other towns. Formerly such
pork was never sent to market, and in some counties it is still unknown. We allude to the more northern of the midland counties,
and those still farther north. A relative farming in Derbyshire, and
on a visit to the author, expressed his surprise at the smallness and
delicacy of the dairy-fed pork placed upon our table. His idea of
fresh pork was limited to spare-ribs, and griskins of bacon hogs ;
and he deemed the destruction of young porkers for food utter folly.
He forgot, perhaps never reflected that these younglings, by quick
returns and good profits, remunerated the farmer, miller, or dairy
man far more than they would have done if kept to be bacon hogs
and fed up to the proper pitch.

"We have sufficiently demonstrated the value of the pig as one
of the flesh-producing animals which man has reclaimed. Throughout the whole of Europe, and the greater portion of America, the
flesh of the hog, fresh, salted, or cured, is in constant demand ; nor
less so the lard, which is required by the cook, by the apothecary,
and by the perfumer.

"No part of the hog, as we have said, is useless; not even its
bristles or its skin.

"The bristles of our fine-bred races are perhaps of no value—
they are generally short, slender, and thinly set ; but in the coarser
breeds, they are long and strong, firm and elastic. The export of
bristles alone from Russia and Prussia into our country, forms no
inconsiderable item. We need not detail their various uses.

"With respect to the hide of this animal, it is, when tanned, of a
peculiar texture, and very tough. It is used for making pocket-
books, and for some ornamental purposes, but chiefly for covering
saddles. The numerous little variegations in it, and which constitute
its beauty, are the orifices whence the bristles have been removed."
—MARTIN.

The establishment of agricultural societies and cattle-shows formed
the commencement of a new era in the breeding of all domesticated
animals, and especially of swine, which had, previously to that epoch,
been very much neglected. There cannot be a doubt but that the

competition, the assembling together of breeders from all counties
and even from abroad, the comparison of the different animals
brought together, and the conclusions drawn in many minds, tend
materially to the elucidation and advancement of the science of breeding. Persons resident in remote localities are apt to set up for themselves some particular standard of excellence, and make it the whole
aim of their endeavors to obtain and develop certain points in an
animal, and having done this they rest satisfied; but when the
annual cattle show places before them other and evidently superior
animals, they perceive how much too limited, and often how erroneous, have been their views, and set to work afresh to improve upon
the knowledge thus acquired.

But there is no good without its attendant evil. It was, doubtless,
originally intended by those who established the distribution of
prizes for certain kinds of stock, that the prize animal should be the
most excellent as to its points, the most useful to the farmer, breeder, and butcher, and altogether the most profitable; but not that it
should be the fattest! It is reported that, on Hannah More being
asked what was the use of cattle-shows, she replied, " To induce people to make beef and mutton so fat that nobody can eat it." This
certainly is the *abuse* of them, and in no class of animals is it carried
to such an extent as in swine. The greedy propensities of the poor
animal are worked upon; he is shut up, often in darkness, and fed
and suffered to gorge himself until he can scarcely move or breathe,
and often dies of suffocation, or is obliged to be killed, from the simple exertion of being brought to the show in the most easy and careful manner. A premium would be far better bestowed upon the
most useful and profitable animal, the one most likely to make good
bacon or pork, than on these huge masses of obesity, whose superabundance of fat is fit for little else but the melting-pot. As much
money is often wasted on one of these monsters as would purchase
food for half a dozen really profitable animals. And to what purpose ? Simply to test the elastic power of a pig's skin ? " No,"
reply the advocates of this species of monomania, " but to discover
which breeds can be fattened to the greatest size in the shortest time,
and on the smallest amount of food." And to this plea we can only
reply, that while we admit the value of such knowledge, we think it
might be attained without the sacrifice of a fine animal, at much less
expense, and far more satisfactorily. Let the animals be fat, but do
not let them be a mere bladder of lard, " of shape undefined," every
point lost and buried. It is fine and profitable breeds we require,
not monstrosities. The grand aim of agricultural societies is to pro-
mote the improvement of the breeds, and consequently the profit of
the breeder, and general advantage. We trust that this will shortly
be fully understood and carried out, and the cattle-shows become, as
it were, model-rooms, instead of mere exhibitions of over-fed, pant-

ing, unshapely beasts. But it is not our feeble voice alone which is raised against this unnatural stuffing: public attention has latterly been much called to this point; and among others, our merry critic Punch, who fails not to lash each passing folly of the age, has, as will be seen by the following epitaph, not been unmindful of this one :—

"Epitaph on a Prize Pig.

HERE LIES
ALL THAT WAS EATABLE
OF A PRIZE PIG.

HE WAS BORN
ON FEBRUARY 1, 1845:

HE WAS FED
ON MILK, POTATOES, AND
BARLEY-MEAL:

HE WAS SLAUGHTERED
ON DECEMBER 24, 1846,
WEIGHING 80st. 9lbs.

STOP, TRAVELLER!
AND REFLECT HOW SMALL A PORTION
OF THIS VAST PIG
WAS PORK SUITABLE
FOR HUMAN FOOD."

Hurtrel D'Arboval, treating of Obesity, says, "There is, however no animal so liable to become over-fat, as the pig, and especially the Chinese and Siamese swine. Naturally inclined to corpulence and gluttony, they easily acquire an enormous bulk; and when fat has once begun to accumulate, the animal eats little, breathes with diffi culty, becomes inert, unable to sustain his own weight, and deficient in sensation. We have seen wretched pigs so fat that they were obliged to be lifted or dragged out of the sty whenever it was neces- sary to move them. We have also made incisions in their buttocks and even taken off portions of skin from their backs, without their betraying any sense of pain. We saw one hog that had lain for a considerable period on one side, too powerless or too inert even to shift its position, and when it was raised, a large hole was perceived in that part of the back which had been undermost. This had been made by rats feeding and gnawing into the fat of the beast, evidently without its being in the least conscious of their proceedings.

"Animals that have been castrated are always more disposed to obesity."

We will now proceed to consider the various modes of keeping and feeding swine and their relative value, and the other incidental matters which may develop themselves as we proceed.

Swine are generally fattened for pork at from six to nine months old, and for bacon at from a twelvemonth to two years. Eighteen months is generally considered to be the proper age for a good bacon hog.

The feeding of pigs will always, in a great measure, depend upon the circumstances of the owner, upon the kind of food which he has at his disposal and can best spare, and the purpose for which he intends the animals. It will also be in some degree regulated by the season, it being possible to feed pigs very differently in the summer to what they are fed in the winter. During the former they can either be sty-fed or pastured, or both; and there is also a greater variety of vegetables and green food for them, as well as of dairy refuse; while in the winter they must be home-fed, and in most cases their diet limited to roots, peas, beans, or other such dried food, and wash composed of the scanty residue of the dairy, or supplied from the house or brewery.

WHEY, MILK, AND DAIRY REFUSE.

For sty-fed pigs the washings of the dairy, as butter and skim-milk, whey, &c., are excellent, and especially whey thickened with barley, or oat, or pea-meal, whey being more nourishing than skim-milk; the animals thrive and make flesh so well on it, that many farmers are of opinion that this mode of employing their sour milk is more profitable than making cheese. But when the swine have once become habituated to this kind of diet it must be continued, as they would fall off if put upon any other. There was a beautiful lot of Coleshill pigs exhibited at the last Smithfield Club Cattle-Show, belonging to the Earl of Radnor, aged twenty-one weeks, which had been fattened on forty-eight bushels of barley-meal and six bushels of potatoes, with an adequate quantity of whey. Wherever, therefore, there are large dairies, swine may be most advantageously kept, the excellence of dairy-fed pork being incontestable.

WASH, GRAINS, AND REFUSE OF BREWERIES AND DISTILLERIES.

The refuse wash and grains, and other residue of breweries and distilleries, may also be given to swine with advantage, and seem to induce a tendency to lay on flesh, but not in too large quantities, or unmixed with other and more substantial food; as, although they gain flesh rapidly when fed on it, the meat is not firm, and never makes good bacon.

Thäer advises that the refuse of brandy-distilleries should always be diluted with water at first, otherwise the animals will reject it, or, if they take it, become giddy, and be unable to keep their feet, afterwards, the quantity of this food may be gradually increased till they are completely accustomed to it. Neuenhahn says that the refuse of the brandy-distillery cannot be given to the pigs too warm, or too soon after its removal from the still, and that it never heats their blood; but that, if it be allowed to get cold and stale, it is rather injurious than beneficial to them. On the other hand, many experienced distillers, who fatten large numbers of hogs, assure us that it requires great attention, and the employment of a man on whose care we can rely, to prevent this residue from being given to the animals while too warm, for it is then that it injures and materially retards their growth. It should be sometimes thick, sometimes diluted with water, and at others mixed with meal or pollard, in order, by thus varying the food, to keep up the appetite of the animals.

RESIDUE OF STARCH MANUFACTORIES.

The residue of the manufacture of starch, the products of the various washings which this precaution involves, and the refuse of wheat, are far superior to brewers' and distillers' refuse. Hogs fed upon these articles fatten more quickly, produce firmer flesh, more substantial bacon, and a greater quantity of lard. At first the animals will often eat these matters with great avidity, and even to excess, and when this is the case they invariably become disgusted and refuse them after a time. The quantity must therefore be carefully regulated, and the troughs kept very clean. If this kind of food be used alternately with one of a different nature, the fattening will be effected with greater certainty. The quantity of this refuse collected at once is often greater than can be consumed at the time, and it is difficult to store it up, because its animal portions so soon putrefy. The only mode of preservation is to dry it, make it into cakes, and bake it.

VEGETABLES AND ROOTS.

Cabbage and lettuce-leaves, turnip-greens, and bean and pea-hauln. may be given to pigs in moderate quantities with advantage, but these substances should be chopped up small and mingled in the wash, as the animals, being very fond of such food, will otherwise devour it too ravenously to be able properly to masticate it.

Almost all our common roots are well adapted for feeding pigs; carrots, turnips, parsnips, beet-root, and last, but not least, the potato, are all exceedingly nutritive, even when given in a raw state, but that cooking tends materially to increase their nourishing powers is a fact well attested by numerous experiments and general experience. Potatoes should be steamed, the other roots boiled. In Guernsey the parsnip is extensively used in the feeding of pigs.

especially from September to Christmas, and eight perches of land, each producing on the average 250 lbs. of this root, are considered as the general allowance for fattening a pig in store order. But the flesh of animals thus fed is not so firm as that of pigs fed on pea or barley-meal with a slight addition of corn, and shrinks when boiled, instead of plumping. Carrots are considered by some persons to fatten swine more rapidly than any other root, and to impart a particularly delicate flavor to the flesh; they may be given raw. Potatoes are, however, the staple food in by far the greater part of England, and the whole of Ireland. They should be steamed, and then mashed with meal or pea-flour in whey or sour milk (where it can be had,) or in wash or clear water, and made of the consistence of porridge. The water in which the potatoes have been cooked should always be thrown away. This root should, however, only be given for a short time, as it is by no means a rapid fattener, and does not make firm good fat,—and never alone if it can be avoided. Turnips should never be given while any other kind of food can be obtained, as their effects are far from beneficial, and often quite the contrary. Beans and peas, both green, dried, and ground, or bruised and macerated, form excellent food. Peas are considered to produce firmer flesh, and to fatten quicker than beans. The gray pea is generally allowed to be the best adapted for swine, and to contain most nutrition. Experiments have been made with the blue pea, but hogs fed on it had always a tendency to diarrhœa. Every part of the pea, the haulm, the cods, and the peas themselves, may be used in feeding pigs. Sir John Sinclair found green beans also very advantageous food for swine; he gives preference to the Windsor bean, and advises that two or three successive crops of them should be sown in order to secure a constant supply from July until September.

In the "*Quarterly Journal of Agriculture*" we find an account of some experiments made with the view of testing the relative fattening powers of carrots, potatoes, peas, wheat, and buckwheat.

Five couples of pigs were separately put up to fatten :—

					Increase of Weight.
To couple 1 was given 55	decalitres of	peas	-	-	315 lbs.
" 2 "	283	"	balls of wheat	-	339 lbs.
" 2 "	96	"	buckwheat	-	374 lbs.
" 4 "	98	"	boiled potatoes	-	284 lbs.
" 5 "	175	"	carrots	- -	394 lbs.

These results of the experiment are, however, unsatisfactory, because it is not mentioned whether the pigs were all of the same age and weight, nor is it stated whether the quantity of food marked in the table was as much as the pigs could consume.

We have always believed that peas were the most nutritious food that could be given to pigs, and this experiment confirms the belief,

as may be seen on comparing the relative increase of weight obtained from the various kinds of food, viz.:—55 decalitres of peas
gave an increase of 22 stone 7 lbs., or nearly 6 lbs. of increase of
pork from 1 decalitre of peas; whereas from boiled carrots only 28
stone 2 lbs. of increase were obtained from 175 decalitres, or about
2½ lbs. from 1 decalitre, giving the advantage over the peas in the
ratio of 2½ : 1. The next most nourishing food is buckwheat, which
nearly gives 4 lbs. of pork from 1 decalitre. Boiled potatoes are
next, giving nearly 3 lbs. of pork from 1 decalitre; and the lowest
quantity of pork is that obtained from the balls of wheat, which is
as low as 1 lb. from 1 decalitre. Flour would no doubt fatten better than wheat, especially if the feeds were made into small dry
balls of dough, and frequently administered.

FRUITS.

With the exception of the acorn we have seldom a sufficiently
abundant crop of fruit of any kind to admit of our making it an
article of food for swine. When England was rich in forest land,
the *mastage* or *pannage* of swine in these localities was a valuable
privilege, for if the animals did not absolutely get fat, they were
kept in fair condition at no expense to the owner beyond that of paying a person to look after them.

Hogs will eat the acorns and beech-mast greedily, and certainly
thrive to a certain extent on this food, so far that it is an easy
matter to fatten them afterwards. Parkinson says:—" When I
lived with my father, acorns were so plentiful in the woods one
year, that they made the pigs sufficiently fat for bacon without any
other food. The flesh was equally as good and as well-flavored as
that of other animals that had been fed on beans and peas." Acorns
that have become dry in the sun and air are far more profitable
than those which are fresh fallen and green; but the way in which
they may be most advantageously employed is to bake or roast
them, and then crush them, and either boil them to a pulp, or pour
boiling water upon them and let it stand until cool; the addition of
a little salt makes an exceedingly palatable food, which the animals
greedily suck up, and which tends far more to fatten them than the
raw acorn would.

Beech-mast eaten alone makes the fat oily and impoverishes the
lean, but when taken in conjunction with acorns the one fruit quali-
fies the other, and the combined effect is good.

In many parts of the Continent where chestnuts are grown in
large quantities they constitute a considerable item in the feeding of
swine, and are exceedingly nutritious, especially when given at the
latter part of the fattening process. They impart firmness and a
delicate flavor to the meat. Few persons give chestnuts in a raw

state; they are either roasted in an oven or macerated in boiling water. The same reason may be given here as will apply to all kinds of roots and fruits, not only when used as food for swine, but also for other animals, and even for the human being; they are rendered more digestible by cooking, divested of their crudeness, and thus better calculated to nourish the system without fatiguing or disordering its powers. Besides which there is a decided saving effected. Some even go so far as to calculate that cooked, or ground, or bruised food, goes as far again as that which is given in its natural state or merely cut up.

In America, where there is an abundance of apples and pumpkins, these fruits are given to swine : we quote an account related by a great breeder of these animals, who attaches much value to these two articles of food, which seems to testify their utility :—

" On the 10th of October twenty swine were put up to fatten, all of which were only in middling store order, in consequence of the scarcity of feed. The cows producing very little wash from the dairy, and the crop of apples being scanty this season, nothing had been given them during summer but a small orchard containing one acre and a-half of land (with the premature apples which fell,) in which was a pond of water, a very essential requisite to hogs, and one to which, under the powerful influence of the sun, they will resort for their chief comfort.

" The above twenty swine were divided into three lots and closely confined ; we proceeded to fatten them by steaming 4 bushels of small potatoes, 12 bushels of apple pomace, 4 bushels of pumpkins, and 1 cwt. of buckwheat cornel, adding a little salt, the whole being well incorporated together while hot from the steamer, with a wooden pounder, and suffered to undergo fermentation before it was used as food : they were at the same time supplied with plenty of charcoal and pure water. While feeding them with the first steamer of the compound, a more than ordinary moisture was observed on their litter, which was occasioned by urine : a knowledge of animal nature convinced the owner that any more than an ordinary flow would weaken the system, and retard the progress of fattening ; and he attributed this evil to the steamed pumpkins acting as a diuretic, stimulating the kidneys and increasing the evacuation of urine. In the next steamer, therefore, 4 bushels of ruta-baga were substituted for the pumpkins, which had the desired effect. This experiment afforded proof that a mixture thus compounded contains a large mass of nutritive material ready prepared for the action of the stomach, and therefore producing flesh more rapidly than any other combination of food made use of. All the waste apples being used up, and there being a greater quantity of soft corn on hand than usual, that was given to the hogs, but instead of their condition improving they fell off, and the owner was under the

necessity of procuring two loads of apple pomace from his neighbors, and commencing the steaming and feeding again; it was
continued with the same good effect until eight days before the
animals were killed, during which latter period they were fed with
sound corn; they were slaughtered on the 1st of December. The
expense of fattening and the produce of pork were as follows:—

	Dr.	Dolls.	Cts.
32 bushels of small potatoes, at 25 cts.		8	00
32 bushels of ruta-baga, including pumpkins, at 25 cts.		8	00
10 bushels of soft corn, at 50 cts.		5	00
10 cwt. of buckwheat, at $1 per cwt		10	00
20 bushels of sound corn, at 80 cts.		16	00
		47	25
	Cr.	Dolls.	Cts.
By 40 cwt. of pork, at $7½ per cwt.		300	00
Deduct expense,		47	00
Balance,		252	75."

It is true that we have not often a superabundance of apples; but
still in years when the crop is plentiful, the windfalls, diseased or
injured apples, and the refuse left after the making of cider, may be
given to the pigs, and will prove a fair substitute for more expensive
food, if not in itself peculiarly advantageous; especially when economy in the keep is more studied than a rapid system of fattening.

Nuts should never be given to swine; they make the fat soft and
greasy, and impart a sweet, unpleasant flavor to the flesh. Pigs are,
however, exceedingly fond of them; so much so, that when they can
get nuts they care little to touch any other kind of food.

GRAIN.

There is nothing so nutritious, so eminently and in every way
adapted for the purpose of fattening, as are the various kinds of
grain; the only drawback is that they are too expensive to be used
to any great extent for this purpose, otherwise no animal should
be considered as properly fattened unless some kind of grain had
been given during the latter part of the time; as nothing tends more
to create a firmness as well as delicacy in the flesh. It has been
calculated that for every bushel, half of peas, and half of barley,
that a hog eats, it gains from nine to ten or eleven pounds of flesh.

Two pigs of about eight months old, were purchased and put up
to fatten on the 23d of December, 1834; they then weighed 316
lbs. They were put into a warm sty and fed on rye and corn-meal,
having three regular feeds per diem, of two quarts each, up to the
following October, when they received three quarts at each feed, or

nine quarts a-day for about a month. From that time until the 7th of December, 1835, a period of five weeks, their feeds were raised another quart, making now twelve quarts a-day. Besides this they had the refuse of the milk of two cows, and occasionally a very little green meat. When slaughtered, they weighed 1134 lbs., which, allowing for one-third of offal, will amount to the gain of about 3½ lbs. of live weight per day. They ate in the whole, fifty bushels of rye and corn ground; in cold weather it was scalded and given to them warm, and in the summer, put into the trough and milk poured upon it. (*The Cultivator*, vol. ii.)

There are also repeated instances in which the animals have increased in weight 2 lbs., 2¼ lbs., and even 3 lbs. a day, while fed on barley-meal only, or barley-meal and peas, or potatoes; the relative prices, however, of grain and pork will always decide the question of the advantage of this mode of feeding far better than volumes of experiments or comments.

Barley and oats are considered to be best adapted for fattening swine. Some persons give the preference to oats, and where the grain is given whole they certainly are more digestible and less heating; but ground barley or barleymeal is universally allowed to be the most nutritious of all food.

There are various ways of giving grain to swine:—Raw and dry, roasted or malted, bruised and macerated, boiled, green, and *growey* or germinating wheat; and, lastly, ground to meal or farina. Of these the first two are the least advantageous, as the grain is then often but imperfectly masticated, and consequently produces indigestion. Wherever it is thus given the animals must be well supplied with water. A little whole grain given once a-day, or every other day, to pigs fed on barleymeal, is considered to be beneficial and add to the firmness of the flesh.

Macerated grain is better, or rather would be if the animals would eat it freely, which they seldom will do. Its fattening properties are increased if, after maceration, it is suffered to lie and germinate, and then dried or malted; or left to stand in the water until the whole turns sour.

Many persons consider that grain boiled until the husk bursts is better adapted for feeding swine in this form than when ground, and is likewise more economical; the only difference, however, in this latter respect, will depend upon whether the expense of having it ground be greater or less than that of the fuel necessary to boil it.

It is our opinion that the best, most economical and advantageous form in which grain can be used, is that of meal moistened with water, whey or sour or skim-milk, into a kind of soup or porridge. The fluid, whatever it may be, which is in the first place poured upon it, should never be more than lukewarm, and had better be quite cold; hot or boiling liquid will cause the meal to conglomerate into lumps of paste, not easily dissolved, and very likely to bring on in digestion. The Rev. Arthur Young, in his work on fattening cattle and swine, gives the following directions as to the best method of employing this kind of food :—" The most profitable method of converting corn of any kind into food for hogs, is to grind it into meal, and mix this with water in cisterns, in the proportion of five bushels of meal to one hundred gallons of water; stir it well several times a-day, for three weeks in cold weather, or for a fortnight in a warmer season, by which it will have fermented well and become acid, till which time it is not ready to give. It should be stirred immediately before feeding. Two or three cisterns should be kept fermenting in succession, that no necessity may occur of giving it not duly prepared. The difference in profit between feeding in this manner, and giving the grain whole, is very great, so great that whoever tries it once will not be apt to change it for the common method."

Thäer informs us that ground corn or coarse meal made into sour dough (by mixing the farina or meal with warm water and a little yeast, and then suffering it to stand in a high temperature until it turns sour, which it will do in the course of a day,) is a better and more profitable mode of feeding swine on grain than any other. A portion of the sour dough is then softened with water and given to the pigs, with a small portion of ground corn or barleymeal stirred up in it. The animals relish this food exceedingly, and thrive rapidly upon it; but if the dough is given alone, although they seem to make flesh as quickly, the meat is flabby and the fat porous. Peas might be added instead of the farina or meal, or a little whole barley or oats.

The same author likewise says :—" Some persons appears to be exceedingly successful in fattening their pigs on bread made of coarse rye or barleymeal. They cut this bread in pieces, dry it in an oven, then soak it in water, mash it, and give it to the animals in the form of porridge. Where sour milk or whey can be substituted for water, this food is said to surpass all others for quickness and efficacy in fattening, and for the goodness of the flesh and fat it produces."

Indian corn has latterly been employed in England with great success in feeding swine, and that it is highly nutritive and well adapted for the purpose there can be no question; here, as in most cases, the price will in a great measure decide the advantage or non-advantage of using it.

Maize is equal if not superior to any kind of grain for fattening, and is extensively used on the Continent, in Europe, and in America, where this article can readily be obtained. The best way is to give it quite at the latter end of the fattening period in small quantities, as a handful or a few ears. It may be given in its natural state, as pigs are so fond of it that they will eat up every seed. The pork and bacon of animals that have been thus fed is peculiarly firm and solid.

Rice is another valuable adjunct in fattening swine; we will quote in support of its properties the following account, given by an amateur pig-breeder:—

" We purchased from the government stores several tons of damaged rice at a very cheap rate; with this we fattened our pigs, and such pork I never saw before or since; the fat was as firm and solid as the lean, and the flavor of the meat very superior.

" The way in which the rice was prepared for food was as follows: My copper held forty gallons; in the afternoon it was filled or nearly so, with water; as soon as the water boiled, the fire was raked out, two pails of rice immersed in the water, and the whole covered closely down and left to stand until the morning. On the following day the copper was emptied of its contents, which consisted of a thick jelly, so firm as only to be taken out with a shovel; and on these contents the pigs were fed. The effect was perfect.

"As to the economy of the plan, that of course must be a matter dependent upon circumstances; we found it more profitable than almost any other kind of food we could have given, from the price at which we were able to purchase the rice, and its goodness. From some slight experiments, I am induced to think that equal parts of rice jelly and mashed potatoes would constitute an excellent food."

Another person who tried rice as a food for pigs put up two weighing 70 lbs. each, and fed them entirely on equal parts of boiled rice and steamed potatoes. At first they progressed but slowly, but eventually attained the weight of 210 lbs. each. Their flesh was fine and delicate, the fat white and firm, and the flavor of both was excellent.

Under the head of grain some writers consider beans, peas, and tares; we have already spoken of the first two when treating of vegetables, and given it as our opinion that pea-meal is little if at all inferior to barley and oatmeal. The addition of a few dry peas to the porridge made of barleymeal and whey is advantageous; and many persons consider good pea-soup to be equal to any thing in its fattening powers.

Bran or pollard, unmixed with any farinaceous particles, conduces but little to fatten an animal; it has been considered that fermentation will increase and develop their nutritive properties, but we should be sorry to be compelled to rely solely on either of these two substances.

SOILING AND PASTURING SWINE.

We have already spoken of the advantage of a run at grass to swine of all ages, and permanent pastures are those best adapted to this purpose. Soiling. or feeding pigs on cut green meat, has also its advantages, and is very much practised wherever there are crops and facilities for so doing. The best artificial grasses and green meat for swine are clover, lucerne, chicory, sainfoin, vetches, tares, and bean and pea-haulm. Some persons feed their swine on these matters in the fields ; but it is a far better practice to turn them into yards or small enclosures, and there have the green meat brought to them, as by this means the animals are not able to wander about so much, exhausting their strength, and feeding in a desultory manner, but are kept quiet, and their dung more concentrated, especially if good litter or earth is laid down to receive and absorb it.

This feeding on green meat for awhile cools and purifies the blood, and keeps the animals in fair store condition, though it tends but very little to fatten them : where it is intended that it shall perform that office as well, it must not be simply cut green from the field and thrown to them, but chopped up small and salted, and mixed with the screenings of corn, or pollard, or meal, or roots, and moistened with some kind of wash and left to ferment.

Clover, hay, or dried vetches may be also given to swine, chopped up small, and in wash; the former with undoubted advantage, for clover and lucerne are allowed to be exceedingly nutritive to swine ; but many persons consider vetches, whether green or dried, as heating.

ANIMAL SUBSTANCES.

There cannot be a doubt but that these are highly fattening in their nature, and also that swine, being somewhat allied to the carnivora, will greedily devour them ; but the question is, Do they not tend to make the flesh strong and rank, to inflame the blood, to create in the animals a longing for more of such food, and thus lead them to destroy fowls, rabbits, ducks, and even the litters of their companions ? Many will give blood, entrails, scraps of refuse meat, horse-flesh, and such like, to swine, but we should decidedly discourage such practices ; the nearest approach to animal food we would admit should be pot-liquor, and dairy refuse. Animal food is bad for every kind of swine; and tends to make them savage and feverish, and often lays the foundation of serious inflammation of the intestines.

GENERAL DIRECTIONS FOR FEEDING AND FATTENING.

Regular hours of feeding rank among the first of the rules which ought to be observed; the pigs will soon learn to expect their meals at certain times, and the stomach will be ready for it; irregularity will therefore irritate the digestive powers, and prevent so much benefit being derived from the meal when it does come.

Small meals, and many of them, are preferable to few and large ones, for swine are very apt to gorge and over-eat themselves, or, if any be left in the trough, to return to it by fits and starts until it is all gone; in both cases the digestive functions are impaired, and the process is not fully and beneficially performed. The best remedy for indigestion is to let the animals fast for four-and-twenty hours, and then to give them a small quantity of dry food, as barley or peas, whole and salted, and let them fast four or five hours more before resuming their usual food.

Pigs always eat more when first put up to fatten than they do afterwards; therefore the most nutritious food should be reserved until they are getting pretty fat. And at that period the food must be varied, for the appetite being diminished, it becomes necessary to excite it by variety; and, besides, the same aliment constantly given palls upon the stomach, and is incapable of supplying in itself all the various kinds of nutriment required by the increased and altered state of the body.

It will be found advantageous occasionally to mingle a little sulphur or powdered antimony with the food of swine put up to fatten; about half an ounce once in ten days will usually be sufficient. These medicines tend to purify the blood, facilitate digestion, and maintain the appetite.

An American writer states that he has found gall-nuts, bruised and mingled with charcoal, to act most beneficially on the health of swine while being fattened; and also recommends that they should always be allowed to root in the earth of a small yard attached to the sty each day, and, if they will, eat some of the earth, which will be good for them. An intelligent writer in the " *Quarterly Journal of Agriculture*" states, that on the Duke of Montrose's estate, the pigs have ashes and cinders given them occasionally to correct the acidity of the stomach; and that they are frequently turned out to a piece of ground sprinkled with lime, which they root in and eat; or else, if this is not possible on account of the weather, a little magnesia is now and then mingled in the milk. These simple precautions are always more or less necessary to animals that are highly fed and have little or no exercise, and we should recommend them to the attention of all owners of pigs.

Cleanliness is another indispensable requisite. There is no idea so utterly without foundation as the common one " that pigs love dirt," and that these animals thrive best in the midst of filth. We will quote one anecdote out of the many which have come to our knowledge, in refutation of this absurd opinion :—"A gentleman in Norfolk put up six pigs of almost exactly equal weight, and all in equal health, to fatten; treated them, with one exception, all exactly the same, and fed them on similar food, given in equal quantities, to each, for seven weeks. Three of these pigs were left to shift for themselves so far as cleanliness went, and the other three were carefully curried, brushed, and washed. These latter consumed in the seven weeks less food by five bushels than the other three, and yet, when killed, weighed more by 32 lbs. on the average."

It should be the duty of some one person to keep the skins of the pigs put up to fatten—indeed we would rather say, of all the pigs kept—perfectly free from mud, dust, or filth of any kind; and this will best be done by taking care that they always have clear water to bathe in within their reach, clean litter to lie upon, are occasionally combed and brushed, and that the sty is always kept free from filth. Nothing is so likely to engender lice and diseases of the skin as for it to be suffered to remain in a dirty state. It is true that the maintenance of cleanliness will cost some trouble and expense, but every owner of pigs will best consult his own interests by attention to this point.

The best period for fattening pigs is the autumn; then almost every kind of food is to be had in plenty, as well as in perfection; the weather is neither too hot nor too cold; and the humidity generally prevalent at this season acts beneficially upon the skin and tissues, and as it were lubricates the whole animal economy. Besides, they are ready to be slaughtered at the period when this can be done with most advantage; when the lowness of the temperature allows more time, and consequently enables the owner to turn the flesh to the greatest advantage; whereas in hot weather the meat must be salted or pickled, eaten or disposed of immediately, or it turns off and is spoiled. In the immediate neighborhood of large towns alone will it be found advantageous to fatten pigs so as to have them ready to kill in the summer; there the prices which can often be obtained may compensate the dealer for the difficulty and risk he undergoes; but even the facilities afforded by railways will hardly do this to those who reside in remote localities, as here the expense of the transit has to be added to the other items, and the risk is increased by close packing.

The best kinds of food for fattening pigs are:

Milk or whey mixed with barley, oat, corn, or pea-meal, or with boiled and mashed potatoes.

Potatoes and rice; potatoes and meal of any of the above kinds, or mashed potatoes and whole grain.

Peas given whole, or crushed, or in the form of soup, and either alone or mixed with barley-meal or potatoes.

Carrots and parsnips; and especially boiled carrots, which some persons consider to be the most nutritious and fattening food that can be given to swine.

Pasturage on clover, lucerne, or sainfoin, or a run in the stubble of corn-fields immediately after the crop has been cut and got in.

Beet-root and ruta baga are good; but should only be given when other roots cannot be easily obtained.

And lastly, grain itself, as corn, barley, and oats, but not rye.

An American correspondent gives the following recipe for "an exceeding nutritious food for hogs;" but it is one which circumstances will not often permit us to make use of:—"Boil Irish potatoes, pumpkins, and apples until they are soft; mash them all together, taking care thoroughly to mix and incorporate them, and add a little salt to the compound; swine will be found to relish this food highly, and thrive uncommonly well upon it."

A small portion of salt should always be mingled in whatever food is given, as it tends to stimulate the appetite as well as the digestive functions; and an ample supply of good water for drinking be kept within the reach of every animal.

Indian corn, buckwheat, rice and maize, may doubtless be given with advantage, and are in themselves highly nutritious; but they cannot be reckoned as among the kinds of food generally in use, as, unless under peculiar circumstances, they are too expensive, and not always to be obtained at all.

Turnips, cabbage, lettuce, and beans, are not so much adapted for fattening as the kinds of food above enumerated, although these matters often form valuable additions to the keep of store-pigs.

THE REFUSE OF THE SLAUGHTER-HOUSE.

Martin says: "The hog is an *omnivorous* animal, and will even greedily devour flesh and garbage; and butchers, and even others, are in the habit of feeding their hogs upon blood, entrails, offal meat, and similar matters. It is a disgusting practice, but, besides this, it is essentially wrong; such diet renders the animal savage and dangerous,—a child accidentally straying within the reach of a hog thus fed, would be by no means safe from a ferocious assault; moreover, it keeps the animal in a state of feverish excitement, and leads to inflammatory diseases.

"Again, as it respects the meat, it is rank, coarse, and scarcely wholesome. Hogs are often kept in knackers' yards, where they revel in corruption. What must their flesh be!

THE REFUSE OF THE KITCHEN.

"The same objections do not apply to *pot-liquor* or *kitchen refuse*, for although there is a good portion of fat, bits of meat and skin, and the liquor in which meat has been boiled, still it has been cooked, and is mixed with the peelings of potatoes, carrots, turnips, cabbage leaves, bread, milk, &c., &c., and forms an acceptable mess.

THE REFUSE OF THE DAIRY.

" The *refuse of the dairy* is noted for its importance, both in the fattening of porkers and bacon-hogs. The very term of ' dairy-fed poik' conveys an idea of delicacy; it has a pleasant sound. We associate it with the idea of meat pleasant to look upon and delicious to the taste, and not without cause: true dairy-fed pork is indeed a luxury ; it causes no indigestion and sits easily on the stomach.

" The refuse of the dairy consists of butter-milk, whey, and skim-milk ; and these, mixed with the flour of steamed potatoes, Indian-corn, pea-meal, barley-meal, &c., constitute a diet of the most nutritious quality for fattening. Such food, however, should not be administered to store hogs ; it is decidedly a *fattening* diet, and hogs accustomed to it do not thrive well when it is withheld and inferior food substituted. No one indeed would think of supplying mere store hogs with such luxurious food. On this diet some of the fattest porkers of thirteen, fifteen, or twenty weeks old, have been reared, as well as bacon-hogs under the age of one year.

THE REFUSE OF THE CORN-MILL.

" The large miller finds swine a profitable stock. The very sweepings of the mill are thus made by the miller to return a profit; he may not have to purchase whey, or butter-milk, or skim-milk, from the farmer, but the latter has to purchase barley-meal, &c., from the miller, or at least to pay him for grinding it.

THE REFUSE OF THE STARCH MANUFACTORY.

"Among other substances available for swine is the *refuse of the starch manufactory*, that is, of the grain or potatoes used in the production. It is said to be extremely nutritious, the animals fattening on it with great rapidity, and yielding very firm and substantial bacon. It is apt to cloy the appetite, and should be given alternately with food of a different quality ; indeed, in all cases, alternation of food is highly desirable, as the stomach palls upon one exclusive kind. The best method of preserving the paste deprived of the starch is to dry it. As is evident, it can only be employed locally and not generally ; it is said to be far superior to the refuse grains and wash of the brewery or distillery.

THE REFUSE OF THE BREWERY AND DISTILLERY.

"Hogs are usually kept in considerable numbers by the proprietors of large breweries and distilleries ; nevertheless these refuse grains and wash are not well adapted for sound fattening, unless mixed or alternated with other food, as pollard, barley-meal, &c. It is true that the animals become in good apparent condition, but their fat is flabby, and does not swell on being boiled, as the fat of good bacon ought to do.

"With respect to the refuse of the *distilleries*, especially the wash, it ought to be very cautiously given; if allowed too liberally, the animals reel from intoxication, until they are accustomed to it, and we cannot but think its influence upon the healthy condition of the animals to be injurious.

"This wash is not a natural food; it is not one which they will at first take willingly, nor can we regard it as beneficial; the pigs may indeed become bloated, but not covered with firm solid fat; it must impair their digestive powers, and render the liver torpid and perhaps swollen; mixed with water and barley-meal, or other farinaceous food, it may be admissible, but this is the best that can be said of it.

GREEN AND DRIED VEGETABLES.

"There are many vegetables used in the feeding of pigs, amongst which may be enumerated clover, sainfoin, lucern, chicory, tares, vetches, pea-haulm, cabbages, turnip-tops, &c.; it is desirable that these, when given, should be cut up small, and mixed with the wash, —indeed, simply cut up, with a little salt scattered among it, and occasionally mixed with a little pollard, it constitutes a good diet for store pigs, where the aim is not to fatten them, but to keep them in fair condition. Indeed, it is not advisable to render store pigs too fat or high in flesh; they grow larger, and their symmetry is better developed, by moderate diet than by full feeding, and afterwards, when put up to fatten for bacon, they thrive rapidly on the increased quantity and quality of the nutriment.

"Clover or lucern hay, cut up small and mixed with the wash, is also recommended, and, where it is practicable, an occasional or indeed a frequent run on good grass lands tends to the advantage of the animals. There are some wild plants, as the sow-thistle (*sonchus*) and others, of which swine are very fond; yet it would appear that these animals, omnivorous as they are, are choice in the selection of their vegetable fare, rejecting many plants on which the horse, ox, sheep, and goat will feed with avidity. It is remarkable that, although the hog will champ the fresh green shells of peas, it does not swallow the tough inner lining, and only drains away the saccharine juice, rejecting the rest.

ROOTS.

"Among the roots given to hogs in our island, potatoes take the first place. These should always be steamed and mashed, and mixed with whey or skimmed milk, with the addition of middlings, barley-meal, peas, &c. Hogs, as we have previously intimated, however apparently well fed on potatoes, do not produce firm bacon which swells greatly in boiling. Hence potatoes ought to form a portion only of their diet, nor indeed are they essentially necessary. In the Channel Islands the store hogs are fattened almost entirely upon boiled parsnips, and they attain to an enormous size, yielding good bacon. Among other roots we may mention carrots, turnips, especially Swedish turnips, and beet-root. All these roots should be boiled, but may be given raw, though not so advantageously. Carrots are highly esteemed by many, and no doubt contain a considerable quantity of nutriment, and in addition to meal may be used with advantage, especially when potatoes are dear and scarce, in consequence of a general failure in the crops. They might, even when given alone, with the addition of whey, or butter-milk, or skim-milk, make the animal reasonably fat, as in the instance of parsnip feeding, but we should doubt whether the quality of the bacon would prove first-rate.

" The same observations apply to Swedish turnips, which are extolled by some as superior to potatoes.

" What will be the character of the bacon produced by such diet is another thing; an animal may be made fat, but the fat may be soft, oily, and waste in boiling.

" No roots, without a due admixture of farinaceous food, as pollard, barley-meal, peas, &c., will produce first-rate bacon, and indeed in the finishing-off, or last stage of feeding, it is better to omit the roots altogether, and give only peas, barley-meal, whey, &c. The same observations apply to *pork;* even young delicate dairy-fed pork requires to be finished off on a mixture of farinaceous food with the refuse of the dairy, in order that the meat may acquire a due degree of firmness. In this respect, as well as in age, pork differs from the sucking-pig; in the latter, tenderness and succulency are in the extreme; they render the young creature, when well cooked, one of the most delicate of ' all the delicacies.'

GRAIN AND BEANS AND PEAS.

" To dwell upon the nutritive qualities of grain in general would be useless. The value of barley-meal, middlings, mill-sweepings, &c., in the feeding of hogs, is well known. It is true that this food is expensive, but then it is not used exclusively till the time for finishing off, or need not be; and, what is more, the expense is repaid by the gain of the animal in weight, and by the great superiority of the meat, which will command its price in the market. The rapid increase in the weight of hogs fed upon barley-meal, peas, steamed potatoes, with whey or butter-milk, is astonishing. They have been known to increase at the rate of $3\frac{1}{2}$ lbs. (live weight) per day, and often at the rate of 2 or $1\frac{1}{2}$ lbs. Here is some remuneration certainly for extra expense, even if the finishing off be entirely on meal and skim-milk.

"There is only one legitimate way of giving barley and that is in the form of meal made into porridge with lukewarm milk, whey, or water, to which potato-meal may be added or not, as is deemed desirable. To give the grain in a raw state, or even bruised, or infused in water till it begins to swell and germinate, is, we consider, very disadvantageous; it is, in fact, attended by two evils—in the first place, the greedy animal does not sufficiently grind down the food for the complete extraction of all its nutriment; and, secondly, semi-champed grain is liable to produce indigestion, loss of appetite, and fever. The same effects are produced by mixing the meal with boiling fluid, which converts it into a sort of dough or paste, very unfit for being taken into the stomach.

"Some recommend that the meal be mixed with cold water in large cisterns, the proportion being five bushels of meal to a hundred gallons of water. This mixture must be stirred several times a-day, for a fortnight or three weeks, until an imperfect fermentation takes place, and it becomes acescent. In this state its fattening powers are said to be greatly increased; but the ordinary way is to mix the meal with lukewarm water, or whey, or butter-milk (pea-meal or potato-flour being added or not), and give it in the form of a thick soup to the animals. Next to barley-meal, oat-meal may be ranked in order, and in some counties it is largely given. It may be made into a sort of thick gruel with wash or whey, &c., or it may be mixed with water, set to leaven, and given in an acescent state.

"Maize takes a high rank among the grains used for feeding hogs. It is little, if at all, inferior to barley, and the animals are very fond of it. It may be ground into meal, or given in its natural state, after being soaked for some time in water, either alone, or in a wash, or in gruel. In many parts of Europe, and in America especially, where many varieties of maize or Indian corn are extensively cultivated, the flesh of hogs, and also poultry, fed upon Indian corn, has a peculiarly fine flavor.

"Occasionally *rice* has been used for fattening hogs. One great objection to this article would be its expense, and we should not think it equal to barley-meal, although it abounds in nutriment. The proper way to prepare it is to put the rice into boiling water (two ordinary pailsful to about forty gallons of water), and let the whole stand for several hours till it is cold. The rice will then be found to have swelled amazingly, and to be compacted into a mass so firm as to admit of being taken out by means of a shovel. In this state it may be given to the hogs, either with whey, milk, &c., or by itself; a certain portion of potatoes mashed after steaming may be added. The flesh of hogs fed on rice is said to have proved very superior. *Peas* and *beans*, either in their green state, or dried and bruised, or ground into meal, are among the best articles of food for fattening swine. Pea-meal, or the meal of the gray pea, or gray peas bruised, are in the highest esteem. Pea-meal may be given alone, or added to the barley-meal, or to the steamed potatoes.

"*Buckwheat* is excellent for fattening hogs. With respect to rye little need be said; occasionally hogs are fed upon rye-meal.

SEEDS OF VARIOUS VEGETABLES, FRUITS, &C.

"*Linseed* cake, or oil-cake as it is called, is occasionally given to hogs, and sometimes linseed meal, or steeped linseed, but only in small quantities, and in addition to food destitute of oil, as potatoes, pea-meal, &c. Oil-cake is used largely in the fattening of horned cattle, but whether it is equally advantageous in the fattening of hogs is not very clear.

"*Beechmast* is eagerly devoured by hogs, and in places where this is abundant, it will be well to turn store hogs into it, or collect it for their use. It is an article of diet not to be despised, but as an adjunct and not a principal article. But though hogs thrive on this food, it will not make firm fat, unless largely mixed with acorns.

"A run in oak copses ought not to be neglected at the time of the fall, by a farmer who has the opportunity of sending his store hogs into the wood.

"In England, chestnuts, as food for hogs, are out of the question. This is not the case, however, in many parts of the Continent, where these are abundant, and indeed where they form portions of woods. There the chestnut tree affords an abundant supply, both for men and swine, and the latter are bountifully supplied with it; it is seldom given raw, but roasted or steamed, or parboiled into a pulp, then crushed and divested of the outer shell. By the conversion of it into a potato-like meal, the nutritive qualities of this fruit are greatly improved, and it is thereby better fitted for the digestive action of the stomach.

"With respect to apples, pumpkins, and even peaches, which in some parts of America are lavishly given to swine, we have little to say. Boiled apples mixed with potatoes, Indian-corn flour, or buckwheat, will no doubt prove nutritious, and in America constitute a cheap diet, but the case is different in England. In North Africa the wild-boar makes incursions into the melon-grounds, and we can conceive that melons, abounding with saccharine matter, are grateful to the palate of the wild hog, and so no doubt are apples, pumpkins, and peaches, but they do not enter into the English bill of fare for hogs. At the same time, we object not to the plan of turning hogs into apple orchards in order that they may pick up the fallen fruit.

"We may here notice a few other articles which do not come under any precise head. One of these is *hay-tea*, or rather an infusion of clover, sainfoin, or lucern hay, which is by many recommended as an excellent vehicle for mixing with other food. It may be thickened with potato-flour, steamed carrots, boiled cabbages, barley or oatmeal, and for store hogs, in particular, it is said to be excellent, not only as keeping the animals in first-rate condition, but as saving more expensive kinds of food which must otherwise be given.

"Another article is *salt*. Salt is almost essential to health; it stimulates the appetite, it aids the operation of digestion, and all cattle are partial to it. A little salt should, therefore, be scattered into the food before it is given to the animal.

"We must not here exclude *earth* or *calcareous* matters from our consideration. With the roots which a hog ploughs up in the ground and devours, a small quantity of earth is necessarily swallowed, the calcareous particles of which act beneficially by correcting any acidity in the stomach. Hogs put up to fatten, highly fed, and taking little or no exercise, are very liable to acidity of the stomach, and loss of appetite as a consequence. Many breeders, aware of this, give the animals occasionally ashes or cinders, which they champ and swallow; or turn them out now and then upon a patch of ground, over which lime or chalk has been freely sprinkled, in which they root and pick up morsels, which, with the lime and particles of earth, are swallowed. It is not a bad plan to mix occasionally a little magnesia or chalk in the wash or milk; this will very effectually correct acidity. Here then, we have another reason why a run, from time to time, in the field given to hogs is advisable; with every root, every pig-nut that they swallow, they take in a portion of earth."

CHAPTER XIII.

On the Proper Construction of Piggeries—Ventilation—Description of Mr. Henderson's Styes—Cooking Apparatus—Curious Contrivance for Feeding Pigs—Description of the Piggery at Prince Albert's Home Farm—Description of a Piggery at Lascoed—Advantages of Cleanliness—Pig-keeping in Mexico.

THERE are few things more conducive to the thriving and well-being of swine than airy, spacious, well-constructed styes, and, above all, cleanliness. The old prejudices — that any place was good enough to keep a pig in, and that filth and pig-styes were synonymous terms—are now passed away, and the necessity of attention to this branch of porcine economy generally recognized.

Formerly swine were too often housed in damp, dirty, close,

imperfectly built sheds; this was an error, and a fruitful source of disease, and of unthrifty animals.

In large establishments where numerous pigs are kept, there should be divisions appropriated to all the different kinds of pigs; the males, the breeding sows, the newly weaned, and the fattening pigs should all be kept separate; and it were as well that in the divisions appropriated to the second and last of these four classes, there should be a distinct apartment for each animal, all opening into a yard or enclosure of limited extent. As pigs require warmth, these buildings should face the south, and be kept weather-tight and well drained. Good ventilation is also important, for it is needless to expect animals to make good flesh and retain their health unless they have a sufficiency of pure air. The blood requires it to give it vitality and free it from impurities, as much as the stomach requires wholesome and strengthening food, and when it has it not, becomes vitiated, and impairs all the animal functions.

> " The blood, the fountain whence the spirits flow,
> The generous stream that waters every part,
> And motion, vigor, and warm life conveys
> To every moving, breathing particle,"

becomes contaminated by those aërial poisons given out by the decaying vegetable matter, rotten or damp litter, accumulations of dung, and animal exhalations engendered by ill-ventilated styes. These noxious gases are inhaled by the breath, and absorbed by the skin, until they enter the circulation, and impair its vivifying fluid. It is by the action of the atmospheric air that venous blood is converted into arterial, freed from all its impurities, and rendered fit to sustain all the vital functions; hence it must be at once evident that if this important agent is in the first place contaminated, its action must be impaired and its effects empoisoned. Besides, bad smells and exhalations injure the flavor of the meat.

Damp and cold floors should also be guarded against, as they tend to induce cramp and diarrhœa; and the roof so contrived as to carry off the wet from the pigs.

The walls of a well-constructed sty should be of solid masonry; the roof sloping, and furnished with spouts to carry off the rain; the floors either slightly inclined towards a gutter made to carry off the rain, or else raised from the ground on beams or joists, and perforated so that all urine and moisture shall drain off. Bricks and tiles are much used for the flooring of styes, but are objectionable, because, however well covered with litter, they still strike cold; wood is far superior in this respect; as well as because it admits of those clefts or perforations being made which we have just recommended, and which not only serve to drain off all moisture, but admit fresh air as well. The value of the litter and dung as manure, must always be borne in mind, and all things ɔo arranged that none of it shall be wasted.

The door of each sty ought to be so hung that it will open inwards or outwards, so as to give the animals free ingress and egress; and to do this it should be hung across from side to side, and the animal push it up to effect its entry or exit; for if it were hung in the usual way it would derange the litter every time it opened inwards, and be very liable to hitch. If it is not intended that the pigs shall leave their sty, there should be an upper and lower door, the former of which should always be left open when the weather is warm and dry, while the latter will serve to confine the animal.

There should also be windows or slides which can be opened oɪ closed at will, to give admission to the fresh air, or exclude rain oɪ cold.

Mr. Henderson's description of his styes is more lucid and practicaɪ than mere vague directions, we will therefore give it in his owɪ words :—" The plan which I recommend is as follows. Have a housɐ thirty feet by fifteen, with four doors all opening outwards, and three partition walls through the house, viz., a wall between each of the doors, dividing the house into four compartments. The two middle ones I use for eating-rooms, and the others for sleeping-apartments, having an inner door between each eating and sleeping-apartment. By this plan the keeper is enabled to get the eating-chambers swept out, the troughs cleaned, and the food put into them without disturbing the swine or being disturbed by them. There should be a division wall having a door in it through each sleeping-apartment; in the hinder part should be the litter; and the front and smalleɪ compartment, through which the animals must pass to get to their food, may be used by them as a kind of necessary, for these animals will never defile their beds if they can avoid it.

" The following is the most convenient manger for their food. Let it be as long as the house is wide, and fixed against the middle wall; in form similar to a horse manger, but not so deep, and it must be divided into twelve divisions by partition boards four feet in length or height, and a little broader than the manger is wide; thus a number will feed as well and as quietly together as two or three. Before every meal the trough should be well washed and the place swept, and once in the day a little fresh litter placed in the sleeping-chambers. Each of these sleeping and eating-rooms may be temporarily divided into two, should it be requisite. The sleeping-rooms should be dark, as animals fatten much more rapidly when they lie down and sleep after each meal than they do when they wander about. There should be a square yard to each piggery, well paved and drained, as should the styes also be; and where it is possible, an enclosure or a small piece of ground adjoining is exceedingly useful.

" Those who have space to admit of it will find it advantageous to have five apartments instead of four, and in the fifth or central one to have a boiler to prepare the food, and chests and lockers to contain the various stores."

Parkinson advises that in the yard or enclosure before every piggery should be a "rubbing-post, or, what is still more beneficial, two posts having a pole between them similar to a horse's leaping-bar, but not revolving; this pole should be raised or let down to the height of the pigs, as the rubbing of the animals against it causes a freer circulation of blood, the same as the flesh-brush does to human bodies."

In all large establishments there should be a proper apparatus for cooking, mixing, and preserving the food. For this a boiler and steamer will be requisite, and some two or three tanks which may be made of bricks plastered over on the interior to prevent leakage, and fixed in the ground. Wherever it can be managed, the troughs should be so situated that they can be filled and cleaned from the exterior without interfering with or disturbing the animals at all, and for this purpose, the following very simple contrivance has been recommended:—"Have a flap or door with swinging hinges made to hang horizontally over the trough, so that it can be moved to and fro, and alternately be fastened by a bolt to the inside or outside of the manger. When the hogs have fed sufficiently, the door is swung inwards and fastened, and so remains until feeding-time, when the trough is cleaned and refilled without any trouble, and then the flap drawn back and the animals admitted to their food." Some persons cover the trough with a lid having as many holes in it as there are pigs to eat from it. This is by no means a bad plan, for then each pig selects his own hole and eats away without interfering with or incommoding his neighbor.

We are indebted to the kindness of a friend for the following account of the Royal piggery, at the Home Farm at Windsor. It consists of an oblong slated shed, of sufficient length and breadth to contain about two dozen sties, of somewhat larger dimensions than ordinary pig-sties, and arranged in two rows with a broad walk between them, from which the spectator looks into the sties on the right and left of him. Each sty has an in-door and an out-door apartment, the former having a wooden coverlid to it, going upon hinges like the lid of a cornbin, instead of a roof, which may be raised to any height in hot or close weather, so as to admit any influx of air required, or even be thrown back if necessary. The sties are paved with brick, both within and without doors, and their floors slightly declivitous.

The following is a description of a piggery at Lascoed Pont Senny, planned and executed by Mr. J. Donaldson, land steward to A. M. Storley, Esq., Brecon, South Wales:—This piggery is constructed for the purpose of breeding and feeding on a scale to suit a farm of six hundred acres of turnip soil in an inland situation, where convenient markets render easy the disposal both of fat and lean stock. There are seven sties at the end of the steaming-house which accommodate a boar and six brood sows, which are calculated to produce yearly one hundred pigs, sixty of which will be fattened from September to April in fifteen sties, placed in two parallel rows, and made to contain two hogs in each apartment. The rest are sold as stores. The yearly rental is from 200*l*. to 250*l*. according to the prices of the produce. The steamed food consists of potatoes and meal, with grain to finish, and is conveyed to the sties along a paved road or path, in a small four-wheeled wagon. The steamer also cooks potatoes for the working horses, and chaff for milch cows, and thus applies the original cost to several purposes, and fully employs a man. The store pigs are fed in summer with clover and vetches, and in winter with roots either raw or steamed. Water is brought to the steaming-house in a pipe from the farm-yards, which are all supplied by ball-cocks from elevated casks fed by a forcing-pump. A pipe underneath conveys the water from the potato-washer to the pond in the store-yard, where it passes to the lower curve of the yard, and then meeting with the collected moisture of the whole area of the piggery, falls through an iron grate into a paved culvert, and is conveyed to the manure-pit, to which the liquid of the farmery is collected and brought by a drain; along the side of the road are sheds opening into the store-yard. The cost of erecting a piggery like this will vary from 80*l*. to 100*l*., according to the price of labor and materials, and to whether the roofs be tiled or slated. The steaming-house has an upper floor to serve as a store-house for grain, meal, roots, &c.

The piggery should always be built as near to that part of the establishment from which the chief part of provision is to come as possible, as much labor will thus be saved. If the dairy is to supply this, let it be as near as may be to that building; or if it is to come from a brewery or distillery, then let it be near to them.

Care must also be taken to preserve the dung and urine, and some place fixed in which these matters can be stored for manure. Wher ever the swine are regularly and well managed, this will not be difficult, for the animals will always, if they can, lay their dung at a distance from the place where they sleep or feed. A small paved yard, somewhat sloping, and with a gutter to serve as a receptacle, will best answer this purpose, and thence it can be daily removed to the proper heap or tank.

We have been told of a gentleman who keeps only a few pigs for his own use, and has a double sty for them, by which means he is enabled to keep them exceedingly clean and sweet. Every morning the pigs are changed from one into the other, so that each sty remains unoccupied for four-and-twenty hours, during which time it is thoroughly cleaned out, and of course becomes well aired, and free .

from all unpleasant smell. And well do we remember the pleasure with which we used to view the pigs and sties of an old friend of ours, now no more. A door leading out of his beautiful flower-garden brought us to those equally well-tended objects of his pride. The sties were always kept whitened on the inside; the sloping floor carried off all moisture to a deep gutter running between the sty and the square-paved yard, each of which inclined towards it; a trough ever stood with water clear as crystal for them to drink, and the animals themselves were, by washing, currycombing, and perfect cleanliness about them, as neat and sleek as a lady's lap dog. They were, in fact, pet pigs. Nor are we without pleasurable reminiscences of delicate spare ribs, loins, and legs of pork, and delicious sucking-pigs.

Washings, combings, and brushings, are valuable adjuncts in the treatment of swine; the energies of the skin are thus roused and the pores opened, consequently the healthful functions are aided, and that inertness so likely to be engendered by the lazy life of a fattening pig counteracted. We cannot close this chapter without quoting the following account of the mode of keeping pigs in Mexico :—

"Fine breeds of these useful animals are kept by many persons of wealth, as an article of trade, in the city of Mexico; and the care and attention paid to their cleanliness and comfort so far exceed any thing I have seen elsewhere, that a short account may be useful by furnishing hints to our farmers, brewers, distillers, &c., by whom large numbers of these valuable animals could be and are conveniently kept. The premises where the business is carried on are extensive, consisting in general of a good dwelling-house, with a shop, slaughter-house, and places for singeing the pigs, large bowls for rendering the lard, salting and drying-rooms, and lard-rooms, with wooden bins for containing the rendered fat, which is an article of great consumption in Spanish cookery, being used as a substitute for butter. There is also a soap manufactory, in which the offal fat is manufactured, and apartments where the blood is made into a kind of black-pudding, and sold to the poor. Behind all these are the sties for the hogs, generally from eight hundred to one thousand in number, which occupy a considerable range of well-built sheds about thirty feet deep, with the roofs descending very low, and having the entrance through low arches, before which is an open space the whole length of the yard, and about twenty-four feet wide, in the centre of which is a kind of aqueduct built of stone, and filled with clear water supplied from a well at the end of the premises. The hogs can only put their noses into this water through holes in the wall, which prevents their dirtying it, as it passes through the whole division of the yard. This is the only liquid given them, and their food is maize or Indian corn, slightly moistened, and scattered at stated hcurs on the ground, which in the yard, as well as the place where they sleep, is kept perfectly dry and clean.   They are attended by Indians with every possible care.   There is a cold bath on the premises, which they are obliged frequently to use, as cleanliness is considered essential to their acquiring that enormous load of fat from which the principal profit is derived.   Their ease and comfort seem also in every respect to be studiously attended to; and the occupation of two Indian lads will cause a smile on the countenances of my musical readers, when they are informed that they are employed from morning till night in settling any disputes or little bickerings that may arise among the happy inhabitants of this community, either in respect to rank or condition, and in singing them to sleep. The boys are chosen for the strength of their lungs, and their taste and judgment in delighting the ears and lulling the senses of this amiable harmonic society; they succeed each other in chanting during the whole day, to the great delight and gratification of their bristly audience, who seem fully to appreciate the merits of the performers."   Martin says:—

"Any place is thought good enough for a pig, no matter how dark, damp, or filthy it may be, and in such places we have seen pigs kept.   But what has been the consequence?—Diseases of the skin, swellings of the joints, dullness, and loss of eager, healthy appetite; often, after being slaughtered, the intestines are found infested by parasitic worms. So far from any place being good enough for a pig, much of the animal's health and ultimate profit-ableness depend on the domicile in which it is kept.   For those who keep only one or two pigs, a well-built wind and waterproof sty or shed for a dormitory, in an inclosure for air and exercise as large as convenient, will suffice.   The feeding-trough should be made of stone, as wooden troughs are liable to be gnawed, and are often knocked over when half full of food by the snout of the pig, either by accident or in wantonness.   It would be well also to give the animal access to a stone receptacle of clean water; for though much water should not be given to a pig during the progress of fattening, still the animal should never be allowed to suffer from thirst; nothing tends more than thrist to derange the digestive organs, and prevent the animal from thriving.   The floor of the whole sty and yard should be well paved with brick, and incline to a drain, both for the sake of dryness and facility of cleaning.   The manure, liquid as well as more solid, should be put into a manure-pit for the future benefit of the garden.   A sufficient quantity of straw should be spread on the floor of the dormitory, and all should be clean, even the trough, which should be washed out every day. The door should be made to open inwards; otherwise, if not very strongly secured, it is liable to be forced open by the animal, and much mischief may be done in the garden before any one is aware of it.   Pigs are very fond of rubbing their sides and shoulders against convenient objects, and this, as it excites the circulation of the blood in the vessels of the skin, is very beneficial ; hence, a short stout post driven into the ground, by one of the side walls of the little yard or inclosure, would be a serviceable and unexpensive addition.   The sty should not be exposed to the cold, damp winds; at the same time, it should be shaded from the mid-day glare of a hot summer's sun. Such a sty as we have described, a cottager may build for himself : it will cost little, excepting his own labor.   His objects are the comfort of the animal, and the saving of the manure; and the latter object, in particular, is too often neglected, as is also the cleanliness of the sty altogether.

"The above remarks apply more especially to the cottager, but are not quite applicable, excepting as far as principle goes, to the farmer, who finds it profitable to keep many pigs, or the brewer, or distiller, or milk-merchant, upon whose establishments great numbers of these animals are kept.   The farmer may find a range of simple styes similar to what we have just described to be convenient, with larger accommodations for breeding sows, and an exclusive and well-secured domicile for the boar.   The young pigs, and porkers, with the sows, will have the advantage of a farm-yard or large straw-yard, in which they may indulge themselves according to their natural instincts.   They must of course be stied up for fattening ; but before this process commences they may be turned into the cut wheat fields in autumn, or into the oak copses (if there be such,) not however without being under surveillance.   The air and the moderate exercise taken in searching for a scanty but excellent kind of food, will render their repast when driven home in the afternoon most acceptable.   The farmer, however, and the brewer or milk-merchant (we mean the great milk-dealers in the neighborhood of London,) are differently situated.   In the latter cases, a well-arranged series of airy, cleanly styes is imperative, especially for pigs above the size of sucklings, for even in such establishments the latter may be allowed some degree of liberty.   System and order should prevail.   There should be a proper place in which to mix and boil the food, with one or more large coppers and straining apparatus.   The food should be mixed in square brick tanks, sunk in the ground and cemented, in order that no filtration of the more fluid parts may take place.   If there is only one tank there should be a partition in it.   From the boiling-house there should be an immediate communication with the styes, under cover if possible— but an out-house close to the styes, with a loft for roots, &c., may be made available.   Each sty should open into a small yard behind, inclosed with a low wall or paling, but with a strong door.   There should be separate styes for breeding sows, for porkers, and fatten-ing hogs. Not more than three or four of the latter should be in one sty. The food should be given in troughs, in a separate com-partment from that in which the hogs lie down, and no litter should be allowed there. The floor should be of brick or stone; should be frequently washed clean, and the troughs should be cleaned out before every meal. Any of the food left from the last meal should be taken out and given to the store pigs. A very convenient con-trivance for keeping the troughs clean is to have a flap or door made with hinges, so that it can swing, and alternately be fastened by a bolt to the inside or outside edge of the trough. When the hogs have fed sufficiently, the door is swung in, and the trough easily cleaned out. It remains on the inside till feeding time, when the food is poured in without any impediment from the greedy hogs, who cannot get at it till the door is swung out. This simple con-trivance saves a great deal of trouble, and is easily adapted to any common sty. It is a great advantage to be able to inspect the styes without going into them; and this is effected by placing them under a common roof, which may conveniently be a lean-to to the boiling-house or any other building, with a passage between them.

" Where numerous pigs are kept, it will be advantageous to have a double row of styes, with a paved alley between them; there should be good drainage, by which all refuse is carried off to a manure-pit, and the greatest cleanliness should be maintained. Six breeding sows, giving each two litters per annum, will produce yearly upwards of a hundred pigs ; of these, fifty or sixty may be fattened at the latter part of autumn, through the winter, and during the months of February and March, for bacon ; the younger brood may be killed as porkers, or sold off as stores. With respect to the steaming apparatus, it will be found available for other animals on the farm, as horses, &c., to which steamed potatoes and other roots may be profitably allowed.

" The breeding sows should be kept each by itself in a large and commodious sty, and the store and fattening pigs should have their respective tenements. Some recommend that the floor of the sleep-ing-shed be made of planks, as bricks are cold and apt to induce cramp or diarrhœa ; certainly wood is preferable to bricks. Where bricks are used, they should be set in cement, in order that no filtration may take place through the interstices, and thereby keep the soil underneath in a state of wetness, whence noxious gases will necessarily arise and generate disease, to the great loss of the farmer. Another thing is desirable, namely, that the roof of the sty, whether composed of slates, tiles, or slabs of stone, should have a gutter in order to carry off the rain ; this may be easily contrived, and at little expense, and will often keep the sty from being flooded."
—Martin.

CHAPTER XIV.

Pigs, Profit of, to the Butcher—Sucking-pigs—Pork-butchers—Pig-killing at Rome—Pickling
Pork—Bacon : Mode of Curing in Hampshire—Buckinghamshire—Wiltshire—Yorkshire—
Westphalia—America—Brine a Poison for Pigs—Quantity of Bacon, Ham, and Salt Pork
imported during the last Three Years—Importation of Swine—Pigs'Dung as Manure.

THERE is perhaps no animal so entirely profitable to the butcher
as the pig. Scarcely an atom of it but is useful. The offal is so
small as not to be thought of in comparison with that arising from
cattle and sheep. The feet, the head, and even portions of the intestines are saleable for food and eagerly purchased by epicures; the
scraps and trimmings of the meat make delicious sausages, pork pies,
and other such savory dishes; brawn, too, is another of the delicacies
we owe to the much despised pig; the fat, or lard, is invaluable to
cooks, confectioners, perfumers, and apothecaries; pigs' bladders
meet a ready sale; the skin is available for pocket-books and several
purposes; and the bristles form by no means an inconsiderable item
in the tables of imports and exports, and are used by shoemakers,
as well as in the manufacture of brushes, &c. Lastly, the flesh in
the form of fresh or pickled pork, ham, and bacon, constitutes the
chief food of thousands of human beings in all parts of the globe.

In France, from one-half to two-thirds of the meat consumed by
the poorer and middling classes of the provinces is pork. In Ireland,
the peasantry and many of the middle-men scarcely know the taste
of any other kind of meat. In most of our Channel Islands pork
constitutes the staple animal food of the laboring classes and small
farmers; and in America, and especially among the new settlements
and back-woods, it is often the only animal food for the first few
years of the settler's life.

SUCKING-PIGS.

In our own country, "sucking-pigs" too are in great esteem, and
will, at their season, fetch a very high price. Charles Lamb, in one
of his inimitable "Essays of Elia," declares, "Of all the delicacies
of the whole *mundus edibilis,* I will maintain this to be the most
delicate.

"I speak not of your grown porkers—things between pig and
pork—these hobbydehoys; but a young and tender suckling, under
a moon old, guiltless as yet of the sty; with no original speck of
the *amor immunditiæ,* the hereditary failing of the first parent, as
yet manifest; his voice as yet not broken, but something between
a childish treble and a grumble, the mild forerunner or *præludium*
of a grunt.

"*He must be roasted.* I am not ignorant that our ancestors ate them seethed or boiled; but what a sacrifice of the exterior tegument!

" There is no flavor comparable, I will contend, to that of the crisp, tawny, well watched, not over-roasted, *crackling*, as it is well called; the very teeth are invited to their share of the pleasure at this banquet, in overcoming the coy, brittle resistance, with the adhesive oleaginous—Oh, call it not fat!—but an indefinable sweetness growing up to it—the tender blossoming of fat—fat cropped in the bud —taken in the shoot—in the first innocence—the cream and quintessence of the child-pig's yet pure food; the lean, no lean; but a kind of animal manna, or rather, fat and lean (if it must be so) so blended and running into each other, that both together make but one ambrosian result, or common substance.

" Behold him while he is doing! it seemeth rather a refreshing warmth than a scorching heat that he is so passive to. How equally he twirleth round the string. Now he is just done. To see the extreme sensibility of that tender age; he hath wept out his pretty eyes — radiant jellies — shooting stars. See him in the dish, his second cradle; how meek he lieth! wouldst thou have this innocent grow up to the grossness and indocility which too often accompany maturer swinehood? Ten to one he would have proved a glutton, a sloven, an obstinate, disagreeable animal, wallowing in all filthy conversation—from these sins he is happily snatched away.

> Ere sin could blight or sorrow fade,
> Death came with timely care.

" His memory is odoriferous: no clown curseth, whilst his stomach half ejecteth the rank bacon; no coalheaver bolteth him in reeking sausages: he hath a fair sepulchre in the grateful stomach of the judicious epicure, and for such a tomb might be content to die.

" Pig—let me speak his praise—is no less provocative of the appetite than he is satisfactory to the criticalness of the censorious palate. The strong man may batten on him, and the weakling refuseth not his mild juices.

" Unlike to mankind's mixed characters, a bundle of virtues and vices, inexplicably intertwisted and not to be unravelled without hazard, he is—good throughout. No part of him is better or worse than another. He helpeth, as far as his little means goeth, all around."

Sucking-pigs should be killed at from a fortnight to three weeks old. The Chinese breed furnishes the most delicate and delicious "porklings." They should be stuck; all the blood suffered to drain out; scalded and scraped gently; and the bowels taken out, and the inside sponged dry and clean.

The alterations latterly effected in the breeds of swine have tended materially to improve pork, and to render it more sought for and valued. We can recall to mind when the thought of pork was associated in our minds with visions of coarse-grained meat and oily fat, and with forebodings of a fit of indigestion. Nothing could tend more effectually to banish such fancies than a sight and taste of the small, fine-grained joints, delicate as poultry, and of excellent flavor, which have taken the place of those ungainly legs and Brobdignagian loins and hands of "olden times."

And with the improvement of the meat has grown an increased demand for it. Formerly, ay, as lately as within the last five and twenty years, the trade of "pork-butcher" was unknown in almost all our country towns, even in those of some considerable importance; it is no longer so; there are now few places of any size or note which have not on an average one pork-butcher to every two or three meat-butchers; and in all smaller places pork is generally to be procured wherever other meat is sold.

PORKERS.

'Supposing the brood to be weaned at the age of eight or nine weeks, those destined for porkers may be allowed the range of the paddock or straw yard for three or four weeks, being at the same time regularly fed on the refuse of the mill and dairy. Where, as in the case of market gardeners and other such, a degree of liberty cannot be allowed, we recommend that the sty-yard be as roomy and extensive as possible. During the last ten days or fortnight, the feeding may be pushed, and more barley-meal, pea-meal, and milk allowed. Too many pigs should not be kept together in the same sty, nor should they be of unequal ages, as the larger are apt to persecute their younger co-mates, and drive them from the trough. Porkers are killed at different ages, varying from about three months to seven months old. We consider that the true dairy-fed pork is in perfection when the animal does not exceed the age of about three months, or ranges from three to four months. Large pork is apt to be coarse and over fat, and consequently not so digestible as younger meat, and is therefore not so much sought for in the London market. It bears a lower price than small pork; and though the pig weighs heavier, still, taking the extra keep into consideration, it is perhaps not more profitable. On such points as this, however, the breeder will always consult his own interest, and study the demands of the market.

STORE HOGS.

"Of store hogs little need be said—they are intended either for sale, or as future bacon hogs. They should be kept in fair condition, not too low, and their health should be attended to; they should be allowed to run in the fields or in the woods and copses, when the beechmast or acorns are falling, and be regularly and moderately fed at certain intervals, say in the morning and evening; knowing their feeding times, by habit, they will never willingly be absent, and wherever they may ramble during the day, their return at the appointed time in the evening may be safely calculated upon. After their evening meal they should be secured in their sty, and snugly bedded up.

HOGS FATTENING FOR BACON

"Bacon-hogs (we here except breeding sows, destined after two or three litters for the butcher) are generally put up to fatten at the age of twelve or eighteen months. Under the term bacon-hogs, we include the barrows and spayed females chosen by the breeder or feeder for fattening, after the age admissible as porkers. In the fattening of bacon-hogs much judgment is requisite. It will not answer to over-feed them at first; under such a plan they will lose their appetite, become feverish, and require medicine. *They should be fed at regular intervals;* this is essential; animals fed regularly thrive better than those fed at irregular intervals, nor should more food be given them at each meal than they will consume. *They should be sufficiently satisfied, yet not satiated.* It would be as well to vary their diet; midlings, peas, potato-meal, and barley-meal may be given alternately, or in different admixtures with wash, whey, butter-milk, skim-milk, and the occasional addition of cut grasses, and other green vegetables; a little salt should be scattered in their mess—it will contribute to their health, and quicken their appetite; a stone trough of clean water should be accessible, and the feeding-troughs should be regularly cleaned out after every meal. The sty should be free from all dirt, and the bed of straw comfortable; indeed, it is an excellent practice to wash and brush the hides of the animals, so as to keep the skin clean, excite the circulation of the cutaneous vessels and open the pores. Pigs thus treated will fatten more kindly than dirty, scurfy animals put upon better fare. This essential point is greatly neglected, from the too common idea that the pig is naturally a filthy brute, than which nothing can be more untrue; it is the keeper who is filthy, and not the animal, if he constrain a pig to wallow in a disgusting sty.

"Too many pigs should not be fed in the same sty; three are sufficient, and they should be, as far as possible, of the same age;

and the meals should be given frequently, but only in moderation at each time,—over-gorging is sure to cause indigestion, and the only remedy for this is abstinence; a little sulphur occasionally mingled with their food is useful. When the store hogs are first put up (and we must suppose them in moderate condition), the food should only be a few degrees superior to that on which they have already fed; it should be improved step by step, till the digestive powers are adapted for that of the most nutritious quality; and with this the fattening must be completed.

"A bacon-hog is generally fattened in autumn, and killed about Christmas,—sometimes after Christmas, sometimes a few weeks before. The average length of time required for bringing the animal into good condition, varies from about fourteen to twenty-one weeks, according to size and breed. Some fatten hogs until they are incapable of moving, from the enormous load of fat with which they are burthened, and in order to accomplish this, four, five, or even six months are required. An animal so fed will certainly not pay for its food, nor can it be deemed in health; the heart and lungs will be oppressed, the circulation impeded, and the breathing laborious; sufficient fatness is all that is desirable. A fat hog is a comely, comfortable-looking animal, the embodied type of epicurean felicity; but a bloated, overladen hog is a disgusting object, uneasy and distressed in its own feelings, incapable even of enjoying its food, buried in its excessive fat.

"The quantity of barley-meal, pea-meal, or other farinaceous food (exclusive of wash, skim-milk, &c.) consumed by a hog during the time of its fattening for bacon, will vary greatly according to the size and breed of the animal. Taking the average, and supposing the pig's age to be fourteen or fifteen months, and the animal to be in fair condition, we should say that ten or twelve bushels of meal (that is, barley-meal, pea-meal, &c.) would be sufficient for every useful purpose; well do we know that much less often suffices. But we are supposing the production of first-rate bacon. Porkers, of course, require a less outlay according to their age. A porker ought not to carry too much fat; neither the feeder nor the buyer profit by over-fed pork, though perhaps the pork-butcher may—he retails it per pound to his customers. Our observations, however, do not apply to the respectable dealers in pork in London and its environs, who exhibit the most delicious country-fed meat, and justly pride themselves upon an article of consumption which brings them the first-rate custom.

"With respect to the estimated tables relative to the increase in weight of hogs, under certain modes of feeding, and under given quantities of food, we hold them to be utterly fallacious. The feeder's means, the produce of his grounds, the breed he adopts, and the proportion of attention he bestows on the porcine part of his stock, which will be regulated by his profit therein, will make all the difference, and must be taken into the account. To the farmer (we speak not of others), the profit to be derived by him from feeding porkers or bacon-hogs will depend upon *suitability*, or the apposite union of circumstances connected with the locality, convenience, and staple returns of his land. It is one thing to keep a few pigs for home consumption, and another to keep them as a source of income."—MARTIN.

PIG-KILLING.

A pig that is to be killed should be kept without food for the last 12 or 16 hours; a little water must, however, be within his reach. Mr. Henderson advises that in order to prevent the animal from struggling and screaming in the agonies of death, it should in the first place be stunned by a blow on the head. Some advise that the knife should be thrust into the neck so as to sever the artery leading from the heart, while others prefer that the animal should be stuck through the brisket in the direction of the heart, care, however, being taken not to touch the first rib. The blood should then be suffered to drain from the carcass, and the more completely it does so, the better will be the meat, say our English pork-butchers, but those of some parts of the Continent disagree with them, probably because there the pig's flesh is eaten for the most part fresh, or spiced, or cooked in other savory modes, and but seldom pickled or dried, therefore the superabundance of blood in it communicates to it a juicy richness agreeable to their palates.

Mr. Waterton gives a very graphic description of the slaughter house for swine at Rome, and the proceedings of the pig-killers :—

"As you enter Rome at the Porta del Popolo, a little on your right is the great slaughter-house, with a fine stream of water running through it. It is, probably, inferior to none in Italy for an extensive plan and for judicious arrangements. Here some 700 or 800 pigs are killed on every Friday during the winter season. Nothing can exceed the dexterity with which they are despatched. About 30 of these large and fat black pigs are driven into a commodious pen, followed by three or four men, each with a sharp skewer in his hand, bent at one end, in order that it may be used with advantage. On entering the pen, these performers, who put you vastly in mind of assassins, make a rush at the hogs, each seizing one by the leg, amid a general yell of horror on the part of the victims. Whilst the hog and the man are struggling on the ground, the latter with the rapidity of thought pushes his skewer betwixt the fore-leg and the body quite into the heart, and then gives it a turn or two. The pig can rise no more, but screams for a minute or so and then expires. This process is continued until they are all despatched, the brutes sometimes rolling over the butchers, and sometimes the butchers over the brutes, with a yelling enough to stun one's ears. In the mean time the screams become fainter and fainter, and then all is silence on the death of the last pig. A cart is in attendance; the carcasses are lifted into it, and it proceeds through the street, leaving one or more dead hogs at the different pork-shops. No blood appears outwardly, nor is the internal hæmorrhage prejudicial to the meat, for Rome cannot be surpassed in the flavor of her bacon or in the soundness of her hams."—*Essays on Natural History.*

PREPARING THE DEAD PIG.

As soon as the hog is dead, if it is intended for pork let it be laid on a board or table, and scalded with water nearly but not quite on the boil, and well scraped to get off all the hair and bristles. Bacon-hogs may be singed by enveloping the body in straw and setting the straw on fire, and then scraping it all over; but when this is done care must be taken not to burn or parch the cuticle. The next thing to be done is to take out the entrails and well wash the interior of the body with luke-warm water so as to remove all blood and impurities, and afterwards dry it with a clean cloth; the carcass should then be hung up in a cool place for eighteen or twenty hours to become set and firm.

On the following day the feet are first of all cut off, so that they shall not disfigure the hams or hands, and plenty of knuckle shall be left to hang them up by; the knife is then inserted at the nape of the neck and the carcass divided up the middle of the back bone; the head is then separated from each side close behind the ears, and the hams and shoulders taken off and trimmed; some take out the chine and upper part of the ribs in the first place, but almost every locality has its peculiar way of proceeding.

PICKLING PORK.

For pickling pork the sides should be rubbed over with sugar and salt, and then laid in a brine-tub, in which a thick layer of salt has already been strewn, and a slighter one of sugar; the pork must be cut into such pieces as will admit of its lying quite flat in the tub; the rind must be placed downwards, and between each layer of pork a layer of salt and sugar. When the tub is quite full, a layer of salt sufficiently thick to exclude the air must be spread over the whole, and the tub covered closely up and left for a week or ten days; if by this time the brine has not begun to rise, warm water should be sprinkled over the top layer.

Pork pickled in this way will be ready for use in about three months, and with proper care will be as good at the end of two years as it was when first begun. The sugar is considered to impart a finer and richer flavor than saltpetre, although the latter is most commonly used. There is no reason why both sugar and saltpetre may not be advantageously combined with the salt in pickling pork, as well as in salting beef, for in this latter process there can be no question that a pickle composed of three parts salt, one part saltpetre, and one sugar, is the very best that can be used, making the meat tender, juicy, well flavored, and fine colored.

CURING BACON.

Bacon is the next form in which we eat pig's flesh. There has been some dispute as to the derivation of this word; some authors have suggested that it may be a corruption of the Scotch *baken*, (dried,) while others suggest that it is derived from *beechen*, as the finest flitches were considered to be those furnished by animals that were fattened on the fruit of the beech-tree, and this opinion is borne out by the fact that in the old Lancashire dialect the word bacon is both spelt and pronounced *beechen*. A bacon hog will in general be fit for killing at about a twelve-month old, when he will weigh some 200 or 240 lbs.; those persons who care most about the hams will find it answer their purpose best not to let the animals be too fat, or so fat as a bacon-hog, and after having taken off the hams to cut up the carcass for fresh or pickling pork.

There are various methods of curing bacon and hams, practised in the different counties of England, as well as in Scotland, America, and the Continent. We will proceed to describe a few of the best and most successful.

In Hampshire and Berkshire the practice is to choose a dry day, when the wind is blowing from the north, and kill the hog early in the morning (it having fasted the day before.) When dressed hang him up in some airy place for 24 hours, then proceed to cut him up. This being done, lay the flitches on the ground, and sprinkle them with salt lightly, so let them remain for six or eight hours; then turn them up edgeways, and let the brine run off. In the mean time take two or three gallons of best salt, and two ounces of saltpetre, pounded very fine, and well mixed together; and the salting bench being made of the best seasoned oak, proceed to salt the flitches by rubbing in the salt on the back side of the flitch. This being done, turn the inside upwards, and lay on the salt about a quarter of an inch in thickness: in like manner treat every flitch. On the third day afterwards change the flitches, viz., take off the uppermost and reverse them, at the same time lay on salt a quarter of an inch in thickness. There will be no need of rubbing as before-mentioned, neither should the saltpetre be repeated, otherwise the lean of the bacon will be hard. The changing and salting should be done every third day for six successive times, when the bacon will be sufficiently salt. Then proceed to rub off all the stale briny salt, and lay on each flitch a covering of clean fresh bran or sawdust, and take it to the drying loft. It should be there hung by means of crooks fastened in the neck of the flitch, and remain for fourteen or sixteen days. The fuel most proper for drying bacon is cleft oak or ash, what is commonly called cord wood.

In Buckinghamshire, as soon as the flitches are cut from the hog they lay them on a form or table in a slanting position, and, supposing the whole hog to have weighed 240 or 280 lbs., take a quarter of a pound of saltpetre, pounded very fine, and sprinkle it all over the flitches, rubbing it well into the shoulder parts especially ; they then suffer them to remain twelve hours, after which they should be rubbed dry, and in the mean time seven pounds of salt mixed with one pound and a quarter of coarse brown sugar put into a frying-pan and heated on a clear fire, stirring it well that it may all be of the same temperature. This mixture, as hot as the hand can possibly bear it, may now be rubbed well into the flitches, which are then put one upon the other and laid in a salting-pan or other contrivance, in order that the brine may form and be kept from wasting. The bacon must be kept in this situation four weeks, turning it and basting it well with the brine twice or thrice a week. At the expiration of this time take it from the brine, hang it up to dry, and smoke it, if preferred, which in the absence of a regular smokehouse may be done as follows:—Hang up the bacon in a chimney or other orifice, then underneath put down a layer of dry straw, upon this a layer of mixed shavings, keeping out those from deal or fir, next a good layer of sawdust and some juniper-berries, or branches where procurable, and over all a mantle of wet straw or litter, which makes the fire give out much smoke without burning away too rapidly. This smoking must be repeated three or four times, or till the bacon appears thoroughly dry, when it may be hung up in the kitchen, or any dry place convenient.

In Kent the hog is *swaled* or singed, in preference to scalding and scraping the skin, as this latter process, it is considered, tends to soften the rind and injure the firmness of the flesh. The flitches are rubbed with dry salt and saltpetre in the proportion of one-third of the latter to two of the former, and laid in a trough, and there each one sprinkled over with this mixture. Here they continue for three weeks or a month, according to their size, during which time they are taken out once in two or three days and well rubbed with the brine and turned.

They are dried before a slow fire, and this process occupies about the same time that the salting has done. When it is completed the flitches are either hung up in a dry place, or deposited on stone slabs until wanted for domestic use.

In Somersetshire and Wiltshire, the following is the common process :—

When the hogs are prepared, the sides are first laid in large wooden troughs and sprinkled over with rock salt, and there left unmoved for four-and-twenty hours, in order to let all the blood and other superfluous juices be completely drained off from them.

After this they are taken up and thoroughly wiped, and some fresh bay-salt, previously heated in an iron frying-pan, is rubbed into the flesh until it has absorbed a sufficient quantity. This rubbing is continued for four successive days, during which the flitches are usually turned every second day. Where the large hogs are killed it becomes necessary to keep the flitches in brine for three weeks, and after that interval to turn them out and dry them in the common manner.

In the county of Westmoreland, which is celebrated for the flavor of its hams, the following method prevails :—First they are thoroughly rubbed, usually with bay-salt alone, after which some curers advise that they shall be closely covered up, while others leave them on a stone for the purpose of draining off the brine. At the expiration of five days this friction is repeated with equal diligence, but the bay-salt is then combined with somewhat more than an ounce of saltpetre to each ham. They are next suffered to lie about a week either in hogsheads among the brine, or on stone benches, after which they are hung up in the chimney to dry. In this last part of the process there is a difference of practice. By some they are suspended so that they shall be dried solely by the heat arising from the fire below, without being exposed at all to the smoke, while by others they are hung up in the midst of the smoke, whether this arises from coals or peat.

In Yorkshire, after the pig has been killed, it is allowed to hang twenty-four hours previous to being cut up ; one pound of saltpetre is then rubbed into a twenty-stone pig, (of fourteen pounds to the stone,) and one and a half or two stones of common salt, taking care that it is well rubbed in ; it is then put into a tub kept for the purpose. After having lain a fortnight it is turned over, and a little more salt applied—say half a stone ; it then remains a fortnight longer in the pickle-tub ; whence it is taken and hung up in the kitchen, where it remains two months to dry, but should the winter be far advanced, and dry weather set in, a shorter period might suffice. After being taken from the top of the kitchen, the inside is washed over with quicklime and water, to preserve it from the fly ; it is then removed into a room not used by the family, away from heat, and where it will be kept perfectly dry, and is ready for use at pleasure. The smoking system is rarely adopted.

Mr. Henderson, in his "*Treatise on Swine,*" gives the following account of the mode of curing bacon and hams in Scotland :—

"In killing a number of swine, what sides you may have dressed the first day, lay upon some flags or boards, piling them across each other, and giving each flitch a powdering of saltpetre, and then covering it with salt. Proceed in the same manner with the hams themselves, and do not omit giving them a little saltpetre, as it opens the pores of the flesh to receive the salt, and besides, gives the ham a pleasant flavor, and makes it more juicy. Let them lie in this state about a week, then turn those on the top undermost, giving them a fresh salting. After lying two or three weeks longer, they may be hung up to dry in some chimney or smoke-house. Or, if the curer chooses, he may turn them over again, without giving them any more salt; in which state they may lie for a month or two, without catching any harm, until he has convenience for drying them. I practised for many years the custom of carting my flitches and hams through the country to farm-houses, and used to hang them in their chimneys, and other parts of the house, to dry, some seasons to the amount of five hundred carcasses. This plan I soon found was attended by a number of inconveniences, yet it is still common in Dumfriesshire.

"About twenty years ago, I contrived a small smoke-house of a very simple construction. It is about twelve feet square, and the walls about seven feet high. One of these huts requires six joists across, one close to each wall, the other four laid asunder at proper distances. To receive five rows of flitches, they must be laid on the top of the wall. A piece of wood strong enough to bear the weight of one flitch of bacon, must be fixed across the belly end of the flitch by two strings, as the neck end must hang downwards. The piece of wood must be longer than the flitch is wide, so that each end may rest upon a beam. They may be put so near to each other as not to touch. The width of it will hold twenty-four flitches in a row, and there will be five rows, which will contain one hundred and twenty flitches. As many hams may be hung at the same time above the flitches, contrived in the best manner one can. The lower end of the flitches will be within two and a half or three feet of the floor, which must be covered five or six inches thick with sawdust, which must be kindled at two different sides. It will burn, but not cause any flame to injure the bacon. The door must be kept close, and the hut must have a small hole in the roof, so that part of the smoke may ascend. That lot of bacon and hams will be ready to pack up in a hogshead, to send off, in eight or ten days, or a little longer if required, with very little loss of weight. After the bacon is salted it may lie in the salt-house, as described, until an order is received.

"I found the smoke-house to be a great saving, not only in the expense and trouble of employing men to cart and hang it through the country, but it did not lose nearly so much weight by this process. It may be remarked, that whatever is shipped for the London market, or any other, both bacon and hams, must be knocked hard and packed into a sugar hogshead, or something similar, to hold about ten hundred weight. Bacon can only be cured from the middle of September until the middle of April."

The annexed system is the one usually pursued in Westphalia :—

"Six pounds of rock salt, two pounds of powdered loaf sugar, three ounces of saltpetre, and three gallons of spring or pure water, are boiled together. This should be skimmed when boiling, and when quite cold poured over the meat, every part of which must be covered with this brine. Small pork will be sufficiently cured in four or five days; hams, intended for drying, will be cured in four or five weeks, unless they are very large. This pickle may be used again and again, if it is fresh boiled up each time with a small addition to the ingredients. Before, however, putting the meat into the brine, it must be washed in water, the blood pressed out, and the whole wiped clean.

"Pickling-tubs should be larger at the bottom than at the top, by which means, when well packed, the pork will retain its place until the last layer is exhausted. When the pork is cool it may be cut up, the hams and shoulders reserved for bacon, and the remainder salted. The bottom of the tub or barrel should be covered with rock salt, and on it a layer of meat placed, and so on until the tub is filled. The salt should be used liberally, and the barrel filled with strong brine boiled and skimmed, and then cooled.

"The goodness and preservation of hams and shoulders depends on their smoking as well as their salting. Owing to some misconstruction of the smoke-house, and to the surface of the meat not being properly freed from saline matter, or other causes, it not unfrequently happens that during the process of smoking, the meat is constantly moist, and imbibes a pyroligneous acid taste and smell, destructive of its good qualities.

"The requisites of a smoke-house are, that it should be perfectly dry; not warmed by the fire that makes the smoke; so far from the fire, that any vapor thrown off in the smoke may be condensed before reaching the meat; so close as to exclude all flies, mice, &c., and yet capable of ventilation admitting the escape of smoke.

"The Westphalian hams, the most celebrated in Europe, are principally cured at and exported from Hamburg. The smoking of these is performed in extensive chambers, in the upper stories of high buildings. Some are four or five stories high, and the smoke is conveyed to these rooms from fires in the cellar through tubes, on which the vapor is condensed, and the heat absorbed, so that the smoke is both dry and cool when it comes in contact with the meat. They are thus kept perfectly dry, and acquire a color and flavor unknown to those smoked in the common method.

"Hams after being smoked may be kept any length of time by

10

being packed in dry ashes or powdered charcoal, or by being kept in the smoke-house if that is secure against theft, or a smoke is made under them once a-week. When meat is fully smoked or dried, it may be kept hung up in any dry room by slipping over it a cotton bag, the neck of which is closely tied around the string that supports the meat, and thus excludes the bacon-bug, fly, &c. The small part of a ham or shoulder should always be hung downward in the process of smoking, or when suspended for preservation."— *Albany Cultivator.*

The following method of curing bacon—which has been practised in Virginia and Kentucky by one person with perfect success for five-and-thirty years, during which time he states that he has cured on the average from six to eight thousand pounds every year, or, in the whole, the enormous quantity of from a hundred to a hundred and twenty-five tons—will conclude what we have to say on this division of our subject.

" The hogs should be killed when the weather is sufficiently cold to ensure that when they are hung up, after having been cleaned, they shall not only become quite cold to the touch, but feel hard and stiff. They should be killed on one day, and cut up and salted on the next. When the weather is very cold they should be hung in a cellar or somewhere where they are not likely to become frozen, but if there be no danger of this, let them hang in the open air.

" The process of cutting up is too well known to need description ; nothing further need be said than that the backbone or chine should be taken out, as also the spare-ribs from the shoulders, and the mouse-pieces and short-ribs or griskins from the middlings. No acute angles should be left to shoulders or hams. In salting up in Virginia, all the meat except the heads, jowls, chines, and smaller pieces, is put into *powdering-tubs* (water-tight half-hogsheads). In Kentucky, large troughs, ten feet long and three or four feet wide at the top, made of the *Liriodendron tulipifera*, or poplar-tree, are used. These are much the most convenient for packing the meat in, and are easily caulked if they should crack so as to leak. The salting-tray, or box in which the meat is to be salted, piece by piece, and from which each piece, as it is salted, is to be transferred to the powdering-tub or trough, must be placed just so near the trough that the man standing between can transfer the piece from one to the other easily, and without wasting the salt as they are lifted from the salting-box into the trough. The salter stands on the off-side of the salting-box. Salt the hams first, the shoulders next, and the middlings last, which may be piled up two feet above the top of the trough or tub. The joints will thus in a short time be immersed in brine.

" Measure into your salting-tray four measures of salt (a peck measure will be found most convenient,) and one measure of clean dry sifted ashes; mix and incorporate them well. The salter takes a ham into the tray, rubs the skin with this composition and the raw hock end, turns it over, and packs the composition of salt and ashes on the fleshy side till it is at least three-quarters of an inch deep all over it, and on the interior lower part of the ham, which is covered with the skin, as much as will lay on it. The man who stands ready to transfer the pieces as they are salted takes up the piece, and deposits it carefully, without displacing the composition, with the skin side down, in the bottom of the trough. Each succeeding ham is thus deposited side by side, so as to leave the least possible space unoccupied.

" When the bottom is all covered, see that every visible part of this layer of meat is covered with the composition of salt and ashes. Then begin another layer, every piece being covered on the upper or fleshy side three-quarters of an inch thick with the composition. When your trough is filled even full in this way with the joints, salt the middlings with salt only, without the ashes, and pile them up on the joints so that the liquefied salt may pass from them into the trough. Heads, jowls, backbones, &c., receive salt only, and should not be put in the trough with the large pieces.

" Much slighter salting will preserve them if they are salted upon loose boards, so that the bloody brine from them can pass off. The joints and middlings are to remain in and above the trough without being re-handled, re-salted, or disturbed in any way, till they are to be hung up to be smoked.

" If the hogs weighed not more than 150 lbs., the joints need not remain longer than five weeks in the pickle ; if they weighed 200 or upwards, six or seven weeks is not too long. It is better that they should stay in too long rather than too short a time.

" In three weeks, jowls, &c., may be hung up. Taking out of pickle, and preparation for hanging up to smoke, is thus performed : —Scrape off the undissolved salt (and if you had put on as much as directed, there will be a considerable quantity on all the pieces not immersed in the brine ; this salt and the brine is all saved ; the brine boiled down, and the dry composition given to stock, especially to hogs.) Wash every piece in lukewarm water, and with a rough towel clean off the salt and ashes. Then put the strings in to hang up. Set the pieces up edgewise, that they may drain and dry. Every piece is then to be dipped into the *meat-paint*, and hung up to smoke. The meat-paint is made of warm, not hot, water and very fine ashes stirred together until they are of the consistence of thick paint. When they are dipped in this, they receive a coating which protects them from the fly, prevents dripping, and tends to lessen all external injurious influences. Hang up the pieces while yet moist with the paint, and smoke them well."

POISONOUS PROPERTIES OF BRINE.

It is a fact worthy of notice that the brine in which pork or bacon has been pickled is poisonous to pigs. Several cases are on record in which these animals have died in consequence of a small quantity of brine having been mingled with the wash, under the mistaken impression that it would answer the same purpose and be equally as beneficial as the admixture of a small quantity of salt.

IMPORTATIONS OF BACON, HAM, AND SALTED PORK.

From a reference to the accounts furnished by the Board of Trade, it appears that there have been imported during the last three years,

		1844.	1845.	1846.
BACON	cwts.	36	54	2,768
HAMS	"	6,732	5,462	11,252
PORK, Salted :				
Of British Possessions .	"	2,153	1,517	72,519
Foreign . . .	"	28,627	38,128	
Fresh	"	63	133	133
Total of Pork . .	"	30,843	39,878	72,652

And of these articles there were entered for home consumption,—

		1844.	1845.	1846.
BACON	cwts.	36	54	2,768
HAMS	"	3,568	2,602	8,385
PORK, Salted :—				
Of British Possessions .	"	248	172	72,519
Foreign . . .	"	1,073	1,289	
Fresh	"	63	133	133
Total of Pork . .	"	1,384	1,594	72,652

These tables demonstrate the enormous increase in the importation of these staple articles of food which has taken place since the abolition of the Tariff of 1842 and the substitution of the new one. The alteration of duties is as follows:

	In 1842.			New Tariff.	
	s.	d.		s.	d.
On Bacon from Foreign Countries	14	0 per cwt.		7	0 per cwt.
British Possessions	3	6 "		2	0 "
Ham from Foreign Countries	14	0 "		7	0 "
British Possessions	3	6 "		2	0 "
Salted Pork from Foreign Countries	8	0 "		0	0 "
British Possessions	2	0 "		0	0 "

Previous to 1842 the duty on bacon and ham amounted to 28s. and 7s. per cwt., and that on pork to 16s. and 4s.; swine were then prohibited; but when, by the Act 5 & 6 Vict. cap. 47, they became admissible, there were imported,—

In 1842.	In 1843.	In 1844.	In 1845.	In 1846.
415	361	269	1,598	3,443

Here again we find the same wonderful increase. In 1845 seven times the number are imported that were brought over in 1844; and in 1846 the import of 1845 is doubled. Yet there is no diminution created in the provision trade by this extraordinary increase in that of live animals, but, on the contrary, it too increases in 1845, and is again doubled in 1846. And the increase of demand is proportionate with that of the supplies.

The accounts of one branch of our imports will this present year, however, in all probability, show a material defalcation in the amount; we allude to those arising from Ireland, whence a large number of the pigs which come to our markets are supplied, and where the present state of dearth has caused numbers of these animals to be destroyed. This fact ought to stimulate our native breeders to increased exertions. In from 1820 to 1825 there was on the average from 204,380 to 338,218 cwts. of bacon and hams imported yearly into England from the sister country. Since the last-named period there has been no decrease; but, the trade between Ireland and Great Britain having been placed on the footing of a coasting-trade, and these articles having been imported without specific duties, it is not so easy to ascertain the precise amounts brought over; they may be, however, estimated at about 500,000 cwt. per annum.

The keeping of swine is fast becoming something more than a mere means of disposing of offal and matters which would otherwise be wasted; and we trust that the value and lucrativeness of this branch of rural economy will soon be fully acknowledged, and that swine will be duly estimated among farmers and breeders. The next step must of necessity speedily follow: men of science will no longer deem them beneath their notice; their habits, instincts, and ailments will be properly studied; individuals as well as the world will be benefited; and a new and important field of knowledge thrown open.

Yet another source of profit accruing from swine, and we close
this chapter.

PIG'S DUNG AS MANURE.

The manure proceeding from the pigsty has been often much
undervalued, and for this reason,—that the litter has been considered
as forming the principal portion of it, whereas it constitutes the least
valuable part; and, indeed, where all due attention is paid to the
cleanliness of the animals and of their dwellings, it can scarcely be
regarded as manure at all, at least by itself.

It is the urine and the dung which are valuable; and these are
now generally allowed to be peculiarly so, and to constitute no inconsiderable items in the profits arising from the keeping of swine.
These matters are, from the very nature of the food of the animals,
exceedingly rich and oleaginous, and materially benefit cold soils
and grass-lands. But, as with most other things relative to swine,
this has also been too much neglected; the animals have been suffered to wander about at will, voiding their dung and urine in waste;
or, when confined, the sty perhaps furnished no means of collecting
and saving it. We will venture to prophesy that the partial alteration of system which is now gradually spreading will speedily lead
to amendment in this point also; and the dung from the piggery
will be husbanded with a care little inferior to that bestowed on the
fold, stable, or cow-house dung.

Martin says: "There is another point relative to the hog, which we
must not omit to notice. We allude to the value of the solid and
liquid manure. This has been, and still is, too much neglected.
Nevertheless, this manure is really of importance, being peculiarly
adapted for cold soils and grass lands. It should always be collected
as carefully as that of the stable or cow-house, and husbanded in
the same way. Those who keep extensive piggeries will soon find
the advantage of this plan, which, besides the profit arising from
the manure itself, will necessitate the keeping of the piggery in a
state of cleanliness. A dirty sty or yard is a disgrace to the owner;
it is the source of disease, and it involves the waste of manure of
first-rate quality. The cottager who keeps a pig or two will find
the utility of this manure in his garden, and, by due attention, he
will prevent the litter or bedding of straw from becoming a mass
of filth; thus in two ways effecting a saving."

CHAPTER XV.

The Medicines used in combating the Maladies of Swine.

THE medicines generally used in the treatment of swine are neither numerous nor complicated. There are, doubtless, many others, besides those enumerated in the following list, which might be employed with advantage, and which will, as the diseases of these domesticated animals become more studied, be discovered and made use of.

The caution requisite in the administration of all medicines has been already alluded to in Chapter X.; force should as seldom as possible be had recourse to.

It must be borne in mind that the doses here given are taken on the average, and must always be proportioned to the size, and constitution, and state of health of the animal. In all cases of actual disease, the best and most economical plan will be to have recourse to some good veterinary surgeon within reach. The life of many a valuable animal will thus be saved, for the mere amateur in surgery is always liable to blunder in the choice of remedies, as well as in the application of them, and will often create evils far greater than those he is endeavoring to cure.

ANTIMONY.—Seldom given by itself. In conjunction with sulphur, forms an efficient cooling and cleansing medicine ; and with sulphur and hog's lard, or palm or train-oil, constitutes the common mange-ointment.

ARSENIC.—Useful in mange, and other cases of diseases of the skin. From one ounce to an ounce and a half, dissolved in a gallon of water, will form a solution of sufficient strength.

CALOMEL.—A dangerous drug, and one better left alone. In cases of emergency, however, it may be given in conjunction with an equal portion of tartarized antimony. From two to three grains of each will constitute an active emetic.

CREOSOTE.—Useful in cases of virulent cutaneous eruptions.

CROTON OIL.—A powerful purgative, and one that should only be had recourse to in cases of obstinate constipation. From one to three drops may be given

DIGITALIS.—A valuable sedative medicine in cases of fever.

EPSOM SALTS.—A very useful and efficient purgative, suitable to most cases of common occurrence. From half an ounce to an ounce and a half may be ordinarily given.

GENTIAN.—An excellent stomachic; every aperient draught should contain a portion of this or the next-mentioned matter

GINGER.—Also a good stomachic, and a tonic as well. From three scruples to a drachm and a half may be given of this and the preceding drug.

LINSEED OIL.—Valuable as an occasional purgative, especially where there is much intestinal inflammation.

MERCURIAL OINTMENT.—Used for mange and scabs, in conjunction with the sulphur ointment. The proportions are one part of the former to eight parts of the latter.

NITRE.—An excellent cooling medicine in all cases where there is tendency to fever. From one to two drachms may be given dissolved in the water the animal drinks.

PALM OIL.—The best emollient to form the basis of all ointments for cutaneous eruptions.

SALT.—A valuable adjunct in purifying the blood, and maintaining the animals in good condition. A small quantity should be regularly mingled with the food.

SULPHUR.—A good cooling medicine, and the best gentle aperient for ordinary use we have. It also constitutes the chief ingredient in mange-ointment.

TARTAR EMETIC.—Useful as an emetic.

VINEGAR.—Valuable in all cases requiring cooling fomentations.

TOBACCO.—A decoction of this plant efficacious and soothing in cases of mange and cutaneous eruptions, especially when mingled with equal parts of digitalis.

TURPENTINE.—A destructive agent in cases of worms : it may be given to swine without danger.

INDEX.

10*

Wild boar exempt from leprosy, 140 ; extinction of, in Great Britain, 48, 87 ; the parent stock of our domesticated breeds, 46 ; prolific in Morocco, 56 ; reintroduction into England, 48 ; small number of litters, 48 ; tamed, 40, 57 ; in America, 57; in France, 52 ; in Germany, 52, 53 ; in India, 54 ; in Morocco, 56 ; in Sweden, 54.

Wiley, Mr. Samuel, his pigs, 78.

William, IV., King, his Suffolk boar, 81.

Wiltshire pigs, 84.

Worms in the intestines, 133.

Y.

Yorkshire breed of swine, 78.

Z.

Zoological definition of the pig. 11.

Breinigsville, PA USA
17 January 2011
253480BV00004B/28/P

9 781163 897249